# The Cuban Embargo under International Law

The United States embargo against Cuba was imposed over fifty years ago initially as a response to the new revolutionary government's seizure of US properties, which was viewed by the US as a violation of international law. However, while sanctions can be legitimate means of enforcing established norms, the Cuban embargo itself appears to be the wrongful act, and its persistence calls into question the importance and function of international law.

This book examines the history, legality and effects of US sanctions against Cuba and argues that the embargo has largely become a matter of politics and ideology, subjecting Cuba to apparently illegitimate coercion that has resulted in a prolonged global toleration of what appears to be a serious violation of international law. The book demonstrates how the Cuban embargo undermines the use of sanctions world-wide, and asks whether the refusal of world governments to address the illegality of the embargo reduces international law to tokenism where concepts of sovereign equality and non-intervention are no longer a priority. Despite the weaknesses of international law, Nigel D. White argues that in certain political conditions it will be possible to end the embargo as part of a bilateral agreement to restore normal relations between the US and Cuba and, furthermore, that such an agreement, if it is to succeed, will have to be shaped by the broad parameters of law and justice.

As a fierce re-evaluation of international law through the story of a country under siege, this book will be of great interest and use to researchers and students of public international law, international relations, and US and Latin American politics.

**Nigel D. White** is Professor of Public International Law at the University of Nottingham in the United Kingdom.

# Routledge Research in International Law

# The Cuban Embargo under International Law
## El Bloqueo

Nigel D. White

Routledge
Taylor & Francis Group

LONDON AND NEW YORK

First published 2015
by Routledge
2 Park Square, Milton Park, Abingdon, Oxfordshire OX14 4RN

and by Routledge
711 Third Avenue, New York, NY 10017

First issued in paperback 2016

*Routledge is an imprint of the Taylor & Francis Group, an informa business*

*British Library Cataloguing in Publication Data*
A catalogue record for this book is available from the British Library

*Library of Congress Cataloging-in-Publication Data*
White, Nigel D., 1961– author.
The Cuban embargo under international law: el bloqueo/
Nigel D. White.
    pages cm. – (Routledge research in international law)
    Includes bibliographical references and index.
    ISBN 978-0-415-66817-0 (hardback) –
    ISBN 978-0-203-79604-7 (ebk)
    1. Sanctions (International law)
    2. Economic sanctions, American – Cuba.
    3. Embargo – Cuba. I. Title.
    KZ6373.W47 2014
    341.5′82 – dc23                                            2014020056

ISBN 13: 978-1-138-21530-6 (pbk)
ISBN 13: 978-0-415-66817-0 (hbk)

Typeset in Garamond by
Florence Production Ltd, Stoodleigh, Devon

# Contents

# Preface

International law is replete with rules but their enforcement against outlaw states and, indeed, more generally, the impact of such rules on the behaviour of such states, is often minimal. Sovereign equality between independent states is at the heart of the international legal order, but the disparities in power between states is the reality of international relations and, inevitably, leads to politics and ideology prevailing over law and justice. The advent of international organisations may have improved the governance of international relations in many technical and less politicised areas, such as telecommunications and cultural heritage but, in matters where states' interests are strongest – concerning security and hegemony – such bodies have limited relevance, especially when one of the protagonists is a permanent member of the Security Council. In these conditions, while there may appear to be universal rules of international law promulgated in treaties and moulded by custom (increasingly helped by consensus resolutions in the United Nations), a combination of an absence of specificity in those rules and a lack of collective enforcement machinery signifies that powerful states can take the law into their own hands and, in so doing, abuse it. The line between law-enforcers and law-violators blurs and international law is seen as a sorry excuse for behaviour rather than a noble expression of the ideals of humanity.

In recent years we have seen Russia act in this way in Georgia in 2008 and in the Ukraine in 2014, continuing the pattern of Soviet interventions in its hemisphere – in Hungary in 1956, Czechoslovakia in 1968 and Afghanistan in 1979. The United States has a long history of such interventions not only within its own hemisphere – Guatemala in 1954, the Dominican Republic in 1965, Grenada in 1983, Panama in 1989, but also beyond it – in Afghanistan in 2001 and Iraq in 2003. From the mid-1960s to the late-1980s Cuba was squeezed by this superpower struggle for unachievable control of the planet, epitomised in the Cuban missile crisis of 1962, when the world reached the brink of existential nuclear war.

But before the revolution of 1959, Cuba was caught within the web of US hegemony; and post-1959 US policy has been driven by an instinctive desire to bring Cuba back within the fold. The revolution in Cuba, with its strong rejection of US imperialism – an aspect of which was the nationalisation of significant US-owned properties and assets – was followed by an increasingly punitive US embargo and, certainly in the early years of the revolution, other forms of intervention (including the use of force) by the US. With the end of Soviet support for Cuba in the early 1990s, the opportunity for normalising relations between the two states seemed to have been lost and, instead of holding out a hand of friendship, the US saw a chance to end the Communist regime in Cuba, and tightened the embargo further. The embargo ceased to be about punishing Cuba for its nationalisation of US-owned property, indeed it ceased to be justifiable in terms of protecting the security of the United States, since without Soviet support Cuba was no longer a threat to the US. Instead, with the end of the Cold War, the embargo became a means of coercing Cuba towards democracy; and the fight became one revolving around differing understandings of self-determination and human rights. The US had one view of these fundamental aspects of international law and Cuba another.

The purpose of this book is to focus on the embargo and its position under international law as both a violation of laws and a means of enforcing others. By placing the embargo within the wider context of the bilateral relationship between the US and Cuba, which stretches back to the late nineteenth century, the book unearths the potential worth of international law in such apparently barren conditions where politics and ideology appear to be supreme.

# Table of cases

THE HENLEY COLLEGE LIBRARY

# Table of abbreviations

| | |
|---|---|
| AAWH | American Association for World Health |
| AJIL | American Journal of International Law |
| BYBIL | British Yearbook of International Law |
| CANF | Cuban American National Foundation |
| CELAC | Community of Latin American and Caribbean States |
| CIA | Central Intelligence Agency |
| EJIL | European Journal of International Law |
| FAO | Food and Agriculture Organisation |
| FLN | National Liberation Front (Algeria) |
| FMLN | Farabundo Marti National Liberation Front |
| GDP | Gross Domestic Product |
| IACHR | Inter-American Commission on Human Rights |
| ICAO | International Civil Aviation Organisation |
| ICC | International Criminal Court |
| ICJ | International Court of Justice |
| ICLQ | International and Comparative Law Quarterly |
| ICTY | International Criminal Tribunal for the Former Yugoslavia |
| ILC | International Law Commission |
| ILM | International Legal Materials |
| ILR | International Law Reports |
| Iran-USCT | Iran-US Claims Tribunal |
| JCSL | Journal of Conflict and Security Law |
| LJIL | Leiden Journal of International Law |
| MPLA | Popular Movement for the Liberation of Angola |
| NAFTA | North American Free Trade Organisation |
| NAM | Non-Aligned Movement |
| NATO | North Atlantic Treaty Organisation |
| NGO | Non-Governmental Organisation |
| OAS | Organisation of American States |
| OECS | Organisation of Eastern Caribbean States |
| PCIJ | Permanent Court of International Justice |
| RIAA | Reports of International Arbitral Awards |
| SCR | Supreme Court Reports (Canada) |

| SFRY | Socialist Federal Republic of Yugoslavia |
| UDHR | Universal Declaration of Human Rights |
| UK | United Kingdom |
| UNCIO | United Nations Conference on International Organisation |
| UNESCO | United Nations Educational, Scientific and Cultural Organisation |
| UNGA | United Nations General Assembly |
| UNITA | National Union for the Total Independence of Angola |
| UNSC | United Nations Security Council |
| UNSG | United Nations Secretary General |
| UNTS | United Nations Treaty Series |
| US | United States (of America) |
| USSR | Union of Soviet Socialist Republics |
| WHO | World Health Organisation |
| WMD | Weapons of Mass Destruction |
| WTO | World Trade Organisation |

# 1 Introduction

## 1.1 The relevance of international law

The story of the Cuban embargo appears to be the story of international law, whereby coercion by means of unilateral trade and other sanctions against a country does not seem to be the attempted enforcement of international law, but rather the violation of it. Although the original reasons for the US imposition of measures in 1960 included responding to violations of international law by the revolutionary government in Cuba, its maintenance over five decades appears almost exclusively a matter of ideology and politics. The concept of sanctions, normally seen as legitimate means of enforcing established norms, appears to be turned on its head. The punishment (the embargo) seems to be the wrongful act, which has not been curbed or fully confronted by the rest of the world. Indeed, the continuing act of apparently illegitimate coercion becomes the norm, making it very difficult to identify when sanctions are lawful or not, potentially undermining other such measures (for example measures taken against Iran for its violations of the Nuclear Non-Proliferation Treaty 1968). Only limited critical responses to the Cuban embargo have been undertaken by other countries or organisations (for example the EU's response to the extraterritorial effects of the US Helms-Burton Act of 1996), so that the end result is a fifty-year toleration of what appears to be a serious violation of international law.

What does this say about the importance and function of international law in the modern era, indeed the very existence of international law? Is it enough to say that some or even most governments recognise the illegality of the embargo (as evidenced by regular condemnation in the UN General Assembly)? Doesn't that reduce international law to mere tokenism or is such a low-level function enough when dealing with the world's remaining superpower? Indeed, should we reconsider the fundamentals of international law and take a more pragmatic view, one which recognises the imbalances of power and no longer pays lip-service to sovereign equality and non-intervention? This book considers these fundamental questions about international law and the international order through a detailed examination of the story of a country under siege.

The book is a sustained legal analysis of the embargo through its various iterations; but it also places it at the centre of a long-standing bilateral dispute between the two countries. The dispute is not simply about how to conduct and control trade, but also concerns different conceptions of security, intervention, human rights and self-determination. To this end the thesis is not only to dissect the embargo in terms of its legality, but also to place its removal at the centre of a potential rapprochement between the two governments involving a restoration of normal conditions between two sovereign states based on mutual respect and cooperation. It will be shown that in the context of a bilateral relationship between two countries, international law can set the framework for a peaceful solution that involves recognising, addressing and remedying past wrongs in a constructive way.

Effective dispute settlement is a feature of a legal order that does not simply consist of primary rules setting standards of behaviour, but of a more rounded legal system where there are secondary rules of recognition, change and adjudication.[1] A system of primary rules alone is one that is uncertain, static and relies on diffuse pressure to maintain it.[2] International law does suffer from these structural defects, especially when compared to national legal systems, but we should understand that it is a legal order of a different nature, which is at its most rudimentary when considering inter-state disputes. Even though the international legal order falls short of a complete legal system it does have the potential to facilitate settlement even in the most intractable disputes. In order to understand international law it is always necessary for the actor, interpreter or observer to come to terms with the relationship between politics and law that is so intrinsic to the study of international law, its legitimacy and effectiveness. In international relations, law is a facet of politics in a much more intimate and complex way than in many domestic legal and political systems where there has developed, over time, a rule of law. Although the international rule of law is increasingly referred to,[3] this book demonstrates that it is clearly an aspiration as opposed to a reality. This is arguably so even in sectors of international law where there appears to be effective dispute settlement (such as the world trading system).[4]

While rights and duties of states under international law can readily be identified, there is often a lack of clarity as to their content, with general principles such as that of self-determination having greater indeterminacy than others. Furthermore, despite the development of secondary rules on liability

---

1   H.L.A. Hart, *The Concept of Law* (Oxford: Clarendon, 1961) 77–96.
2   Ibid.
3   See for example UNGA Res 68/116 (2013), 'The rule of law at the national and international levels'.
4   See generally D. Cass, *The Constitutionalization of the World Trade Organization: Legitimacy, Democracy and Community in the International Trading System* (Oxford: Oxford University Press, 2000).

(or 'responsibility' in international legal terminology) there remains uncertainty as to how rights can be asserted and duties enforced. Indeed, one of the most problematic issues in international law is that although it has largely (but not completely and not without controversy) banned the use of military force to settle disputes, it still allows for, indeed arguably encourages, self-help in the shape of unilateral enforcement using a variety of non-forcible measures. Furthermore, the weaknesses of international laws signify, according to the pragmatists, that they are outweighed by political concerns and interests.

A pragmatic approach justifies the Cuban embargo as a legitimate defence of US rights and interests. While the pragmatic view sees international law as peripheral and no barrier to the pursuit of sovereign interests, scholars from post-colonial countries would argue that it is important to confront the reality that international law actually embodies the inequalities in international relations, reflecting its imperial and colonial origins. Given Cuba's dependence on the United States prior to the revolution of 1959, this view has resonance for the subject of the book. The critical view has been developed to put forward the idea of unequal sovereignty whereby a great power is not so limited by international law as a 'normal' state would be and, further, has far more rights than a 'pariah' state, which, for example, cannot hide behind the principle of non-intervention.[5] Given Cuba's alleged 'outlaw' status – at least from the US perspective – this literature has relevance and is discussed in the book.

In contrast to these and other power-focused theories, the universal approach will also be considered. This portrays international law as being legitimately universally applicable to all states and other international legal persons, an approach that recognises the weaknesses of international law but still sees its rules and principles as embodying the values of the international community of states and other actors (values of equality, peace, humanity, and justice), producing a system of law that can be held up against even the most powerful of actors. Although this is the approach favoured by the author and,[6] more importantly, by the International Court of Justice (for instance in the *Nicaragua Case* of 1986),[7] the ease with which international law is brushed aside by powerful states, with very little by way of sanction, needs to be taken seriously and requires a critical re-evaluation of the universal approach to international law.

The Cuban embargo is shown to embody the weaknesses and contradictions at the heart of international law; it poses a series of questions about

---

5 G. Simpson, *Great Powers and Outlaw States: Unequal Sovereigns in the International Legal Order* (Cambridge: Cambridge University Press, 2004).

6 N.D. White, *Advanced Introduction to International Conflict and Security Law* (Cheltenham: Elgar, 2014) 31–6.

7 *Case Concerning Military and Paramilitary Activities in and Against Nicaragua (Nicaragua v United States)*, (1986) ICJ Rep 14.

international law that are addressed as a test-case for the normative relevance and legitimacy of international law. Throughout the book international law is not seen simply as a set of universal rules, but as part of an on-going process,[8] enabling progress to be made towards dispute settlement within a normative framework established by international law, but also one which allows for a significant degree of political choice. Indeed, it will be argued, adapting Koskenniemi's analysis,[9] that in case of highly politicised disputes, law is normally shaped by politics, but there are occasions when the political context changes where international law comes into its own and shapes political choices.

## 1.2　A note on sources

The history of Cuba, which features in the earlier chapters of the book, is based on a number of secondary accounts, but particularly revolves around two authoritative accounts: Marifeli Pérez-Stable's, *The Cuban Revolution*,[10] and Richard Gott's *Cuba: A New History*.[11] The two books are widely referred to in the literature and the information within them has been used to form the basis of a legal analysis of events. These histories have been supplemented by the excellent political history of the embargo by Patrick J. Haney and Walt Vanderbush, *The Cuban Embargo*.[12] The legal analysis that dominates later in the book is largely based on an examination of numerous primary documents (treaties, meetings, resolutions, legislation, cases, state practice . . .), supplemented by secondary sources, where available. The literature is primarily English language based.[13]

---

8　R. Higgins, *Problems and Process: International Law and How We Use It* (Oxford: Clarendon Press, 1994).

9　M. Koskenniemi, 'The Place of Law in Collective Security', (1996) 17 *Michigan Journal of International Law* 455.

10　M. Pérez-Stable, *The Cuban Revolution: Origins, Course and Legacy* (2nd edn, Oxford: Oxford University Press, 1999).

11　R. Gott, *Cuba: A New History* (New Haven: Yale University Press, 2004).

12　P.J. Haney and W. Vanderbush, *The Cuban Embargo: The Domestic Politics of an American Foreign Policy* (Pittsburgh: University of Pittsburgh Press, 2005).

13　A selection of Spanish literature: F. Calzón, 'El embargo a debate: Persistir en el embargo', (1998) 1 *Revista hispano cubano* 54; F. Calzón, 'USA-Europa: los Estados Unidos y el embargo contra Cuba', (2003) 17 *Revista hispano cubano* 30; J.R. Cárdenas, 'El embargo a debate: La política de los Estados Unidos hacia Cuba: Una defensa', (1998) 1 *Revista hispano cubano* 46; M. Falcoff, 'Presente y future en las relaciones Estados Unidos-Cuba: un ejercicio de análisis y especulación', (2003) 173 *Foro internacional* 693; A. Liriano de la Cruz, *Cuba, El Caribe y el post embargo* (Santo Domingo: FLASCO, 2005); A. Leyva de Varona, *Propaganda y realidad: análisis del embargo económico de los Estados Unidos contra la Cuba castrista* (Washington DC: Fundacion Nacional Cubano Americana, 1994); R.A. Nuccio, 'El embargo a debate: Castro es quien mantiene aislada a Cuba', (1998) 1 *Revista hispano cubano* 55; S.K. Purcell, 'La Ley Helms-Burton y el embargo estadounidense contra Cuba', (2003) 173 *Foro*

The purpose in assimilating these various sources is not to provide an alternative history of Cuba, rather a historical account of the bilateral relationship between Cuba and the US and the legal relations established (and broken) by it. Those legal relations are partly bilateral but are, in the main, part of a multilateral, arguably universal, set of rules, which bind both parties. Care clearly has to be taken not to impute obligations to the two countries that they do not have, for instance, under human rights treaties. However, while the US and Cuba do not have many reciprocal treaty obligations under human rights law, they are both subject to that cruder, but essential element of international law, custom. Custom though suffers, by its very nature, from indeterminacy and is often contested but it is worthwhile here reprising the orthodox understanding of it as forming a core component of universal international law.

From an orthodox perspective customary international law has both an internal and an external aspect. Customary law is what states do while accepting that they are under a duty or have a right to do so (*opinio juris sive necessitates*).[14] *Opinio juris* is best understood as the internalisation of a norm by a state so that when it is asserting its rights or following its duties, in relation to other states, its agents will make declarations to that effect; or when other states are not acting in accordance with their obligations it will condemn those states for breaching customary norms. *Opinio juris* is an essential element of customary law and it is this element that explains the continued validity of the norm prohibiting the use of force as a rule of custom. In treaty law there is a parallel principle – *pacta sunt servanda* – which explains the obligatory force of treaties.[15]

It is informative to consider the most debated customary international law, namely that prohibiting the use of force, to uncover its continued validity and, moreover, relevance even in the face of clear violations of the norm. This is best illustrated by an example from the Cold War when the superpowers seemed to use force whenever their spheres of influence were under threat. For example, in 1979, the Soviet Union invaded Afghanistan but claimed that the Afghan government had requested Soviet intervention pursuant to a treaty of friendship between the two states, to protect it from external

---

*internacional* 704; J. Roy, 'Las dos leyes Helms-Burton: contraste de la actitud de los Estados Unidos ante la Unión Europea y ante Cuba', (2003) 173 *Foro internacional* 719; S. Seriocha Fernandez Pérez, *Las nacionalizaciones cubanas y el bloqueo de los Estados Unidos: una historia ajena a la guerra fría* (Madrid: Escuela Diplomatica, 2000); I. Vásquez and L.J. Rodríguez, 'Es hora de levanter el embargo contra Cuba', (1999) 4 *La Ilustración liberal: revista española y americana* 44; A. Zaldívar Dieguez, *Bloqueo: el asedio económico más prolongado de la historia* (La Habana: Capitán San Luis, 2003).
14  Article 38(1)(b) Statute of the International Court of Justice 1945, which refers to 'general practice accepted as law'.
15  Article 26 Vienna Convention on the Law of Treaties 1969, which states that 'Every treaty is binding upon the parties to it and must be performed by them in good faith'.

intervention. The argument was, in essence, one of collective self-defence, with the Soviet Union arguing that it had been requested to send troops to protect Afghanistan from being a victim of a violation of the customary rule prohibiting the use of force between states.[16]

The Soviet contention was clearly spurious since the request for assistance came from the very regime that the Soviet troops had just installed, but it illustrates that even though the Soviet Union was prepared to use force to achieve regime change it was not prepared to say it had the right to do so. Furthermore, the Soviet actions were roundly and regularly condemned by the rest of the world in the form of General Assembly resolutions, which were adopted annually until Soviet withdrawal from Afghanistan in 1989.[17]

This very important point received the highest judicial endorsement in 1986 in the *Nicaragua Case*, when the International Court of Justice confronted the argument that state practice was not in conformity with the prohibition of the use of force:

> The Court does not consider that, for a rule to be established as customary, the corresponding practice must be in absolute rigorous conformity with the rule. In order to deduce the existence of customary rules, the Court deems it sufficient that the conduct of States should, in general, be consistent with such rules, and that instances of State conduct inconsistent with a given rule should generally have been treated as breaches of that rule, not as indications of the recognition of a new rule. If a State acts in a way *prima facie* incompatible with a recognised rule, but defends its conduct by appealing to exceptions or justifications contained within the rule itself, then whether or not the State's conduct is in fact justifiable on that basis, the significance of that attitude is to confirm rather than weaken the rule.[18]

Indeed, the prohibition of the use of force is not only a rule of custom but is widely recognised as a peremptory rule of international law (*jus cogens*) from which no derogation is allowed.[19] *Jus cogens* are the most fundamental norms of international law. The prohibition of violence except in clear self-defence or under the authority of a central body is perhaps the most important hallmark of any society but, moreover, underpins any legal order. In a sense, the prohibition on the use of force can withstand many violations simply because without it any attempt to construct an international legal order would be doomed to failure. However, there must come a point when violence

---

16  UNSC 2190th meeting (1980).
17  Starting with UNGA Res ES-6 (1980).
18  *Nicaragua Case* (n.7) at 98.
19  A. Orakhelashvili, *Peremptory Norms under International Law* (Oxford: Oxford University Press, 2006) 50–1.

is so widespread and appears to be spiralling out of control that the validity of the whole legal order is called into question.[20]

When it comes to the Cuban embargo as an example of non-forcible action, however, the relative certainties provided by the UN Charter, customary and, indeed, peremptory prohibition on the use of force, find no equivalence. There is no equivalent prohibition in the Charter or in custom prohibiting economic coercion, particularly when it is justified as a valid response to a prior violation of international law. Again we can see the reasons why the Cuban embargo, representing as it does a serious rupture in normal inter-state relations, makes for an excellent case study into the relevance and function of international law.

One final point of clarification, although Cubans refer to the embargo as *el bloqueo* it is not technically a blockade within the terms of traditional international law. Stephen Neff relates the art of blockade as practised by the North against the South in the American Civil War of 1861–5 in the following terms as:

> The physical presence of a line of ships encircling an invested area – with the number of ships required to be large enough to satisfy the requirement of effectiveness (i.e., to make captures on a systematic, rather than merely a sporadic, basis). A blockade is therefore a kind of fence or stockade – although composed not of posts and railings but of naval vessels.[21]

Even the 'quarantine' imposed against Cuba by the United States during the Cuban Missile Crisis in 1962 was not robust enough to constitute a blockade in the classical sense.[22] Nonetheless, the embargo against Cuba is more than just stopping trade between the US and Cuba, it involves trying to block other states from trading with Cuba as well, hence justifying the term *el bloqueo* in a non-technical sense. It is worth noting, in this regard, that in order to make its economic squeeze against the Confederate states effective, the Union had to extend its measures to include export controls to prevent supplies getting from North to South (via third countries).[23] The North saw this as a fundamental aspect of its freedom to trade (or not to trade),[24] a view that the United States has adopted in its dealings with modern day Cuba.

20 H. Kelsen, *Principles of International Law* (New York: Rinehart and Winston, 1967) 551–88.
21 S. Neff, *Justice in Blue and Grey: A Legal History of the Civil War* (Cambridge, MA: Harvard University Press, 2010) 187.
22 D. Guilfoyle, *Shipping Interdiction and the Law of the Sea* (Cambridge: Cambridge University Press, 2009) 192–3.
23 Neff (n.21), 192–3.
24 Ibid., 193.

## 1.3 Argument in outline

The early part of the book considers the history of Cuba, essentially from a bilateral perspective. This is premised on the fact that it is the bilateral relationship between the US and Cuba that is at the heart of the history and development of Cuba, first briefly in the shape of US occupation (1898–1902), then US imperialism (1902–1959) and, from 1959, antagonism between the two countries. This aids understanding the nature of the bilateral dispute in more profound terms than solely focussing on the conflicting arguments about legal rights and wrongs. The whole history of Cuba has been shaped by what Marifeli Pérez-Stable calls 'mediated sovereignty'.[25] Antony Anghie helps us understand that this form of sovereignty is common among developing states that eventually escaped colonialism and imperialism.[26]

Antony Anghie's thesis is apposite to our analysis of the unfolding history of Cuba. Although Anghie mainly concentrates on the history and process of African independence, his analysis of colonialism and decolonisation can readily be applied to Cuba. Anghie writes that the 'acquisition of sovereignty by the Third World was an extraordinarily significant event; and yet, various limitations and disadvantages appeared to be somehow peculiarly connected with that sovereignty'.[27] Anghie deploys 'Third World' as a term for 'non-European societies and territories which were colonized from the sixteenth century onwards by European Empires, and which acquired political independence since the 1940s'.[28] Cuba's original colonial master, Spain, did not hand the country back to its people, but handed it over to the United States in 1898. It was the United States that gave Cuba its independence in 1902, but it was a limited and disadvantageous form of independence, making Anghie's analysis relevant. Although only occupying Cuba for a short period of time, the United States briefly took on the mantel of colonial master and granted independence with strings attached.

The history of Cuba is a history of the struggle for self-determination of the Cuban people – initially from Spain, then from the United States and, finally, from Soviet Communism. From the US perspective, national security and self-interest would strongly suggest that it was ludicrous to expect the US government to permit the continuation of an ideologically and strategically-opposed Communist dictatorship in its backyard.[29] US President Johnson reflected this thinking in the early period of the Cuban revolution in relation to another intervention in the Caribbean, in the Dominican

---

25　Pérez-Stable (n.10), 7.
26　A. Anghie, *Imperialism, Sovereignty and the Making of International Law* (Oxford: Oxford University Press, 2004).
27　Ibid., 2.
28　Ibid., 3.
29　M. Glennon, *The Fog of Law: Pragmatism, Security and International Law* (Chicago, IL: Stanford University Press, 2010) 27.

Republic in 1965, when the President declared that the 'American nation cannot permit the establishment of another Communist dictatorship in the Western Hemisphere'.[30]

The US policy of intervention in Cuba from 1960 onwards is but a component of its Cold War interventionism in the region, principally in Guatemala in 1954, the Dominican Republic in 1965, Grenada in 1983, and Panama in 1989. Both superpowers engaged in parallel policies during the Cold War, with the Soviet Union intervening in Hungary in 1956, Czechoslovakia in 1968, and Afghanistan in 1989. In the post-Cold War era Russia has intervened in the former Soviet republics of Georgia in 2008 and Ukraine in 2014, while the US engaged in military actions further from its territory in Afghanistan in 2001 and Iraq in 2003. In these circumstances it is legitimate to raise the question of whether international law has any relevance to major powers when they act militarily to protect their essential national interests.[31] It has been said that in these conditions 'law does not deal with such questions of ultimate power – power that comes close to the source of sovereignty'.[32] It is worth noting that this comment was made by Dean Acheson in the context of the Cuban Missile Crisis of 1962.

The opening chapters help to set up one of the central questions the book seeks to answer: whether, in these conditions, it is possible or indeed desirable to have a universal set of rules regarding international rights and wrongs, or are laws so indeterminate and weak as to be irrelevant in controlling behaviour since they oscillate between explanations for behaviour and attempts at controlling it?[33] The opening chapters range widely across issues of colonialism, self-determination, sovereignty, intervention, and international law and its enforcement, but these are the building blocks upon which the analysis in the book is based. Inevitably the opening chapters will throw up more questions than they answer, but the remainder of the book is dedicated to trying to answer some of the most fundamental questions about international law, about its purpose and function – in simple terms to address that oft-heard lament – 'what is the point of international law?'.

Delving deeper into the complexity of the relationship between Cuba and the US reveals that there is a series of relationships: first one best described as colonialism by the US, which then blurs into one of imperialism; and finally one of sovereign inequality whereby Cuba, according to the US at least, has limited sovereignty. These phases reveal that Cuba's sovereignty is acquired incrementally and, even then, not completely at least in the Westphalian sense of the term. However, from the Cuban perspective the Cuban story after the

---

30  (1965) 52 US Dept. of State Bulletin 745.

31  Simpson (n.5).

32  D. Acheson, 'Response to Panel: The Cuban Quarantine – Implications for the Future', (1963) 14 *American Society of International Law Proceedings* 14–15.

33  Koskenniemi (n.9), 489.

1959 Revolution represented the highpoint of the assertion of Cuban independence, sovereignty and self-determination. For a relatively brief period of time, until the early 1970s, the revolutionary government embodied the will of the people and this potent combination of government and people enabled Cuba to defend itself from direct and indirect US intervention. However, to ensure Cuba's longer-term defence, the revolutionary government turned to the Soviet Union for economic and military assistance. Soviet influence, in turn, undermined the political independence of Cuba, moving it from a genuine form of popular continuing revolution towards Marxism and all the structuralism and doctrine that such an ideology entailed but, more importantly, shifting it from dependence on the US to dependence on the USSR. In the light of this, consideration is given to the change in emphasis in international law, which started in the Cold War but flourished after its ending. This has involved a move from external self-determination in the form of securing independence from colonial and other similar forms of domination, towards internal self-determination, to the extent of debating the representative nature of national governments. Having achieved independence from the US, and therefore having achieved external self-determination, we need to consider Cuba's continuing respect for the right of self-determination during the period of Soviet influence and thereafter.

The Cuban revolution was not only striving to consolidate its own self-determination in the 1960s, it became involved in exporting its revolution by forcible intervention, first in Latin America and then in Africa. History shows that it was not until 1962, after the US embargo had been imposed, that the Cuban revolutionaries 'made a conscious decision to put their revolutionary theories into practice and to actively promote guerrilla warfare in Latin America' – 'encouraged by Guevara, Castro made plans to accelerate history'.[34] However, Cuban military involvement in Latin America in 1962–7 was on a small-scale being confined to Argentina, Bolivia and Venezuela. In this period, the largest intervention was in Africa and consisted in sending just over 100 Cuban soldiers under Che Guevara to the Congo in 1965.[35] Cuba also sent advisers to train MPLA fighters in Angola and sent arms to the FLN fighters in Algeria, helping those movements fight colonial powers (Portugal and France).[36] Guevara's expedition to Bolivia in 1967 to support a guerrilla movement in that country ended in his capture and execution.

Cuban interventions, like the US embargo and its other external interventions, appear to be evidence that both states are guilty of taking the law into their own hands. The US was punishing Cuba for its expropriation

---

34  Gott (n.11), 215–16.
35  Ibid., 219.
36  Ibid., 220–1.

of US-owned property and for its interventions in Latin America and Africa, and Cuba was trying forcefully to help peoples towards self-determination along Cuban lines. This highlights the contrast between the apparent equality of sovereign states before the law or, more accurately, before the International Court of Justice, and the inequality in the world outside the Peace Palace in The Hague, where the Court has its seat. If we consider the role of power in international law we have to confront the argument of the pragmatist that many rules of international law are simply 'paper rules', which do not act as any real constraint on the behaviour of powerful states. Such states are not just the superpowers or other major powers but can be determined states, like Cuba, whose external influence was greater than might be expected.

The restriction on self-help in modern international law, embodied in the doctrine of countermeasures, is contrasted with the real world of economic coercion. Although the Cuban embargo does not appear to accord with the doctrine of countermeasures and, therefore, is a *prima facie* breach of international law, there is a considerable amount of state practice where punitive economic and other forms of coercion are applied on a regular basis as a means of enforcing perceived rights. Consideration is given in this book to the pragmatic challenge to the restricted legal framework that has been constructed around self-help in the post-1945 world order.

Detailed examination is undertaken of the US domestic legal basis of the embargo by looking at the Presidential Executive Order that initiated it and the subsequent pieces of legislation that supplemented and strengthened it. The obstacles, both political and legal, that block the lifting of the embargo are reconsidered. It will be seen that the embargo has ceased to be driven by the external policies of the US towards the Cuban government but is almost entirely driven by US domestic policy under the influence of the exile Cuban community in the US, particularly in Florida. However, the purposes of the embargo remain overtly the enforcement of international law; although the norms being enforced have changed from those protecting US-owned property and assets in Cuba to those protecting human (especially democratic) rights of Cubans.

It is essential to consider the embargo in fact as well as in law before we can measure its impact upon Cuba, the Cuban people and other actors (other countries, individuals and corporate actors). Is the embargo coercive and punitive viz-à-viz Cuba as a state so that its ability to exercise both external and internal sovereignty is undermined, and does it significantly impact upon health and other elements of the life of the Cuban people? The book includes an evaluation of various studies on the impact of the embargo, particularly on health. The embargo is evaluated under international law not only in isolation but more broadly as a significant part of a wider dispute (arguably conflict) between two states that is (or should be) governed by the law of nations, understood as international law applicable to nation states. The issue is treated as a dispute between the US and Cuba in order to establish and evaluate the legal positions of both parties. Every effort is made to analyse these positions fairly and impartially in order to establish the reasons behind the imposition and continuation of the embargo. Was it a response to Cuban intervention in other Latin American countries; a protest about the abuse of human rights by the Castro government; an attempt to promote democracy within Cuba; a response to the expropriation without compensation of the property and assets of American citizens and companies by the revolutionary government of Fidel Castro; or simply an ideologically driven measure initiated in an era when fear and hatred of Communism was at its height? Do any of these claims justify what appears to be an illegitimate intervention in the sovereign affairs of Cuba? On the other hand doesn't the United States have the freedom to choose its trading partners? The extra-territorial extension of the embargo to cover foreign companies trading with Cuba is also considered in terms of the traditional international legal concept of jurisdiction. Given that the Helms-Burton Act of 1996 was enacted following the shooting down of two private aircraft belonging to Cuban exiles by the Cuban air force, it is essential to examine each episode in the history of the embargo, as well as considering it as a whole.

An evaluation of the Cuban response to the embargo is undertaken by considering whether Cuba sees itself as a victim of a violation of international law and, if so, whether it (or its allies) has attempted to take any legitimate countermeasures against the United States. The book unearths the extent and significance of the legal dispute by considering the dialogue between the two governments and whether the issue is debated in terms of legality and responsibility, countermeasures and sanctions. Did the United States see the Helms-Burton Act of 1996 as a lawful countermeasure taken in response to the downing of the two aircraft? Such an examination will reveal the importance (or not) of international law by assessing the significance of the legal debate within the wider political and ideological dispute. The relevance and role of self-help measures, recognised in international law, is revealed and the limitations of such measures are identified.

According to the orthodox approach universal international law is maintained by a consistent critical reaction of the community of states to breaches of its norms. An examination is undertaken of how other states and actors have reacted to the embargo, by looking principally at the debates in the UN General Assembly and the Organisation of American States, and the resolutions produced therein. Along with the legality of US decisions to impose the embargo against Cuba and to maintain and increase its coverage, consideration is given to the potential violations of human rights law that may be attributable to the United States due to the embargo's prolonged maintenance and potentially devastating impact. This concerns both peoples' rights (principally the right to self-determination) and individual rights (for instance to freedom of movement, health and education). Pinpointed is the extent of human rights violations but these raise the problematic issue of attribution of such wrongful acts, since the Cuban government has also been extensively criticised for its human rights violations (and not just by the US), and under international law responsibility for the protection of human rights falls primarily on the territorial state (Cuba).

Both Cuba and the United States have patchy records in terms of their commitment to human rights treaties rendering an evaluation of violations by these states difficult. Cuba has only recently (in 2008) signed (but not yet ratified) the two international covenants on human rights, meaning that the analysis of Cuban obligations under human rights law must primarily rest on customary international law. While the United States ratified the Covenant on Civil and Political Rights in 1992, it has only signed the Covenant on Economic, Social and Cultural Rights (in 1977), meaning that it is not bound by the latter. Given that the main impact of the embargo is on economic and social rights (although there are freedom of movement issues as well), again the human rights obligations of the United States are primarily customary ones. There are question marks about the extra-territorial extent of both treaty and customary human rights. Moreover, given the Covenants were only adopted in the mid-1960s, there are further issues about when, if at all, some or all of the rights contained therein became customary, bearing in mind the dispute goes back to 1959. This makes it essential to understand the customary status of the Universal Declaration of Human Rights, adopted by the UN General Assembly in 1948,[37] an instrument containing both types of rights.

Despite the lack of commitment to human rights treaties by Cuba and, to a lesser extent, the United States, in a wider sense the nature of the conflict between the two countries is a conflict over human rights, since the United States accuses Cuba of denying its citizens basic civil, political and democratic rights, while the US embargo potentially violates the fundamental economic, social and cultural rights of the Cuban people. Both sides claim that the right of self-determination of the Cuban people is being violated by the other. In essence the conflict reflects profound differences in the understanding of modern international law, and goes to the heart of the conflict in human rights law and its claims to universality.

The book then turns to address the issues of state responsibility in the context of the imposition of the embargo and its human rights impact, including the oft-overlooked issue of whether breaches of international law for which a state is responsible actually lead to access to justice (in terms of satisfaction, reparations or compensation) for the victims of such violations. The issue is whether international law's function is to act as the conscience of the world, pointing to wrongful acts when they occur, but not in helping in any significant way those directly injured, or whether it is also an instrument for justice for victims of internationally wrongful acts.

The traditional view of international law is that an injured state can seek to establish the responsibility of the violating state and require it to remedy

37  UNGA Res 217A (1948).

its transgression, but the enforcement of that liability remains problematic. The International Court of Justice remains dependent upon consent, while other international mechanisms available to the victim state are equally underdeveloped. The attempts by the governments of both countries to utilise these mechanisms, as well as the other options open to them are considered towards the end of the book. The book not only looks at the issue of access to justice from the traditional perspective of the countries involved, but also from the viewpoint of the Cuban people for violations of their right to self-determination, individuals (Cuban and American citizens) for human rights violations and loss of property, American companies for unlawful expropriation, and companies from other countries for the unlawful application of extra-territorial sanctions. The book provides valuable insights into the progress international law has made in providing access to justice to victims of violations of international law.

International law helps us identify the wrongs committed by both sides, but it does not automatically provide any evolved mechanisms for resolving the dispute. Going back to treating this as an inter-state dispute, admittedly not a traditional one about territory, but a modern one about self-determination – the ability of a state, people or individuals to determine their future – it is possible to envisage international law providing a framework within which negotiations take place and peaceful settlement is achieved. Cuba views its self-determination as an issue of continuing independence, sovereignty and non-intervention, while the United States sees this as an issue of individual freedom of choice so that self-determination is an issue of participation and democracy. Furthermore, the US views itself as having a right in seeing the principle of self-determination upheld in Cuba. In such a modern dispute over the nature of statehood and sovereignty it is necessary to revisit and revive traditional methods of dispute settlement – diplomacy, conciliation, mediation, arbitration, and judicial settlement. This is supplemented by emerging literature and ideas on dispute settlement and transitional justice, which involve concepts of restoration and reconciliation, as well as reparations and possible retribution. Here it will be essential to gauge the possibilities of achieving a settlement based on respect for international law within the hitherto crushing limitations of the political context, with its Cold War lineage, which governs relations between the two countries. In such a hostile environment, the possibilities for agreement based on principles of international law as a result of 'deliberative diplomacy',[38] are explored.

While the underlying approach of the book is based upon the universal view of international law, each chapter is critical of the limitations of this approach. The final chapter is an assessment of these limitations and the prospects for international law in its still largely unevolved state. The presence

---

38 S. Wheatley, *The Democratic Legitimacy of International Law* (Oxford: Hart, 2010) 138.

of numerous primary rules of international law imposing obligations on states and other international legal persons disguises the fact that although there are secondary international rules of recognition, change, adjudication and enforcement, they are weak and disputed. Indeed, even the primary rules themselves often lack coherence, especially between the traditional norms of the law of nations which emphasise state sovereignty and non-intervention; and modern human rights laws, some of which pull in the opposite direction. It is argued that until both primary and secondary rules are strengthened, providing for greater clarity and relevance, as well as greater access to effective remedies for victims, international law is in danger of being a minor factor or irritant in the decision-making processes of governments. However, there may be lessons to be learnt from updating dispute settlement techniques using ideas of restoration and reconciliation found within transitional justice but also, upon closer examination, woven into the fabric of international law itself.

# 2 Cuba's struggle for independence

## 2.1 Introduction

This first substantial chapter considers the history of Cuba, essentially from a bilateral perspective. The premise is that it is the bilateral relationship between the US and Cuba that lies at the heart of the history and development of Cuba, first in the shape of a brief US occupation (1898–1902), then a period of US imperialism (1902–1959) and, from 1959, on-going antagonism between the US and Cuba. This facilitates understanding the nature of the bilateral dispute in more profound terms than reviewing conflicting arguments about legal rights and wrongs. The history of Cuba has been shaped by what Marifeli Pérez-Stable calls 'mediated sovereignty'.[1] In Chapter 3 Antony Anghie's work is used to help explain that this form of sovereignty is common among developing states that eventually escaped colonialism and imperialism.[2]

The history of Cuba is a history of the struggle for self-determination of the Cuban people – initially from Spain, then from the United States and, finally, from Soviet Communism. From the US perspective, national security and self-interest both strongly suggest that it would be ludicrous to expect the US to permit the continuation of an ideologically and strategically-opposed Communist dictatorship in its backyard.[3] US President Johnson reflected this thinking in the early period of the Cuban revolution in relation to another intervention in the Caribbean, in the Dominican Republic in 1965, when the President declared that the 'American nation cannot permit the establishment of another Communist dictatorship in the Western Hemisphere'.[4]

---

1 M. Pérez-Stable, *The Cuban Revolution: Origins, Course and Legacy* (2nd edn, Oxford: Oxford University Press, 1999) 7.
2 A. Anghie, *Imperialism, Sovereignty and the Making of International Law* (Oxford: Oxford University Press, 2004).
3 M. Glennon, *The Fog of Law: Pragmatism, Security and International Law* (Chicago, IL: Stanford University Press, 2010) 27.
4 (1965) 52 US Dept. of State Bulletin 745.

The US intervention in Cuba is part of a pattern of interventions undertaken by the superpowers during the Cold War (military interventions were principally by the US in Guatemala in 1954, Dominican Republic in 1965, Grenada in 1983 and Panama in 1989; and by the Soviet Union in Hungary in 1956, Czechoslovakia in 1968, and Afghanistan in 1979) and continued in the post-Cold War era by Russia in Georgia in 2008 and Ukraine in 2014, and by the US in Afghanistan in 2001 and Iraq in 2003. It is legitimate to question whether international law has any real relevance to the United States or other major powers in these circumstances,[5] recalling the words of Dean Acheson in the Cuban Missile Crisis of 1962, when he argued that the issue of the quarantine imposed by the US to prevent missiles from reaching Cuba from the Soviet Union was 'not a legal issue', given that the 'power, position and prestige of the United States had been challenged by another state; and law does not deal with such questions of ultimate power – power that comes close to the source of sovereignty'.[6]

This chapter sets up one of the central questions the book seeks to answer: whether, in these conditions, it is possible or indeed desirable to have a universal set of rules regarding international rights and wrongs of Cuba and the United States. Alternatively, are international laws so indeterminate and contradictory that they constantly oscillate between explanations for behaviour and attempts at controlling it?[7] This chapter, and the three that follow, range widely across issues of colonialism, self-determination, sovereignty, intervention, and international law and its enforcement, but these are the building blocks upon which the analysis in the book is built. Inevitably the opening chapters will throw up more questions than they answer, but the remainder of the book will be dedicated to trying to answer some of the most fundamental questions about international law, about its purpose and function – in simple terms to address that oft-heard lament – 'what is the point of international law?'.[8]

## 2.2  A bilateral history

Cuba was 'discovered' by Christopher Columbus. On 3 December 1492 Columbus described the scene in front of him – 'I climbed a mountain and saw a plain sown with *calabaza* and so many other vegetables that it was a

---

5  G. Simpson, *Great Powers and Outlaw States: Unequal Sovereigns in the International Legal Order* (Cambridge: Cambridge University Press, 2004).

6  D. Acheson, 'Response to Panel: The Cuban Quarantine – Implications for the Future', (1963) 14 *American Society of International Law Proceedings* 14–15.

7  M. Koskenniemi, 'The Role of Law in Collective Security', (1996) 17 *Michigan Journal of International Law* 455 at 489.

8  M. Koskenniemi, 'What is International Law For?' in M. Evans (ed.), *International Law* (3rd edn, Oxford: Oxford University Press, 2010) 32.

joy to behold. In the centre of the plain was a large village . . . houses looking like tents in a camp, without regular streets but one here and another there. Within they were clean and well-kept, with well-made furniture. All were of palm branches, beautifully constructed'.[9] It was not until 1511 that the Spanish conquest of Cuba began under Diego de Velásquez. Initial conflict between Spanish settlers and the indigenous population (Tainos) reduced the numbers of the latter significantly. The Spanish relied on the remaining Tainos for slave labour, until necessity forced them to bring in large numbers of black African slaves.[10] This was followed by a policy of increasing the proportion of white Spanish settlers, which continued after independence from Spain in 1902. By the 1930s Spanish immigration, including Fidel Castro's father Ángel, had led to the country being dominated by white Spanish, with the black component of the population being reduced to 30 per cent, and the indigenous Tainos to virtual extinction.[11]

Cuba remained a Spanish colony until 1898 when, after the Spanish/American war, Spain gave up title to it in the Treaty of Paris. Article I of the Treaty stated that:

> Spain relinquishes all claims of sovereignty over and title to Cuba. And as the island is, upon its evacuation by Spain, to be occupied by the United States, the United States will, so long as such occupation shall last, assume and discharge the obligations that may under international law result from the fact of its occupation, for the protection of life and property.[12]

Cuba was then subject to American occupation for four years until it gained independence in 1902. From this bare history, it would appear that the United States acted as liberator and, indeed, in the Cuban conflict of 1898 US troops fought alongside indigenous Cubans struggling for independence. The US military occupation was expressly stated to be temporary and only lasted for four years,[13] enough time to secure Cuba and to ensure it could stand alone as an independent state.

Another history shows that the main Cuban rebel forces (the Liberation Army), in a rebellion that had lasted intermittently for thirty years, had already

---

9 In D. Murphy, *The Island that Dared: Journeys in Cuba* (London: Eland, 2008) 89.

10 The population of the island in 1544 was 7,000, consisting of 5,000 Tainos, 800 black slaves and 660 Spanish settlers. By 1650 the population had only increased to 30,000, while the huge increase in sugar production and the slaves needed to achieve this meant that by 1842 the population had reached 1 million, 45 per cent of which were black slaves – R. Gott, *Cuba: A New History* (New Haven: Yale University Press, 2004) 20, 35, 46.

11 Gott (n.10), 6–7.

12 http://avalon.law.yale.edu/19th_century/sp1898.asp (accessed 14 May 2014).

13 Gott (n.10), 102.

partially defeated their brutal Spanish colonial masters by 1897.[14] It was fear
of an unfriendly government being set up by these forces that led the United
States to intervene as an imperial power not as a liberating one.[15] The Cuban
rebels 'watched bleakly from the sidelines as their victory was taken from
them'.[16] Indeed, the seeds of US intervention can be traced back to the 1820s
when Spain had withdrawn from the Latin American mainland and also from
Spanish Florida, but clung on to Cuba. It was at this point, with Florida
joining the United States, that the US realised that 'Cuba had drawn ever
closer' to its frontiers.[17] US President Monroe enunciated the Monroe Doctrine
in 1823, warning European powers against further colonisation upon Spanish
withdrawal, which meant that the US had 'put down markers in the 1820s
regarding its future interest in Cuba'.[18]

The occupation of the island by the US between 1898 and 1902 was to
'safeguard order, property, and privilege'.[19] Cubans only participated as
observers in the Treaty of Paris of 1898 that ended the war and, in 1902,
Cuban independence was granted by the US subject to a number of conditions
including a prohibition on alliances with any other country, a perpetual lease
of Guantánamo Bay, and a reservation allowing the United States to intervene
in Cuba (embodied within the US by the Platt Amendment of 1902, which
was incorporated as an annex to the Cuban constitution).[20] The US occupiers
had retained Spanish administrators, who continued in their positions after
independence, and whose presence was bolstered by an influx of US-educated
Cuban exiles and US citizens.[21]

In the light of these historical facts it is true to say that Cuban 'independence
was compromised'.[22] The influence of the Platt Amendment 'lasted long after
it was formally abrogated in 1934, and it continued to echo in the global
perceptions of the United States a century later, notably in the wording of
the Helms-Burton Act of 1996'.[23] A further US intervention in 1906 led
to a further three years of occupation (1906–1909) during which the Cuban
army was reorganised and re-equipped in order to improve security on the
island, and there were a number of US military interventions thereafter.[24]

---

14  Ibid., 74.
15  Pérez-Stable (n.1), 4.
16  Gott (n.10), 98.
17  Ibid., 57.
18  Ibid., 59.
19  Pérez-Stable (n.1), 37.
20  Gott (n.10), 111. Cuba retained 'ultimate sovereignty' over the Guantánamo naval base –
    see Agreement of the Lease to the United States of Lands in Cuba for Coaling and Naval
    Stations, 23 February 1903, US-Cuba T.S. No. 418.
21  Gott (n.10), 104–5.
22  Pérez-Stable (n.1), 4.
23  Gott (n.10), 110.
24  Pérez-Stable (n.1), 38: Gott (n.10), 111.

Nevertheless, 'continuous intervention did not beget stable government capable of maintaining order and defending foreign capital', rather it 'provoked growing nationalist demands'.[25] Although the Platt Amendment was repealed in 1934, Cuban political and economic dependence on the US remained.

Before the Cuban revolution of 1959 that brought Fidel Castro to power, the economic relationship between Cuba and the United States ensured that Cuba was dependent upon its vastly larger neighbour. Foreign, mainly US-based ownership of most of Cuba's natural wealth, principally sugar, meant that Cubans did not benefit at all from independence until the 1920s when they acquired majority ownership in the sugar industry, by which time profits were falling. By the 1950s sugar was still the most important export (mainly to the United States), but output remained at the same levels as the 1920s, while the population of Cuba had doubled in this period.[26] According to Pérez-Stable the 'centrality of sugar reinforced a vicious circle: without sugar there was no Cuba, and there was no sugar without the US market'.[27] It was only in 1959 that 'nearly one hundred years of struggle for national sovereignty' was ended.[28] However, that year marked the beginnings of an uneasy relationship with the Soviet Union. Without Soviet support the Cuban revolution would not have survived in the face of continued US hostility.[29]

Between 1902 and 1959, Cuban sovereignty was effectively 'mediated', meaning that Cuba was dependent both politically and economically upon the United States. 'Cuba before the revolution was rather unique in Latin America' in that the 'sugar monoculture appeared to cast Cuban society in the mould of a foreign-dominated, enclave economy'.[30] Although the years of US occupation were short, the US used them to ensure that the Cuban economy would remain dependent upon the United States, initially through ownership of the sugar industry but then, more importantly, through the openness of the Cuban economy to US capital and investment.[31] In the early years of the post-1902 new Cuban Republic 'almost everyone of importance and influence possessed direct experience of living in the United States'. By 1910, 60 per cent of rural properties were owned by US corporations and individuals.[32] Continued US influence ensured that successive Cuban governments did not challenge this relationship of subservience or attempt to change the nature of the economy by, for instance, moving it away from its dependency on sugar.

25  Pérez-Stable (n.1), 39.
26  Ibid., 5.
27  Ibid.
28  Ibid.
29  Ibid., 10.
30  Ibid., 14.
31  Ibid., 15–35. US influence on the sugar industry is traced back to the 1850s by which time the US already bought most of Cuba's sugar – Gott (n.10), 67.
32  Gott (n.10), 14–15.

Any moderate attempt to do this was met by US threats to reduce the amount of sugar imported by the US. Nonetheless, there was some evidence that between the end of the Second World War and the revolution of 1959 other sectors of the economy were developing – cattle, tourism, gambling and oil extraction – but again this was due to the inflow of US capital and expertise.[33]

## 2.3  Revolution as self-determination and self-defence

Before the US intervention in 1898, José Martí, a heroic figure in Cuban and Latin American revolutionary history, argued that Cuba should not only fight for freedom from Spain but should resist annexation by the United States, a growing world power which, he argued, saw Cuba as a 'desirable possession'.[34] In an early expression of that desire for self-determination he wrote in 1891 that the 'hands of every nation must remain free for the untrammelled development of the country, in accordance with its distinctive nature and with its individual elements'.[35] The Cuban nation struggled to achieve this even after its independence from Spain in 1898 and the ending of US occupation in 1902.

As a history of Cuba from 1902 to 1959 shows, Cuba was dependent upon the US, both politically and economically. Cuban sovereignty had not been established in the strong Westphalian sense of a state having complete independence from other states,[36] an independence which, if present, would have enabled the Cuban people to exercise their right to self-determination and follow their own political and economic path. Although elections were held in this period, they were typically corrupt and their outcomes were subject to US approval. The first President of Cuba, President Estrada, a Cuban exile and US citizen, was elected unopposed.[37] The last President before the revolution of 1959, General Batista, called elections in 1954 but he was unopposed and simply used the outcome to legitimate his rule.[38] By 1958 Batista's rule was coming under heavy pressure from an armed insurrection led by Fidel Castro that had started in a very small way on 26 July 1953. Castro was captured and put on trial in October 1953. He defended himself and his captured comrades 'basing his case on the illegality of the regime and the inherent right of the citizen to rebel against an illegal government'.[39]

---

33  Pérez-Stable (n.1), 15–35.
34  In Gott (n.10), 87.
35  Ibid., 84.
36  *Island of Palmas Case* (1928) 2 RIAA 829 at 838.
37  Gott (n.10), 113.
38  Pérez-Stable (n.1), 53.
39  Gott (n.10), 150.

Fidel Castro's speech at the Court of Appeals of Santiago de Cuba in October 1953 not only asserted the 'right of rebellion against tyranny',[40] but also pointed to the denial of self-determination incorporated into the Cuban constitution of the time:

> The Constitution is understood to be the basic and supreme law of the nation, to define the country's political structure, regulate the functioning of its government agencies, and determine the limits of their activities. It must be stable, enduring and, to a certain extent, inflexible. The Statutes fulfil none of these qualifications. To begin with, they harbour a monstrous, shameless, and brazen contradiction in regard to the most vital aspect of all: the integration of the Republican structure and the principle of national sovereignty. Article 1 reads: 'Cuba is a sovereign and independent State constituted as a democratic Republic.' Article 2 reads: 'Sovereignty resides in the will of the people, and all powers derive from this source.' But then comes Article 118, which reads: 'The President will be nominated by the Cabinet.' So it is not the people who choose the President, but rather the Cabinet. And who chooses the Cabinet? Article 120, section 13: 'The President will be authorized to nominate and reappoint the members of the Cabinet and to replace them when occasion arises.' So, after all, who nominates whom?[41]

After inviting the Court to: 'Condemn me. It does not matter. History will absolve me',[42] Castro was convicted and sentenced to fifteen years, although he was given an amnesty following Batista's unopposed election in 1954.[43] Castro and his followers returned from self-imposed exile in Mexico in a small motor yacht, the *Granma*, on 2 December 1956. Just over two years later he had orchestrated an increasingly effective guerrilla campaign that led to Batista fleeing the country.

The overthrow of General Batista by rebel forces on 1 January 1959 did not lead overnight to a Marxist dictatorship, the process was gradual, and even then fell short of the brutal, externally-imposed dictatorships of Eastern Europe. The period immediately after the revolution is described by Pérez-Stable:

> The overthrow of Batista brought radical nationalism to power, and Fidel Castro and the *rebeldes* owed allegiance only to *el pueblo cubano*. Over the next two years struggles between the *clases populares* and the *clases económicas*

---

40  F. Castro, *History Will Absolve Me: Speech at the Court of Appeals of Santiago de Cuba October 16, 1953* (Havana: Editora Política, 2002) 59.

41  Ibid., 55–6.

42  Ibid., 64.

43  Gott (n.10), 151.

as well as confrontations with the United States radicalized the revolution. Remembering 1898 [when the US started its occupation] and 1933 [when General Batista seized power], the revolutionaries of 1959 refused to compromise; instead, they mobilized the working class and the *clases populares* and forged a new consensus based on national sovereignty and social justice.[44]

The revolutionary government did not have a precise vision for the future, but the vast majority of the Cuban people were behind its vision for a truly independent Cuba in which the social injustices of the previous half-century would be addressed – 'their program was one of economic growth, more equitable distribution of wealth, honest government, due process of law, and the pursuit of national interests'.[45] The new leadership eschewed elections since these had been discredited as a method of securing genuine representative Cuban government in the past; instead it claimed, with justification, that it represented the 'new popular *conciencia*', and that this was the best way of securing democracy in Cuba.[46] To achieve this, however, power was initially centralised in the first cabinet, and was consolidated in the executive thereafter, driven by the need to seize control of the major means of production and, in part, by the need to strengthen national defence as counter-revolutionary activities increased.[47] Nevertheless, in the period 1959–60, '*el pueblo* and the government appeared to be one'.[48]

In the initial post-revolutionary period, 1959–60, the United States and its supporters in Cuba (the *clases económicas*), with a 'sudden appreciation of democracy' for Cuba, started to demand that elections be held immediately.[49] In September 1959, the Organisation of American States (OAS) seemed to rebuke Cuba and US intervention seemed imminent.[50] In these conditions, Castro's initial attempt to find a middle path between capitalism and Communism (which he labelled 'humanism') was abandoned in the face of increasing US hostility – 'had Cuba not been ninety miles from the United States, the revolution might have found that elusive middle ground'.[51] Centralisation of power – economic, political and military – was seen as essential to preserve the revolution and the independence of Cuba. US-owned assets and companies were being nationalised in 1959, and despite a visit by Castro to the United States in that year, the State Department and the CIA

44   Pérez-Stable (n.1), 60.
45   Ibid., 61–2.
46   Ibid., 66, 77.
47   Ibid., 66, 72.
48   Ibid., 74.
49   Ibid., 75.
50   Ibid., 76.
51   Ibid., 78.

decided that it was 'impossible to carry on friendly relations with the Castro government', and began to 'devise means to help bring about its overthrow and replacement by a government friendly to the United States'.[52]

A trade agreement between the Soviet Union and Cuba quickly followed, with nationalisations of American oil and other companies gathering pace. When the Land Reform Act came into force in June 1959, which basically restricted private land ownership to 1,000 acres, compensation was offered to foreign owners on the basis of the 'landowners' own assessments of value, as recorded on their tax forms over the years',[53] assessments which grossly underestimated their value but, in the context of Cuba's reclamation of its land from foreign ownership, had an inherent justice to them. In July 1960 Law 851 led to nationalisation of foreign corporations' assets, including the powerful Bacardi Company, and again compensation was offered on the same basis. 'Eventually most foreign companies (Mexican, Canadian, British, Swiss, French) accepted that Castroism had arrived to stay and took whatever was on offer, always calculated on the basis of taxes previously paid. To this day, however, the Bacardis and the US government have refused compensation on Cuba's terms'.[54]

The US response to the Land Reform Act of 1959 was in the form of a Note of Protest, which stated that the reform would have an adverse effect on the Cuban economy and that the compensation offered was inadequate and should, rather, take the form of 'prompt, adequate and effective compensation'.[55] This was a re-iteration of the famous Hull formula embodying a Western standard for a lawful expropriation of foreign property and assets. It was first formulated in 1940 by US Secretary of State Cordell Hull in a note to the Mexican government following its expropriation of US oil interests:

> the right to expropriate property is coupled with and conditioned on the obligation to make adequate, effective and prompt compensation. The legality of an expropriation is in fact dependent upon the observance of this requirement.[56]

As we shall see in later chapters, there is some debate about the level of compensation that would actually satisfy this standard, although the US was adamant that this was a long way from the Cuban government's standard. As shall be seen a failure to comply with the standards set in the Hull formula would, in principle, convert a lawful expropriation into an unlawful one,

---

52  Ibid., 79.
53  Murphy (n.9), 219.
54  Ibid.
55  Gott (n.10), 180.
56  3 Hackworth, *Digest of International Law*, 662.

requiring reparation either in the form of *restitutio in integrum* (returning the property or interests to the US) or the equivalent in damages (which would include loss of future profits).[57] Certainly Cuba, along with other developing countries, argued against this high tariff, contending that the standard should be a national one and not one set by international law, since states had sovereign right over their natural resources.

In 1962 international opinion settled uneasily on a standard for lawful expropriation between the US and Cuban positions, with the UN General Assembly declaring that, whereas a state had permanent sovereignty over its natural resources and, therefore, had a right to expropriate in order to assert that right, it had to be for public reasons and that appropriate compensation had to be paid.[58] Despite not being adopted by consensus (the vote was 87 to 2 with 12 abstentions), this resolution has been accepted as being the origin of a binding customary norm in a number of influential arbitrations.[59] The national treatment approach to expropriation advocated by the Non-Aligned Movement (NAM) of states within the UN, of which Cuba was a member and strong supporter, was embodied in a 1974 General Assembly Resolution (adopted by 120 votes to 6 with 10 abstentions),[60] but it is commonly asserted that Western states have managed to block the passage of this instance of soft law into a binding norm of customary international law.[61]

In January 1961 President Eisenhower severed diplomatic relations with Cuba. In April 1961, his successor, John F. Kennedy, dispatched a force of Cuban exiles to Cuba, expecting victory as happened in Guatemala in 1954, but the US had underestimated the strength of support for Castro and the military capabilities of his forces. The Bay of Pigs invasion was repelled and many of the exile force captured.[62] Although no US forces played a part in the invasion, the CIA organised the landings that were led by former officers in Batista's army. The effects of the failed invasion were catastrophic for the US, since it effectively helped Castro reinforce his hold over the country, and it also pushed him towards the Soviet camp as a means of ensuring Cuba's defence. It is noteworthy that Castro only declared that Cuba was a 'socialist' country immediately before the Bay of Pigs invasion and, only as a response to the invasion, was he willing to allow his country to be used as a military base for Soviet nuclear missiles under Soviet command and control.[63] The Bay

---

57  *Texaco v Libya* (1978) 17 ILM 1; *Amoco International Finance Corp v Iran* (1987) 15 Iran-USCTR 189.

58  UNGA Res 1803, 'Permanent Sovereignty over Natural Resources' (1962).

59  For example, *Texaco v Libya* (1978) 17 ILM 1 para 87; *Aminoil Case (Kuwait v American Independent Oil Co)* (1982) 21 ILM 976 para 143; *Amoco International Finance Corp v Iran* (n.57).

60  UNGA Res 3281 (1974), 'Charter of Economic Rights and Duties of States', para 2(c).

61  For example, *Texaco v Libya* (n.57), para 88.

62  Pérez-Stable (n.1), 80.

63  Gott (n.10), 200, 202.

of Pigs invasion was also a disaster for those Cubans inside and outside Cuba who wished for annexation by the US, who were henceforward seen as traitors by the vast majority of Cubans.[64] 150,000 Cubans left Cuba for the US in 1960–61.[65] Thereafter, low levels of departures were interspersed with the occasional mass exodus such as the Mariel boatlift, when 125,000 Cubans embarked on small boats in a six-month period in 1980.[66]

Pérez-Stable addresses the question of how a country so dependent upon the United States could manage to completely break that relationship of 'mediated sovereignty' – 'part of the answer was the centralization of power and the elimination of independent political activity. The cold-war provided the other part: an alliance with the Soviet Union'.[67]

> Fidel Castro and the *rebeldes* were committed to *Cuba libre*, and the United States had never encountered such determination from a Cuban government. Consolidating a nationalist revolution led Cuba to socialism, an alliance with the Soviet Union, and permanent hostility from the United States.[68]

Defence of Cuba from the United States became paramount for the revolutionary government necessitating a form of politics that was more akin to military discipline rather than one allowing for the development of political diversity and debate.[69] Richard Gott recalls a visit to Havana in 1963: '"Operation Mongoose", the US campaign to destabilise Cuba in the wake of the abortive Bay of Pigs invasion [of 1961], had recently been abandoned, but terrorist attacks against the island from exile groups in Miami were still frequent'.[70]

## 2.4 Missile crisis

The Soviet Union had itself contributed to massively heightening its proxy Cold War confrontation with the United States by using Cuba as a frontline and then by giving the 'world a collective heart attack by its intemperate decision to station nuclear missiles on the island'.[71] The US response, in the form of a military quarantine to prevent further missiles reaching Cuba, seemed a proportionate measure, although it was an action that was difficult to justify as self-defence, since there was no imminent attack threatened by Cuba or the Soviet Union.[72] Instead, the US based its argument on the fact

---

64  Ibid., 190–1.
65  Ibid., 212.
66  Ibid., 266.
67  Pérez-Stable (n.1), 80.
68  Ibid., 81.
69  Pérez-Stable (n.1), 81.
70  Gott (n.10), 2.
71  Ibid., 10.
72  Article 51 UN Charter. But see M.S. McDougal, 'The Soviet-Cuban Quarantine and Self-Defense', (1963) 57 *AJIL* 597 at 600.

that it obtained a resolution from the Council of the OAS, which recommended that member states:

> take all measures, individually and collectively, including the use of armed force, which they may deem necessary to ensure that the Government of Cuba cannot continue to receive from the Sino-Soviet powers military material and related supplies which may threaten the peace and security of the Continent and to prevent the missiles in Cuba with offensive capability from ever becoming an active threat to the peace and security of the Continent.[73]

Although the US Deputy Legal Adviser, Leonard Meeker, stated that this made the measure compatible with Chapter VIII of the UN Charter,[74] Article 53 of that Chapter clearly states that any enforcement action proposed by a regional organisation can only be taken with the authority of the Security Council and, of course, none such was forthcoming. Nevertheless, the US position was that the OAS resolutions gave the quarantine a clear legal basis. US Attorney General Robert Kennedy wrote that:

> It was the vote of the Organization of American States that gave us the legal basis for the quarantine. It changed our position from that of outlaw acting in violation of international law into a country acting in accordance with twenty allies protecting their position.[75]

In effect the US position was that, although its action in placing a forceful quarantine around Cuba was enforcement action, it was justified enforcement that did not breach the authorisation requirement of Article 53 of the UN Charter because that provision should be interpreted to allow regional enforcement action when the Security Council is silent on the matter – its silence should, in the circumstances, be construed as authorisation.[76]

In the UN, the US convened the Security Council and introduced a draft resolution that had little chance of being adopted.[77] It demanded the immediate dismantling and withdrawal from Cuba of all missiles and other offensive weapons to be overseen by UN observers. Only after affirmation of the removal of the missiles would the quarantine be lifted.[78] The Soviet Union countered with its own, equally uncompromising draft, which called for the

---

73  (1962) 47 US Dept. of State Bulletin 723.

74  (1963) 57 *AJIL* 515.

75  R. Kennedy, *Thirteen Days: A Memoir of the Cuban Missile Crisis* (New York: Norton, 1969) 121.

76  A. Chayes, *The Cuban Missile Crisis* (Oxford: Oxford University Press, 1974) 61.

77  UNSC 1022nd meeting (1962).

78  UN Doc S/5182 (1962).

immediate revocation of the decision to inspect ships bound for Cuba as well as an end to any kind of interference in the internal affairs of Cuba.[79] Although these polarised positions appeared to leave little prospect for resolution, they did overlap in one significant respect: they did call for negotiations to remove the threat to the peace. UN Secretary General U Thant used this common ground to send letters to both Khrushchev and Kennedy in which he called for the voluntary suspension of all arms shipments to Cuba in return for the temporary suspension of the quarantine.[80]

The Cuban Missile Crisis of 1962, like so many elements of Cuba's relationship with the US, seemed to be conducted outside of the parameters of international law.[81] The quarantine did prove effective in deterring further Soviet ships and, after a relatively brief but tense period, Khrushchev offered to withdraw the 'defensive' missiles placed on Cuba in order, he argued, to prevent another invasion, in return for a US promise not to invade the island.[82] As Gott relates: 'successive United States governments kept Kennedy's (never officially revealed) promise not to invade Cuba',[83] even though the US has shown a propensity for military intervention elsewhere in its own backyard – in the Dominican Republic (1965), Grenada (1983), and Panama (1989). Although minor forcible incidents continued, US attention turned to the economic embargo as the means of effecting change in Cuba. The Soviet defence guarantee was only withdrawn from Cuba in 1983,[84] and Soviet troops (about 7,000) were finally withdrawn from the island in 1991.[85]

## 2.5 Representative revolution?

Although reinforcing its grip over Cuba in order to be able to defend the island against US attacks and threats, the proclamations of the Cuban leadership claimed that the revolution of 1959, and the overwhelming support of the people for it, constituted self-determination, although that term was not the rallying cry used. Self-determination is the securing of independence of a people within a country from foreign domination or control (the external aspect), but then requires that the government is representative of the people (the internal aspect). Certainly the regime did not try to accommodate within it those who favoured the old regime or, indeed, annexation by the US. It is difficult to see how the revolutionary government could, since it was so opposed to domination by its northern neighbour. With this caveat in mind

79  UN Doc S/5187 (1962).
80  UN Doc S/5197 (1962).
81  Acheson (n.6).
82  Gott (n.10), 207.
83  Ibid., 208.
84  Ibid., 274.
85  Ibid., 286.

the revolutionary regime did appear to embody the will of the people, at least in the early years. In 1965, Fidel Castro declared that:

> We shall seek our own revolutionary institutions, our own new institutions, stemming from our conditions, from our idiosyncrasy, from our customs, from our own character, from our spirit, from our thought, from our creative imagination. We shall not imitate.[86]

In 1974, his brother Raúl Castro stated that:

> Even without representative institutions, our revolutionary state is and always was democratic. A state like ours which represents the interests of the working class, no matter what its form and structure, is more democratic than any other state in history.[87]

This rhetoric has continued; for example in 1986 an editorial in the newspaper *Granma*, the mouthpiece of the regime, stated that the revolution of 1959 'turned the people into sole owners of their wealth', above all the 'Revolution bestowed upon them, for the first time in their history, the conquest of their full dignity, *conciencia* of their power'.[88]

More recent exclamations of the government emphasise the attempted denial of Cuban self-determination by the United States' continued pressure for regime change. In a speech given to the UN's Human Rights Council, in presenting Cuba's national report, Cuban Minister of Foreign Affairs, Bruno Rodríguez Parrilla, stated on 1 May 2013 that:

> Persistent efforts on the part of the United States to impose a 'regime change' on Cuba are a serious violation of the nation's right to self-determination. These efforts have been unable to prevent the active, democratic and direct participation of its citizens in the construction of constitutional order, in government decisions and in the election of its authorities.[89]

The argument remains essentially that attempted interference in Cuba's internal affairs by the US justifies the Cuban regime's continuation in the (authoritarian) form that it has. Such claims require an examination, in later chapters, of the governmental structures of Cuba in terms of their representativeness of, and accountability to, the Cuban people. Furthermore,

---

86  In Pérez-Stable (n.1), 98.
87  Ibid., 121.
88  2 December 1986 in Pérez-Stable (n.1), 82.
89  Digital *Granma Internacional*, 3 May 2013 – www.granma.cu/ingles/news-i/3may-Speech-Bruno-Rodríguez.html (accessed 14 May 2014).

such analysis considers how these claims have fared before UN and OAS human rights bodies.

Certainly the United States has not accepted Cuban self-determination and 'after 1962 imposed a steep overhead by means of an embargo'.[90] The evidence is that from 1959 to 1965 the government of Fidel Castro and the people of Cuba were of one mind: '*las masas* followed Fidel without vacillations but with convictions. Fidel was a *maestro*: the people trusted him because he expressed their wishes and needs'.[91] Although there were elections to the National Assembly and there were attempts to increase democracy in other ways, the reality was that power was exercised by the executive, in particular power was in the hands of the President, so that after 1971, 'the working class bore the burden of legitimating socialism, but workers did not have the power to make national policies', so that the 'correct proletarian *conciencia* was to abide by party directives and charismatic authority'. In this way Cuban socialism seemed to be similar to that found in many other socialist states where the 'working class wielded power vicariously'.[92] Indeed, it could be argued that during the Cold War, Cuban dependence upon the Soviet Union, both economically and ideologically, undermined the revolutionaries' claims to embody the will of the Cuban people. Ironically, the Soviet Union's willingness to buy Cuban sugar from 1963 meant that the regime abandoned plans for diversification so that the 'Revolution, which had once sought to escape from the tyranny of sugar production, was now tied to it for the foreseeable future'.[93]

However, the authenticity of the social revolution in Cuba in 1959 meant that its form of government, combined with the people's belief in Fidel Castro, were sufficiently robust that the revolutionary government did not fall along with the regimes in Soviet satellite countries and within the Soviet Union itself in the period 1989–91. Increasingly, a growing number of Cuban people were 'acquiescing in public and dissenting in private', although outright dissent was punished.[94] The consequence of having a surviving post-Cold War Communist regime next to the world's remaining superpower was that the United States was even more determined to bring that regime down. But therein lies the paradox at the heart of the bilateral relationship between the United States and Cuba, the more independent (from the United States) Cuba becomes, the more the United States wants to intervene; but the more the United States attempts to intervene in the sovereign affairs of Cuba, the more it helps prolong a government that has lost most of its impetus except for its insistence on independence from the United States. In a sense

90  Pérez-Stable (n.1), 84.
91  Ibid., 99.
92  Ibid., 135.
93  Gott (n.10), 211.
94  Pérez-Stable (n.1), 209.

the self-determination of the Cuban people, begun in 1959, has not been allowed to be completely fulfilled because both the Cuban government and the United States have prevented it. The right of the Cuban people to self-determination has been denied by the Castro government entrenching its power by increasingly coercive means, and the United States has violated the principle of self-determination by continually intervening in the sovereign affairs of Cuba. If only the United States would let Cuba go?

## 2.6 Conclusion

There have been periods of *détente* between the United States and Cuba, though never full rapprochement. Under President Ford, State Department officials undertook secret negotiations with Cuba in 1975. Gott reports that the 'main issues for discussion were the same as always: the US trade embargo, compensation for Cuban losses attributable to the embargo and compensation for US properties nationalised in the early years' of the revolution'.[95] Other secondary issues revolved around the future of the US base at Guantánamo, the reunification of Cuban families, and the release of political prisoners. Further dialogue looked promising but was brought to an end by Cuban intervention in Angola.[96] President Jimmy Carter came to power in 1977 and made several gestures towards Cuba, including ending US reconnaissance flights over the island and reopening diplomatic relations but this was also unproductive due to Castro's involvement in Ethiopia in 1977 in support of the Mengistu regime, and the US failure to prevent terrorist groups sponsored by the exile community from carrying out attacks, most infamously the attack that destroyed a civilian aircraft killing all 73 people on board including the Cuban fencing team over Barbados in 1976.[97] Although by this time many US companies were keen to end the embargo, and most of those that had investments in Cuba in 1959 had long written off those losses, the US had adopted many laws requiring 'prompt, adequate and effective compensation' be paid by Cuba for its expropriations of US property and businesses, and was not prepared to drop these. Castro was also unwilling to make concessions at this stage, as the Cuban economy was successful due to its relationship with the Soviet Union.[98] Castro also tried to by-pass the US government by dealing with the exile community directly, trying to break the link to terrorist groups, leading to his release of several thousand political prisoners in 1978.[99]

History shows that the struggle for Cuban independence itself is dependent upon resolving the 'dispute' between the US and Cuba and in establishing a

95   Gott (n.10), 262.
96   Ibid.
97   Ibid., 261.
98   Ibid., 263.
99   Ibid., 265.

bilateral relationship between the two countries whereby each respects the other's sovereignty. Although this appears to be a straightforward prescription, the term 'dispute' barely touches upon the complexity of the relationship between the two countries. The history of Cuba's struggle and its dependence upon, and then rejection of the US, followed by its reliance on the USSR, brought its rejection of the US within the broader ideological struggle of the Cold War, during which fundamental legal principles such as non-intervention and sovereign equality (embodied in Article 2 of the UN Charter) were pushed to one side by power politics. Having set the scene, it is to these issues that we now turn in greater detail in the following chapters.

# 3 Colonialism, imperialism and pariah states

## 3.1 Introduction

Delving deeper into the complexity of the relationship between Cuba and the US, there are a series of relationships: first one best described as colonialism by the US, which then blurs into one of imperialism; and finally one of sovereign inequality whereby Cuba, according to the US at least, has limited sovereignty allowing the more powerful state to intervene in the weaker one. These phases reveal that Cuba's sovereignty is acquired incrementally and, even then, not completely, at least in the Westphalian sense of the term. Cuba's history is one of struggle for national sovereignty; sovereignty in the sense of independence from interference by other states, and sovereignty in the sense of freedom to choose its own destiny.

Antony Anghie's thesis is apposite to our analysis of the unfolding history of Cuba. Although Anghie mainly concentrates on the history and process of African independence, his analysis of colonialism and decolonisation is readily applicable to Cuba. Anghie writes that the 'acquisition of sovereignty by the Third World was an extraordinarily significant event; and yet, various limitations and disadvantages appeared to be somehow peculiarly connected with that sovereignty'.[1] Anghie deploys 'Third World' as a term for 'non-European societies and territories which were colonized from the sixteenth century onwards by European Empires, and which acquired political independence since the 1940s'.[2] Cuba's original colonial master, Spain, did not hand the country back to its people, but handed it over to the United States in 1898. It was the United States that gave Cuba its independence in 1902, but it was a limited and disadvantageous form of independence, making Anghie's analysis relevant. Although only occupying Cuba for a short period of time, the United States took on the mantel of colonial master and granted independence with strings attached.

---

1 A. Anghie, *Imperialism, Sovereignty and the Making of International Law* (Oxford: Oxford University Press, 2004) 2.
2 Ibid., 3.

The role of international law in this history will be explored throughout the book, but the core ideas of statehood, independence, sovereignty and self-determination, the bread-and-butter of international law, have a darker provenance than assumed in modern literature. As made clear by Sundhya Pahuja: 'The ambivalence of international law's role in the story of decolonisation points to the complex duality of international law being explored . . .: its capacity to be both regulatory and emancipatory, both imperial and anti-imperial.'[3]

The Cuban struggle for national liberation, first from Spain and then the United States, was achieved in 1959, but was arguably then again compromised by its close alliance with the Soviet Union. International law on decolonisation did not start to take shape until the early 1960s and then only within certain colonially defined boundaries. At the time of Cuban struggle against Spain, international law supported colonialism. During the period of US domination (1898–1959), international law continued to support colonialism and imperialism in many different forms, from direct occupation and governance, to looser structures of domination through agreements with local rulers.[4] Even the UN Charter of 1945 was ambivalent on decolonisation, despite its general appeals to self-determination; and it was only in 1960, when the tide of history had turned against exhausted colonial powers, that the UN General Assembly clearly advocated decolonisation. The Cuban struggle therefore straddled the development of modern international law: it cannot be said that Cuba benefited from its principles but it may have helped to shape the corpus of law away from supporting imperialism to, at least, being able to criticise and, in limited cases, control aspects of it. Cuba's struggle reflects a struggle for the legitimacy as well as relevance of international law.

## 3.2 Colonialism

Despite its appearance of a country free from the opprobrium of having been a colonial power, the US, albeit briefly, was a second generation colonial power after it had defeated Spain in a war. The conflict was mainly about the independence of Cuba, although it was fought in both the Caribbean and the Pacific. Under the Treaty of Paris 1898, the US acquired title to Puerto Rico and the Philippines as well as occupier's rights over Cuba. Under Articles II and III of the Treaty, Spain 'ceded' title to the US, while under Article I

---

3  S. Pahuja, *Decolonising International Law: Development, Economic Growth and the Politics of Universality* (Cambridge: Cambridge University Press, 2011) 45.

4  M. Craven, 'Statehood, Self-Determination, and Recognition' in M. Evans (ed.), *International Law* (3rd edn, Oxford: Oxford University Press, 2010) 203 at 212. For a compelling account of the British form of imperialism see Z.B. Ghandour, *A Discourse on Domination in Mandate Palestine* (London: Routledge, 2010).

Spain relinquished 'all claim of sovereignty over and title to Cuba', which would be occupied by the US exercising commensurate powers under international law.

That the US was prepared to assert its title, as a neo-colonial power, over the Philippines was evidenced by the arguments it put forward in the *Island of Palmas Case* of 1928. This was an arbitration between the Netherlands and the US before Judge Huber of the Permanent Court of Arbitration.[5] Although a dispute over a small island, the case has played a pivotal role in shaping international law on how title to territory was acquired by colonial powers under international law. The case remains a central feature of chapters on 'territory' found in most standard textbooks on international law. Disembodied from its historical context students study the methods of acquiring territory as they would a chapter on transferring title to a house in an equivalent text on the law of property.

Although the US lost the case, it was prepared to dispute title to territory (the remote Island of Palmas in the Pacific), on the basis that the US had acquired the island from Spain under the Treaty of Paris of 1898, which brought an end to the Spanish–American War. Under that treaty, Spain had ceded the Philippines to the United States, and the United States believed that the island in question was included in the depiction of the extent of the Philippine Islands in Article III of the Treaty. The island was of little economic or strategic importance, and had a population of less than a thousand, but both the United States and the Netherlands disputed sovereignty.

The judgment of Arbitrator Huber was a masterful treatment of the classical modes of acquiring territory under international law. In essence the US relied on cession from Spain, which itself had acquired the territory by discovery of *terra nullius* (land belonging to no one); and the Dutch relied on prescription, which was the acquisition of territory by continuous and peaceful display of state authority (the early part of which was exercised by the Dutch East India Company, whose acts, according to Huber were entirely assimilated to the Netherlands itself) from 1700 to 1906 (when the dispute arose). The Spanish/US claim to title was based on discovery which, due to its inchoate nature, did not prevail against one derived from a peaceful and continuous display of sovereignty.

The judgment was also very clear in its rationalisation of colonialism, although the term was not used by the arbitrator, his preference being for 'sovereignty'. Sovereignty, according to Huber, signified 'independence in regard to a portion of the globe', where a colonial power exercised the functions of a state to the exclusion of any other state. Unsurprisingly, both states agreed that 'international law underwent profound modifications between the end of the Middle Ages and the end of the nineteenth century, as regards the

5 (1928) 2 RIAA 829.

rights of discovery and acquisition of uninhabited regions or regions inhabited by savages or semi-civilised peoples'. Both parties to the dispute also agreed that a 'juridical fact must be appreciated in the light of the law contemporary with it, and not of the law in force at the time when a dispute in regard to it arises or falls to be settled'. This doctrine of inter-temporal law signifies that although the norms of international law might have changed over the years (eventually in the UN-era to prohibit colonialism), territory gained in the period 1600 onwards was validly acquired so long as the Roman Law-derived rules on acquisition were complied with.[6] The reality is that those Roman legal concepts were adapted by colonial powers to legitimate their conquest of large portions of the globe.

In summary, the law created by colonial powers allowed for the acquisition of territory, and any subsequent dispute was to be judged by that very same law. The consolidation of this customary practice over several hundred years meant that by the nineteenth century, to use Huber's phrase, the number of 'territories without master had become relatively few'. The use of the term 'master' by Huber is apposite given that he also applied modes of acquisition derived from a legal system — Roman Law — that also recognised that property could be acquired over people. In Roman Law there were no universal rights, since slaves had none but their owners had many. In the sixteenth century, Francisco de Vitoria (a Spanish theologian whose influence on international law was profound at the time), despite being portrayed as 'brave champion of the rights of Indians at the time',[7] accepted that there was no universal international law that applied to colonial powers and 'uncivilised' peoples/territories alike.[8] This meant that Spain as a sovereign power could acquire rights over territory (and peoples), while the indigenous peoples had no right to resist them. Indeed, if they did the Spaniards could 'make war on the Indians, no longer as on innocent folk, but as against foresworn enemies and may enforce against them all right of war, despoiling them of their goods, reducing them to captivity, deposing their former lords and setting up new ones'.[9]

The laws of war, which restricted the savagery of armed conflict between civilised states, did not apply to wars waged by civilised states against peoples resisting colonialism. According to the German author, Henrich von Treitschke, writing towards the end of the nineteenth century regarding German colonies in Africa:

6  J. Crawford, *Brownlie's Principles of Public International Law* (8th edn, Oxford University Press, 2012) 220–36.
7  Anghie (n.1), 28.
8  M. Craven, 'Colonialism and Domination' in B. Fassbender and A. Peters (eds), *The History of International Law* (Oxford: Oxford University Press, 2012) 862 at 868.
9  F. de Vitoria, *De Indis at de Ivre Belli Relectiones* (Ernest Nys ed., John Pawley Bate trans., Washington DC, Carnegie Institution of Washington, 1917) 155.

It is mere mockery, however, to apply these principles [of international law] to warfare against savages. A Negro tribe must be punished by the burning of their villages, for it is the only kind of example which will avail.[10]

Cuba was little different from other Spanish colonies in this respect, with well-documented massacres of the indigenous Tainos in the early part of the sixteenth century, and not only of those who fought the conquistadors.[11] Although de Vitoria justified this combination of conquest, enslavement and settlement as a form of natural law, it was a normative system derived from European traditions and religion, and exported to non-European states.[12] In effect, the international customary rules on territory, as accurately summarised by Huber in the *Island of Palmas Case*, allowed 'civilised' states to acquire property rights over 'savages and semi-civilised peoples' and their lands.

In effect, nineteenth-century positivist legal doctrine excluded the 'uncivilised' peoples of the world from the protection of international law.[13] Exploitation, under the guise of paternalism and protection, was in the hands of colonial states. Henry Wheaton (an American jurist and diplomat) stated in 1866 that the law of nations 'with slight exceptions, has always been and still is, limited to the civilised and Christian people of Europe or to those of European origin'.[14] The distinction between civilised/sovereign states and uncivilised/non-sovereign peoples was obvious to the jurists of the time. Thomas Lawrence (a British international lawyer), writing in 1895, declared that it 'would be absurd to . . . require the dwarfs of the central African forest to receive a permanent diplomatic mission'.[15] Such peoples lacked international legal personality as well as the attributes of sovereign statehood (often, but not always, evidenced by their lack of permanent control over territory).

Clearly the norms of international law in this era reflected the power politics of the day, with the dominant and aggressive form of the state imposing its will over areas of the globe that neither matched its form, nor could resist its power. Sometimes European states simply colonised a territory and its inhabitants by conquest, occupation, cession or prescription or, indeed, by securing the agreement of the local leaders, thereby assimilating them into their empires by asserting sovereignty over them. Later in the nineteenth century European states developed more of a civilising form of empire in the shape of protectorates where control was exercised over the territory but not

---

10 H. von Treitschke, *Politics* (Hans Kohn ed., 1963) 300–1.
11 R. Gott, *Cuba: A New History* (New Haven, CT: Yale University Press, 2004) 9, 13.
12 Anghie (n.1), 19–22.
13 Ibid., 39.
14 H. Wheaton, *Elements of International Law* (Boston, MA: Little, Brown and Co, 1866) 15.
15 T. Lawrence, *The Principles of International Law* (Boston, MA: D.C. Heath, 1895) 58.

formal sovereignty.[16] Colonialism blurred into imperialism, or as described by Matthew Craven, *dominium* became *imperium*:

> Colonialism was not just about acquiring things as property, but about turning things into property. If, originally, *dominium* and *imperium* lacked a decisive point of differentiation, not only were they later set apart, but the rationality of *imperium* was increasingly organized around the idea of establishing the conditions for the enjoyment of private property and exchange.[17]

Interestingly by the time of the Berlin Conference of 1884–5 the debate about the basis upon which the division of Africa by European states would occur centred on gaining the consent of local leaders, thereby purporting to bring the division of Africa within the normative (consensual) framework of international law, albeit in a completely self-serving and distorted way. Having said this, any treaties with local leaders prior to the conference were dismissed as possible evidence that such leaders could cede sovereignty by means of treaty, since they were 'too primitive to understand the concept of sovereignty';[18] and the conference itself did not include any African representatives. The result of this was 'to transform Africa into a conceptual *terra nullius*: as such, only dealings with European states with respect to those territories could have decisive legal effect'.[19]

It was the American representative at Berlin, John A. Kasson, who argued for the 'recognition of the right of native tribes to dispose freely of themselves and of their hereditary title'. Mr Kasson went on to say that 'in conformity with this principle my government would gladly adhere to a more extended rule, to be based on a principle which should aim at the voluntary consent of the natives whose country is taken possession of, in all cases where they had not provoked the aggression'.[20] Although this view was not officially adopted, Anghie writes that 'subsequent practice suggests that to the extent that *any* remotely legal explanation could be given to the partition of Africa, it was based on his proposal';[21] though the 'consent' of the local people did not require a genuine act of self-determination, simply formal assent to a treaty given in the face of overwhelming power and superiority. It must not be forgotten that at the time international law recognised treaties of cession (such as the Treaty of Paris discussed above) between Western states imposed by

---

16  Anghie (n.1), 67–90; citing L. Oppenheim, *International Law: A Treatise* (2nd edn, London: Longmans, 1912) 285–6.
17  Craven (n.8), 888.
18  Anghie (n.1), 91.
19  Ibid.
20  Ibid., 93.
21  Ibid., 95.

the victorious power over the vanquished sovereign; it would have little problem in accepting treaties extracted from local leaders by colonial powers. While treaties of cession were acts between two sovereigns with full international legal personality, treaties with local African leaders were agreed between a full sovereign state and an entity recognised only for the purpose of the agreement. A similar approach is found in modern peace agreements, which purport to bind non-state parties to them, thereby according them limited legal personality just for that purpose.[22] Thus, once the consent of the local leaders was given, since it was not a sovereign act, any attempted retraction of that consent by local leaders would not 'restore' the status quo that existed before colonisation. Colonisation thus changed the face of Africa and other areas of the globe permanently.

The Berlin Conference did mark the formal recognition that with colonies and empires came responsibilities; Article 6 of the General Act of 1885 stated that:

> all the Powers exercising sovereign rights or influence in the aforementioned territories . . . bind themselves to watch over the preservation of the native tribes, and to care for the improvement of the conditions of their moral and material well-being, and to help in suppressing slavery.

Unfortunately, such rhetoric did not match reality, evidenced by the atrocious acts committed under the personal sovereignty exercised by King Leopold II of the Belgians over the Congo Free State (the creation of which was one of the outcomes of the Berlin Conference);[23] nor did it disguise the fact that increasing trade was one of the main motivations for empire. The civilising mission was continued in the League of Nations' mandate system created in 1919, though this only applied to the colonies of the nations defeated in the First World War. Britain's empire, for instance, remained largely untouched.

## 3.3 Imperialism

Anghie's compelling thesis is that sovereignty in the Westphalian sense was not simply extended from European states to newly decolonised states, rather colonialism helped to shape a new form of sovereignty for this new wave of independent states, one that is 'rendered uniquely vulnerable and dependent by international law'.[24] He mentions the rules regulating the expropriation of foreign property as one form in which international law enabled the imperial

---

22  S. Sheeran, 'International Law, Peace Agreements and Self-Determination: The Case of the Sudan', (2011) 60 *ICLQ* 423.

23  Anghie (n.1), 97.

24  Ibid., 6.

hold over a newly dependent country to be maintained.[25] Those rules, as we shall see, purported to restrict the rights of the newly independent state to (re)-claim sovereignty over its natural resources, more broadly its economic future. Thus, 'colonialism' as a form of acquiring territory gave way to 'imperialism' as a form of exercising empire over newly decolonised (and ultimately non-liberal) states.[26] The colonial period under which Spain (for many centuries), and the US (for very brief periods of occupation, 1898–1902 and 1906–9) exercised authority over Cuba, gave way to a period (1902–59) of imperial dominance by the US, and dependence of a 'sovereign' Cuba.

Richard Gott analyses the period of Cuban history from 1902 to 1921, during which there were a number of disputed and fraudulent elections, in the following terms:

> American military interventions in Cuba in 1906, 1912 and 1917 had propped up unstable and insecure governments to maintain peace and security. Crowder's intervention in 1921 [to enforce a guarantee for a large loan from US banks following a collapse in sugar prices] was of a new and different order, more directly concerned with the protection of US investments and loans during a difficult period. Cuba had become a significant producer of immense wealth, in whose activities American companies and individuals were deeply involved. Bankers and traders, mill and plantation owners, railroad operators and simple investors, all looked to the United States to protect their interests, Cuba had become a [US] colony in all but name.[27]

The dictatorships of President Machado and then General Batista continued to ensure US domination.[28] The Cuban revolution of 1959 threw off US shackles but led to a period that extends up to the present day, during which the US agitated against the Cuban revolutionary regime, while the Cuban regime fell into a dogmatic, inflexible form of Soviet-influenced governance, as a way of protection against American imperialism.

Anghie questions whether the advent of the United Nations, which endorsed decolonisation in 1960, led to a truly universal international law applicable to Western developed countries and developing states alike. It appears that established sovereign states had a change of heart after the Second World War so that international legal doctrines of decolonisation and self-determination replaced doctrines of *terra nullius* and acquisition of territory. However, Anghie argues that this has not resulted in a truly universal international law. He argues that the relationship between liberal states

---

25  Ibid., 8.
26  Ibid., 11.
27  Gott (n.11), 129.
28  Ibid., 142.

(as the continuation of the sovereign states of the nineteenth century) and non-liberal states (formerly non-sovereign and colonised entities) in the twenty-first century meant that the structures of modern international law resemble those of the late nineteenth century.[29] Liberalism in the twenty-first century is a leitmotif for both universalising human rights and democracy, and for liberalising trade, so that non-liberal states come under pressure to change their form to become liberal states. Human rights law is a vehicle for pushing 'good governance' in developing states, a new form of the 'civilising' mission.[30] That support for good governance was not motivated out of concern for the peoples of developing countries but out of a desire to 'impose "universal standards" that essentially further . . . European/Western interests'.[31] The result was that a newly independent state 'never possessed the absolute power over its own territory and people that was exercised by the nineteenth-century European state'.[32] In other words, newly independent states never acquired Westphalian sovereignty in the sense of independence externally and exclusive competence internally.[33]

While the strong anti-colonial origins of the United States restricted its colonial ambitions in the late nineteenth and early twentieth centuries, it furthered its imperial ambitions by aggressively advocating and coercing states towards becoming liberal states. More recently, it (along with the UK) invaded Iraq in 2003 not to conquer it, but to lead it to better government and enable its people to realise their right to self-determination along Western democratic lines. It is no coincidence, however, that the invasion and subsequent occupation of Iraq led to the economic dominance of Iraq's natural resources by Western companies. Iraq in the period 2003–5 has been described as the 'first contractors' war'.[34] Economic domination very much reflected the approach taken by the US after the Spanish–American War of 1898, which led to the occupation of Cuba, and the promotion of American-subservient, self-government,[35] in which the economy was dominated by US companies and US citizens.

From the end of US occupation in 1902 until the revolution of 1959 Cuba's independence was compromised due to its dependence on the United States.

---

29  Anghie (n. 1), 113.
30  Ibid., 248–9.
31  Ibid., 253.
32  Ibid., 255.
33  A. Anghie, 'Basic Principles of International Law: A Historical Perspective' in B. Cali (ed.), *International Law for International Relations* (Oxford: Oxford University Press, 2010) 46 at 53. In fact as Anghie points out the Peace of Westphalia of 1648, the starting point of modern sovereign states, contained provisions protecting religious minorities within states.
34  A. Stanger, *One Nation Under Contract: The Outsourcing of American Power and the Future of Foreign Policy* (New Haven, CT: Yale University Press, 2009) 99.
35  Anghie (n.1), 280–5; Gott (n.11), 9.

The United States acted as an imperial or neo-colonial power over Cuba in this period. According to the Ghanaian leader, Kwame Nkrumah, the 'essence of neo-colonialism is that the State which is subject to it is, in theory, independent and has all the outward trappings of international sovereignty. In reality its economic system and thus political policy is directed from the outside'.[36] There can be little doubt that this describes the relationship between the United States and Cuba from 1902 to 1959. Although the United States generally eschewed direct colonialism, its method of establishing domination was through achieving overwhelming economic and political influence on states, which resulted in dependence. This was illustrated in the debate about the possession of German and Turkish territories after the First World War. While the US was opposed to becoming a mandatory power in 1919, 'nevertheless, it was implacable in asserting its economic interests by insisting that the "open door policy" be implemented in all mandated territories'.[37]

After 1959, the Non-Aligned Movement of states (of which Cuba became a leading light) was caught between the ideological, economic, and physical (albeit indirect) confrontation between the superpowers, giving those states some choice, although many came under the influence of one camp or another. The choices of Non-Aligned states were limited, evidenced by Fidel Castro's movement from a middle way between the United States and capitalism on the one hand and the Soviet Union and Communism on the other, towards the latter in the face of American hostility. Cuba refused to accept that it came under the American sphere of influence, opting for membership of the opposing camp in order to try and ensure its independence from the United States. Arguably, in so doing, it became dependent upon the Soviet Union,[38] although its distance from the Soviet Union and the fact of the continuation of the Cuban Communist regime after the collapse of the Soviet Union, both suggest that it had retained its independence during its period of Soviet dependence in a more robust way than during the period of American hegemony.

With the end of the Cold War liberal states have promoted democracy and human rights in a selective way in relation to non-liberal states such as Cuba, but not in relation to allies such as Saudi Arabia. Cuba's refusal to bend has led to it being labelled a 'pariah state' by the United States, an issue we will return to when looking at Gerry Simpson's thesis towards the end of this chapter, and again in Chapter 5. Cuba maintained its independence after 1959 more robustly than many other developing and newly decolonised states that

---

36  Cited in J.C. Young, *Postcolonialism: An Historical Introduction* (Oxford: Blackwell, 2001) 46.
37  Anghie (n.1), 143.
38  M. Pérez-Stable, *The Cuban Revolution: Origins, Course and Legacy* (2nd edn, Oxford: Oxford University Press, 1999) 148.

were inevitably disappointed by the lack of real economic and political power that the 'formal acquisition of sovereignty and equality' delivered.[39]

## 3.4  A new international economic order

Newly independent states were not supine in the face of American and Soviet imperial ambitions during the Cold War. Such states used the only real power they had, equality in voting power in the UN General Assembly, to try to change the rules of international law in order to produce a New International Economic Order. As seen in Chapter 2, developing states like Cuba argued that they should only pay compensation as required by national law when nationalising and expropriating foreign property. Developing countries argued that they should not pay full compensation for a lawful expropriation or damages for an unlawful expropriation as required by the rules of international law shaped in the colonial period,[40] in order that they could reclaim sovereignty over their own natural resources without bankrupting themselves. Developed states and their corporations, on the other hand, wanted to continue their domination over the resources and economies of developing countries by making it very difficult for developing countries to nationalise their oil or extraction industries, or expropriate foreign owned hotels etc.

Latin American countries, which had achieved independence earlier than African or Asian states, were at the forefront of this challenge to the established order. Latin American governments argued that foreign companies should not be protected by some sort of international minimum standard, but should be subject to national law, and be treated the same as indigenous companies and nationals. Indeed, newly independent Latin American states, in the early twentieth century, often included a so-called Calvo clause in contracts between governments and foreign companies or nationals. Such clauses provided that foreigners could only rely on local law and remedies to access justice. Such an approach had originally been advocated by the Argentinian writer, Carlos Calvo in 1896.[41] The validity of such clauses was accepted by a US–Mexican Claims Commission in the case of *North American Dredging Company v Mexico* arbitrated in 1926,[42] but such clauses did not take hold as foreign investors and their governments (exercising their right of diplomatic protection for their nationals and companies) sought the protection of international law.

In many respects developing countries failed to change international law. Although they helped to establish the principle that states had sovereignty

---

39  Anghie (n.1), 199.
40  Exemplified in the case before the Permanent Court of International Justice – *Factory at Chorsow*, (1928) PCIJ Series A, No. 17, 48.
41  C. Calvo, *Le Droit International* (5th ed., 1896) vol. 3, s. 1276.
42  (1926) 4 RIAA 26.

over their natural resources,[43] they failed to persuade developed/investor states they should not have to pay a high price for achieving that when, as in most cases, their natural resources were effectively subject to foreign ownership. Developing countries would have to become heavily indebted if they wanted to regain economic sovereignty and keep within the bounds of international law. Although international law has arguably moved away from the requirements of full compensation for expropriation of foreign owned assets, the current standard of 'appropriate' compensation remains disputed although it is clearly an international standard rather than a national one and, therefore, did not help the newly decolonised countries of the 1960s.[44] When the General Assembly introduced the idea of 'appropriate' compensation in 1962,[45] the US expressly stated that it understood this as incorporating the international minimum standard of the Hull Formula of prompt, adequate and effective compensation.[46]

Indeed, in place of public international law governing expropriation, modern international law protects foreign investors in developing countries by the shaping of a complex web of a new form of foreign investment law, governing contracts made between the governments of developing countries and private foreign investors.[47] Such contracts are deemed to be 'internationalised' and, therefore, not subject to the national law of the host state, but are subject to international rules derived from public international law,[48] thus having the opposite effect to the Calvo clause that was popular in Latin America in the early twentieth century. Subjecting such contracts to international legal principles such as *pacta sunt servanda* severely restricts the host governments' sovereign rights to take measures to protect the interests of the country and its people, and thereby contributing to their 'economic powerlessness'.[49] As Anghie states:

> The old international law of conquest creates the inequalities that the new international law of contracts perpetuates, legalises and substantiates when it 'neutrally' enforces the agreements, however one-sided, entered into by sovereign Third World states. It is in this way that the 'old' international law of imperialism, based on conquest, is connected with the new international law of imperialism, based on contract.[50]

---

43  UNGA Res 1803 (1962), 'Permanent Sovereignty over Natural Resources'.
44  *Aminoil Case* (1982) 21 ILM 976.
45  UNGA Res 1803 (n.43).
46  UN Doc A/C.2/SR 835, para 10 (1962).
47  Anghie (n.1), 223. See further Pahuja (n.3), 95–171.
48  *Texaco v Libya* (1978) 53 ILR 389 at 455.
49  Anghie (n.1), 233, 241.
50  Ibid.

In 1959 Cuba expropriated US property without paying the compensation demanded by the US, in effect adopting a national approach to expropriation and compensation and thereby breaching established, though contested, international rules governing expropriation but, in so doing, asserted its independence from the United States. The on-going dispute about Cuban expropriation of American-owned assets will be examined further in a later chapter.

## 3.5 Independence and external self-determination

In the post-colonial era, sovereignty and sovereign equality are closely related to the independence of states and self-determination of peoples. Sovereign independence from colonial or other forms of domination is an expression, in international law, of the exercise of the right to external self-determination by a people in a hitherto dominated or occupied territory or state.[51] The independence of a state means that under international law, at least, it is equal to other states no matter how powerful. Historically, however, self-determination was a political argument and value that helped consolidate the statehood of European countries and the USA in the eighteenth and nineteenth centuries. Although US President Woodrow Wilson deployed self-determination in his Fourteen Points at the end of the First World War, it is inaccurate to view the League of Nations' Covenant of 1919 as a significant development for self-determination as a legal principle.[52]

President Wilson's Fourteen Points were not included in the Covenant, a treaty that very much reflected the British view of Empire. For example, Article 1(2) allowed 'any fully self-governing state, dominion or colony' to become a member of the League if its admission was agreed to by two-thirds of the Assembly. Member states of the League were mainly European and South American states including Cuba as one of the founding members of the League. In the Assembly these states did allow British India, still part of the British Empire, to join, but Indian representatives reflected the British view.[53] Although formally an independent state in this period, Cuba was dependent upon the US, and thus the Cuban representatives in the League period did not carve out a Cuban foreign policy even though the US refused to join the League.[54] While India was dependent upon the UK through the

---

51 UNGA Res 1514 (1960), 'Declaration on the Granting of Independence to Colonial Territories or Peoples', para 5.
52 See Aaland Islands Commission, League of Nations Official Journal, Special Supp. No. 3 (1920) 3.
53 D. Hunter-Miller, *The Drafting of the Covenant Volume I* (London: Putnams, 1928) 261.
54 P. Kennedy, *The Parliament of Man: The Past, Present and Future of the United Nations* (London: HarperCollins, 2006) 13.

medium of empire, Cuba was dependent upon the US through the medium of imperialism.

In the League of Nations, those territories that had belonged to the defeated states that were not colonised by the victorious allies were placed under a mandate system, which in the terms of the Covenant meant that the 'tutelage of such peoples should be entrusted to the advanced nations', and that the 'development and well being of such peoples form a sacred trust of civilisation'.[55] It was not envisaged that such development and tutelage would inevitably lead to an independent state, though of the fifteen territories placed under a League mandate; all but one achieved self-government (mainly through independence) either under the League's Mandate system or afterwards under the UN's Trusteeship system. The one exception is Palestine, so that the Palestinians' (still unrealised) legal right to self-determination dates back to the 1922 mandate, when Britain was the mandatory power.[56]

In limited ways the League period witnessed the beginnings of a right for certain dependent peoples to self-determination, alongside the rights of minorities within established states. But on a more general level self-determination was a political device not a legal right. The UN period witnessed the legal right of self-determination extending beyond certain dependent peoples to all colonial peoples (the UN Trusteeship system replaced the remaining League mandates, while Chapter XI of the UN Charter on Non-Self-Governing Territories applied to all colonies). The general references of the UN Charter to self-determination in Articles 1 and 55 were given some content by Article 73, which provided that member states administering dependent territories should not only respect the culture of the dependent peoples but should develop self-government taking account of the political aspirations of the peoples. This was deliberately unclear as to whether a dependent people had the right to independence.

Portugal, Spain and France claimed that their colonies were part of their metropolitan territories. In response, the General Assembly of the UN, which by 1960, had ceased to be dominated by colonial powers, adopted Resolution 1514, which took the form of a 'declaration' on the granting of independence to colonial countries and peoples. This declaration made it clear that self-determination not only extended to any form of 'blue-water' colonisation, but more broadly declared that 'the subjection of peoples to alien subjugation, domination and exploitation constitutes a denial of fundamental human rights', and 'is contrary to the Charter of the United Nations . . .'. Further, it provided that 'all peoples have the right to self-determination; by virtue of the right they freely determine their political status and freely pursue their economic, social and cultural development'. According to the Declaration,

---

55  Article 22 League of Nations Covenant, 1919.
56  J. Crawford, 'The Right to Self-Determination in International Law: Its Development and Future' in P. Alston (ed.), *People's Rights* (Oxford: Oxford University Press, 2001) 7.

the inadequacy of political, economic, social or educational preparedness could not serve as a pretext for delaying independence. While those provisions can be read quite widely, the declaration then made it clear that it was concentrated on colonial and trust territories by stating that 'immediate steps shall be taken, in Trust and Non-Self-Governing Territories or all other territories that have not yet attained independence, to transfer all powers to the peoples of those territories, without any conditions or reservation, in accordance with their freely expressed will and desire'. The Declaration then made it clear that none of its provisions should be interpreted as allowing the 'partial or total disruption of the national unity and the territorial integrity of a country'. While the earlier part of the resolution could be seen as stretching self-determination beyond the colonial context, the later part is in essence a reassertion of the principle of *uti possidetis*, which resulted in colonial 'administrative boundaries being transformed in the full sense of the term'.[57] In effect the carve-up of Latin America, Africa, Asia and other regions of the world that occurred during the period of colonisation shaped the world of states in the modern period as the principles of international law were adapted to allow for independence within existing colonial boundaries and frontiers.

It is important to realise that self-determination did not simply give decolonising territories the right to political independence: it gave them a right to economic independence, further evidenced by the 1962 UN General Assembly Declaration on Permanent Sovereignty over Natural Resources, which stated that 'the rights of peoples and nations to permanent sovereignty over natural wealth and resources must be exercised in the interest of their national development and of the well being of the people of the State concerned'. The 1962 Declaration, however, protected Western interests by including within it a duty to pay 'appropriate' compensation.[58] When developing states (including Cuba) tried to change the status quo by arguing for a new international economic order primarily by adopting by majority vote the Charter of Economic Rights and Duties of States in 1974,[59] which applied a national standard to issues of compensation, Western states (including the US) not only voted against but were largely successful in preventing this approach from becoming customary international law.[60]

The entrenchment of the principle of self-determination as a legal right in the 1960s (being embodied as an identical right in *both* International Covenants on Human Rights),[61] culminated in the 1970 Declaration on

---

57  *Burkina Faso/Mali Frontier Dispute Case* (1986) ICJ Rep 554 at 566.

58  UNGA Res 1803 (n.43).

59  UNGA Res 3281 (1974). Adopted at 2315th mtg (1974). See also UNGA Res 3201 (1974), 'Declaration on the Establishment of a New International Economic Order'.

60  See for example *Texaco v Libya* (n.48), para 88.

61  Article 1 International Covenant on Economic, Social and Cultural Rights 1966; Article 1 International Covenant on Civil and Political Rights 1966.

Friendly Relations,[62] which included as one of the key principles that of self-determination of peoples – that 'all peoples have the right to freely determine, without external interference, their political status and to pursue their economic, social and cultural development, and that every State has the duty to respect this right in accordance with the provisions of the Charter'. The 1970 Declaration then urged the end of colonialism, ruling out the argument that colonies could be part of the metropolitan territory, but preserving the territorial integrity of existing states. It provided that the 'establishment of a sovereign and independent State, the free association or integration with an independent State or the emergence into any other political status freely determined by a people constitute modes of implementing the right of self-determination by that people'.

Furthermore, the 1970 Declaration did not authorise the break-up of existing states that were 'conducting themselves in compliance with the principles of equal rights and self-determination . . . and thus possessed of a government representing the whole people belonging to the territory without distinction as to race, creed, or colour'. This can be interpreted as supporting a remedial right to secession in the case of a permanently unrepresented minority, ethnic or indigenous group, or an unfulfilled right to self-determination of the whole people if the government is endemically unrepresentative. Otherwise, as the Supreme Court of Canada made clear when discussing and dismissing the claimed right of Quebec to secede, the 'right of self-determination of a people is normally fulfilled through internal self-determination – a people's pursuit of its political, economic, social and cultural development within a framework of an existing state'.[63]

It is clear from the analysis in Chapters 2 and 3 that the US denied the Cuban people's 'right' to self-determination in the period from 1898 until 1959, first by occupation and then by its imperialist policies and actions towards Cuba and its people. Whether this was a denial of a legal right by the US and thus a breach of an obligation under international law is doubtful when bearing in mind that the UN General Assembly only adopted Resolution 1514 in 1960 with its clear declaration of the right to self-determination in the form of independence for colonial territories and peoples subject to alien subjugation, domination and exploitation.[64] Although this has been seen as being the source of a customary norm of international law, there is no unequivocal evidence that the Resolution simply codified existing custom. In 1959, therefore, one year before the Resolution was adopted, it could be argued that the Cuban people did not have a clear legal right to self-determination

---

62  UNGA Res 2625 (1970), 'Declaration on Principles of International Law Concerning Friendly Relations and Co-operation Among States in Accordance with the Charter of the United Nations'.
63  *Reference Re Secession of Quebec* [1998] 2 SCR 217 paras 112 and 126.
64  UNGA Res 1514 (n.51), para 1.

but, bearing in mind that the right to self-determination is an on-going one, it had such within a short period of time. Nonetheless, again we see customary international law does not come to the aid of Cuba in its struggle for national liberation; rather, international law confirms what has already happened.

However, while external self-determination of Cuba happened in 1959 without a clear legal norm that would support its emancipation, self-determination as an on-going right is fulfilled by the newly independent state having a government 'representing the whole people'.[65]

As we have seen in our analysis of the Cuban revolution of 1959 in Chapter 2, the government, although unelected, did largely represent the whole Cuban people, certainly in the period 1959–71, apart from those who favoured the old US-backed regime or those who wished for US annexation. It is difficult to see how the regime could have accommodated these, although its policy of encouraging their departure to the US at least in the early years of the revolution,[66] rather than trying to accommodate them, can be criticised as a failure to be inclusive.

The 1970 UN Declaration on Friendly Relations also prohibited forcible action by states aimed at depriving peoples of their right to self-determination. In resisting such forcible action, the 1970 Declaration states that peoples struggling for self-determination are 'entitled to seek and to receive support in accordance with the Purposes and Principles of the Charter of the United Nations'. Again, if this were a Declaration of existing law, it could be argued that the US attempt to undermine Cuban self-determination in 1961, by backing the Bay of Pigs invasion, violated this principle and, in addition, entitled the Cuban government to seek assistance from the Soviet Union and that such support was not in violation of the purposes and principles of the Charter. However, although the placing of missiles on the island appears to be in accord with the principles of the Charter in that it does not technically amount to a threat or use of force under Article 2(4) of the Charter, it could be said to have been more broadly contrary to the purposes of the Charter by representing a threat to international peace and security (the maintenance of peace and security being the primary purpose of the UN).

## 3.6 Sovereign (in)equality

While Anghie and Pérez-Stable identify a differentiated sovereignty that developing states inherited from their colonial past, Gerry Simpson examines the idea of 'sovereign equality' so often pointed to as the cornerstone of international law and international relations.[67] There is in fact a thin veneer

---

65  UNGA Res 2625 (n.62).
66  Gott (n.11), 213.
67  Crawford (n.6), 448–9.

of state equality (what Simpson labels 'juridical sovereignty'),[68] which disguises hierarchies and hegemonies in international relations. These real inequalities have manifested themselves in recent years when 'the Charter conception of equality has been undermined by the tendency to characterise some states as "outlaws"'.[69] As shall be seen, the group of 'outlaw' or 'pariah' states, at least from the US perspective, includes Cuba.

Simpson traces the dominance of the 'Great Powers', in the Congress of Vienna 1815, the League era, and finally as embodied in the permanent membership of the UN Security Council, and states that 'in each instance, these powers have policed the international order from a position of assumed cultural, material and legal superiority'.[70] Such superiority is also found and justified in the writings of liberal interventionists, such as Francis Fukuyama, and is reinforced by ideas of 'universal' human rights and democracy. Fukuyama wrote in his seminal, but apocryphal, *The End of History and the Last Man* in the immediate euphoria of the end of the Cold War:

> A world made up of liberal democracies then, should have much less incentive for war, since all nations would reciprocally recognize one another's legitimacy. And indeed, there is substantial empirical evidence from the past couple of hundred years that liberal democracies do not behave imperialistically towards one another, even if they are perfectly capable of going to war with states that are not democracies and do not share their fundamental values.[71]

Thus, the theory of democratic peace, where democracies do not go to war with each other, can lead to quite a violent world where democracies and non-democracies go to war. Simpson recognises this condition but sees interventions being based on power relationships, with powerful states (whether democracies or not) intervening in weaker pariah (and therefore undemocratic) states: a 'key prerogative of this position has been the right to intervene in the affairs of other states in order to promote some proclaimed community goal'.[72] The problem that Simpson does not fully tackle is whether the 'Great Powers' can enforce these perceived community norms unilaterally, even avoiding the institutional structures (what he labels as forms of 'legalised hegemony')[73] they have established to continue their domination. American attempts to widen the Cuban embargo, to bring on board its allies for

---

68　G. Simpson, *Great Powers and Outlaw States: Unequal Sovereigns in the International Legal Order* (Cambridge: Cambridge University Press, 2004) 9.
69　Ibid., 5.
70　Ibid., 5.
71　F. Fukuyama, *The End of History and the Last Man* (London: Penguin, 1992) xx.
72　Simpson (n.68), 5.
73　Ibid., 7.

instance, have largely failed,[74] making the embargo a naked example of a Great Power treating Cuba as an unequal sovereign state; a relationship which, following Simpson's thesis, entitles the US to intervene in Cuba.

Furthermore, it is very difficult to claim that the avenues of 'legalised hegemony', such as the Security Council, are used systematically to promote liberal values and liberal interventionism, given that neither the five permanent members, nor the wider Security Council, are a uniform set of (liberal) states. Thus, Simpson is forced to consider the possibility of trying to accommodate unilateral great power interventions. Having said that the Security Council can sometimes be persuaded to authorise Western interventions in pariah states, as with non-forcible measures against Iran for its nuclear programme,[75] or forcible measures against Libya for its brutal attempted repression of rebels during the 'Arab Spring' of 2011.[76] However, on other occasions Russia and China do not succumb to Western pressure for intervention as in Kosovo (1999), or Iraq (2003), or Syria (2011–).

A further problem with Simpson's thesis is that while he establishes the evidence of sovereign inequality, he does seem to overstate the implications of this when he writes: 'put bluntly, the Great Powers are subject to a different set of norms from other states in relation to the permissible limits of self-defence', and further 'outlaw states cannot call on the same juridical resources (territorial integrity and political independence) to constrain acts of force by other states'.[77] Although this is posited as an explanatory judgment and not a normative one,[78] it seems to elide an analysis of patterns of great power behaviour with judgments about the nature of international law. It is, in effect, a claim that because the great powers have behaved in such a way, and continue to do so, such behaviour is law, bringing it close to the behaviourists of the Cold War, who, after analysing the interventions by the superpowers in their respective spheres of influence, concluded that international law reflected a right of hemispheric intervention.[79]

At best a claim can be made that the great powers perceive they have rights (to intervene in their respective hemispheres for instance, or to take pre-emptive action against terrorists based in outlaw states) that other states do not have, and the rest of the world can do very little to stop them. However, unless the major powers channel their power through the forms of 'legalised

---

74  Pérez-Stable (n.38), 204 stating that 'Canada, Europe, and Latin America denounced the embargo and refused US entreaties to make the punitive measure a true international economic blockade'.
75  UNSC Res 1737 (2006).
76  UNSC Res 1970, 1973 (2011).
77  Simpson (n.68), 10.
78  Ibid., 17.
79  I.I. Dore, *International Law and the Superpowers: Normative Order in a Divided World* (New York: Rutgers University Press, 1984).

hegemony' such as the UN Security Council, then such actions are violations of the international legal order, as shaped in 1945 by those very same powers. It is not simply the fact that the majority of states will not support, or may even condemn, such actions that makes them unlawful, it is the fact that they violate even the basic veneer of sovereign equality as found in Article 2 of the UN Charter,[80] which also prohibits the threat or use of force against the territorial integrity and political independence of any state,[81] as well as any intervention in the domestic affairs of any states (unless the UN Security Council takes action under Chapter VII).[82]

It is clearly true that the UN Charter contains within it elements that reflect the idea of sovereign equality, for example, by having a system of one-state-one-vote in the General Assembly, as well as realist considerations of power (as in the need for consensus among the permanent membership of the Security Council). This enables writers to stress one element over the other,[83] but this does not mean that such a system is necessarily unworkable. Sovereignty and sovereign equality must give way to intervention when, for example, the international community is faced with international crimes of immense magnitude such as genocide or threats such as the proliferation of weapons of mass destruction. However, such intervention has to come through the UN and other competent organisations, where the move away from the greater protection of sovereign equality found in the unanimity rules of the League's Covenant towards majority voting in the UN Charter, has enabled that to happen. The voting rules in the Security Council are not so much 'legalised hegemony', but rather represent a realist core within an institutional framework, making it difficult for one major power to hold sway. Of course the permanent five member states, representing the world's police force, are immune from any UN intervention themselves, at least through the Security Council where their position is protected by the veto,[84] and in that sense they have greater rights than other states. However, in the absence of a UN army which, even if Chapter VII provisions were to be fully acted upon, would not truly materialise, powerful states' economic and military capabilities must be harnessed. As US President Roosevelt stated following the Yalta Conference of 1945, when faced with aggressor states, the 'policing powers could then threaten to quarantine the offending state and, if that did not work, to bomb some part of it'.[85] It is interesting to note that at the San Francisco Conference

---

80  Article 2(1) UN Charter provides that the 'Organization is based on the sovereign equality of all its Members'.
81  Article 2(4) UN Charter.
82  Article 2(7) UN Charter.
83  Simpson (n.68), 166–7.
84  Article 27(3) UN Charter.
85  R. Russell, *A History of the United Nations Charter: The Role of the United States 1940–1945* (Washington DC: Brookings, 1958) 98.

which established the United Nations, it was smaller states, especially Latin American states, which, as well as arguing strongly for sovereign equality to be reflected in the UN Charter, called for greater accountability of the Security Council to the General Assembly.[86] It is to these forms of accountability that consideration must be given, rather than black-or-white conceptions of the UN as either a form of hegemony or a sanctuary for sovereign equality.[87]

Simpson's argument is that the major powers, now dissatisfied with the rules of the UN Charter, are reshaping the norms to allow for intervention without Security Council authority (as in Kosovo in 1999 and Iraq in 2003), or as some form of expanded and potential unending right of self-defence (Afghanistan in 2001).[88] This argument is considered throughout the book in relation to the Cuban embargo, where what appears to be a continuing, unending violation of international law, is seemingly not addressed by the international legal order.

## 3.7 Conclusion

Cuban independence and formal sovereignty were achieved in 1902 with the end of US occupation (although its sovereignty was suspended during the second period of US occupation from 1906 to 1909). Formal sovereignty in theory brought with it sovereign equality under international law, but Cuba's imperial domination by the US until 1959 meant that its sovereignty was of a lesser nature than the Westphalian variety enjoyed by developed states including the US. In the period 1952–9 Cuba's political and economic sovereignty was in the hands of US politicians, companies and businessmen.

When the revolution came to power in 1959 Cuba struggled to assert a stronger version of sovereignty, but found that the rules of international law did not favour its reassertion of sovereignty over its natural resources so that its expropriation of US concerns and nationalisation of its sugar industry were not accepted as lawful, although this did not stop the Cuban government from carrying them out. For that it is still being punished by the United States, which has stuck to the Hull Formula for demanding full compensation from Cuba to this very day.

Although the rules of international law did not favour Cuba's choice of economic future, they did provide it with some protection from external intervention in the form of the basic principles contained in Article 2 of the UN Charter. The UN Charter prohibits the use of force unless undertaken under the authority of the Security Council or in self-defence, and neither the Bay of Pigs invasion of 1961 nor the Cuban quarantine of 1962, could be

---

86  Simpson (n.68), 184, 267.
87  Ibid., 192.
88  Ibid., 70–1.

classified in these ways. Cuba was entitled to defend itself, and invite its allies to help it. Its invitation to the Soviet Union to place nuclear missiles in Cuba was, it is argued here, an ill-considered and disproportionate defensive response – one that undermined the purposes of the United Nations in Article 1 of the UN Charter by destabilising peace.

With Soviet military support came political support, which in turn threatened the political independence of Cuba. Once the situation stabilised after the Missile Crisis, the US tightened the embargo on Cuba and treated it as a pariah state, one not deserving of full respect for its sovereignty. Although the US was unable to persuade the UN to its agenda it did receive some support from the Organisation of American States, not only for the quarantine, but for the expulsion of the Cuban government from participation in the organisation. The resolution of the Ministers of Foreign Affairs of the OAS, adopted in January 1962, gave the 'repeated acts' of the Cuban government, as well as its 'alignment with the communist bloc', as the reasons for its suspension.[89] It was only in 2009 that this resolution was deemed to have ceased to have effect by the OAS General Assembly,[90] although Cuba has yet to resume participation in the OAS. However, there was no continuous legalised hegemonic support from relevant security communities for the embargo imposed against Cuba, except for a time by the OAS which supported limited sanctions against Cuba in the period 1964–75 (reviewed in Chapter 6).

Cuba's form of government and entry into the Soviet camp only partly explained its pariah status. Another reason was the Cuban support for rebellions in Latin America and in Africa, reviewed in the next chapter.

---

89  UN Doc S/5075 (1962). Six foreign ministers abstained, which casts doubt on the competence to exclude the Cuban government since the OAS constitution does not contain an exclusion clause – see H.G. Schermers and N.M. Blokker, *International Institutional Law* (5th edn, Leiden: Nijhoff, 2011) 117.
90  OAS AG/RES 2438, 9 June 2009.

# 4 Exporting revolution, importing communism

## 4.1 Introduction

This chapter details the Cuban story after the 1959 Revolution which, as we have seen in Chapters 2 and 3, represented the assertion of Cuban independence, sovereignty and self-determination. For a relatively brief period of time, until the early 1970s, the revolutionary government embodied the will of the people and successfully defended itself from direct and indirect US intervention. However, to ensure Cuba's longer-term defence, the revolutionary government turned to the Soviet Union whose influence, in turn, undermined the political independence of Cuba, moving it from a genuine form of popular continuing revolution, towards Marxism and all the structuralism and doctrine contained within that ideology but, more importantly, shifting it from dependence on the US to dependence on the USSR.

In the light of this, this chapter considers the parallel change in emphasis in international law, which started in the Cold War but flourished after its end, from external independence from colonial and other similar forms of domination, towards internal self-determination. The development of a two-dimensional approach to self-determination derives from transition of the concept from principle to right. As an on-going right self-determination is not just a one-off event which, in the case of Cuba, occurred in 1959, but is a continuing right which aims to ensure that the people of an independent state have a government representing the 'whole people . . . without distinction as to race, creed, or colour'.[1] Having achieved independence from the US and, therefore, having achieved external self-determination, we need to further consider in detail Cuba's continuing respect for the right of self-determination during the period of Soviet influence.

The Cuban revolution was not only striving to consolidate its own self-determination in the 1960s, it became involved in exporting its revolution

---

1 UNGA Res 2625 (1970), 'Declaration on Principles of International Law Concerning Friendly Relations and Co-operation Among States in Accordance with the Charter of the United Nations'.

by forcible intervention, first in Latin America, and then in Africa. History shows that it was not until 1962, after the US embargo had first been imposed, that the Cuban revolutionaries 'made a conscious decision to put their revolutionary theories into practice and to actively promote guerrilla warfare in Latin America'.[2] According to Richard Gott, with the encouragement of Che Guevara, Fidel Castro 'made plans to accelerate history'.[3] However, Cuban military involvement in Latin America in 1962–7 was small-scale and was confined to Argentina, Bolivia and Venezuela. A more significant intervention was in Africa, which initially consisted of sending just over 100 Cuban soldiers under Che Guevara to the Congo in Africa in 1965.[4] Cuba also sent advisers to train MPLA (Popular Movement for the Liberation of Angola) fighters in Angola and sent arms to the FLN (National Liberation Front) fighters in Algeria, helping those movements in their armed struggle against colonial powers (Portugal in Angola and France in Algeria).[5] Guevara's expedition to Bolivia in 1967 to support a guerrilla movement there ended in his capture and execution.

## 4.2  Cuba's early interventions under international law

The interventions by Cuba in Latin America and Africa appeared to violate the principles of the UN Charter, in that sending troops to fight a legitimate government in power amounts not only to an illegal use of force contrary to Article 2(4) of the UN Charter,[6] but also, if it has 'scale and effects',[7] can amount to an 'armed attack', within the meaning of Article 51 (embodying the right of self-defence).[8] This means that such a level of support for rebels or insurgents entitles the attacked state not only to use armed force to suppress the rebellion or insurgency, but also to defend itself against the state sending troops in support of the armed struggle. In principle, an attacked

---

2  R. Gott, *Cuba: A New History* (New Haven, CT: Yale University Press, 2004) 215–16.
3  Ibid., 16.
4  Ibid., 219.
5  Ibid., 220–1.
6  Article 2(4) UN Charter states that: 'All members shall refrain in their international relations from the threat or use of force against the territorial integrity or political independence of any state, or in any other manner inconsistent with the purposes of the United Nations'.
7  *Case Concerning Military and Paramilitary Activities in and Against Nicaragua* (1986) ICJ Rep 14 at para 195. The Court stated: 'The Court sees no reason to deny that, in customary law, the prohibition of armed attacks may apply to the sending by a state of armed bands to the territory of another state, if such operation, because of its scale and effects, would have been classified as an armed attack rather than a mere frontier incident had it been carried out by regular armed forces'.
8  Article 51 UN Charter states that: 'Nothing in the present Charter shall impair the inherent right of individual or collective self-defence if an armed attack occurs against a member of the United Nations . . .'.

state that has the right of self-defence under international law can request help from its allies to act in collective self-defence, either under an *ad hoc* arrangement or an existing defence treaty such as the one creating NATO (the North Atlantic Treaty Organisation) in 1949.

The normative framework on the legality of interventions in intra-state conflicts developed by the International Court of Justice in a case brought by Nicaragua against the United States,[9] concerned support in the late 1970s and early 1980s for rebel movements against governments (in El Salvador and in Nicaragua) that had achieved independence. In contrast, Cuban interventions, at least in Africa, were in support of rebel movements fighting for independence against colonial powers. Thus, it is possible to make an argument to the effect that Cuban support for decolonisation in Africa was in accordance with the 1970 Declaration on Friendly Relations, which ambiguously encouraged 'support' for peoples fighting for self-determination.[10] This, of course, assumes that this seminal General Assembly resolution was declaratory of existing customary law. Such an argument is less convincing in the case of Cuba's interventions in independent states in Latin America no matter how unrepresentative their governments were. While the General Assembly's resolutions during the Cold War lent ambiguous 'support' for national liberation movements struggling for external self-determination, they could not be interpreted to encourage support for interventions against established governments, democratic or otherwise.

The circumstances surrounding Cuba's later involvement in Angola are disputed. One view is that Cuba came to the defence of the MPLA revolutionary movement in Angola in 1975, and thus its intervention can be seen in more orthodox terms of coming to the aid of a government, at its request, to defeat a rebellion by UNITA (National Union for the Total Independence of Angola), an armed movement fuelled by the United States and heavily supported by white South African troops. However, an alternative history would be that Cuban support was incisive in the civil war between the MPLA and UNITA that followed Portuguese withdrawal and helped to secure the victory of the MPLA over its rivals and also to secure the independence of Angola from Portugal. Under this conception Cuba was not acting in collective defence of an established state and government, but was acting to further self-determination in another country by aligning itself with an ideologically compatible revolutionary movement which, with Cuban support, became the established government. A truer version is that it appears that Cuban troops were not sent to Angola until South Africa had directly intervened,[11] making Cuba's action closer to one of collective defence against an armed attack,

9  *Nicaragua Case* (n.7), 14.
10  UNGA Res 2625 (n.1).
11  Gott (n.2), 253–4.

although it was defending a revolutionary proto-government fighting not only for independence, but against rival factions and outside states – not exactly the right of collective self-defence envisaged under Article 51 of the UN Charter but something akin to that. Again Cuba's impact on international relations is profound, challenging traditional boundaries of international law on the back of an evolving right of self-determination.

Cuba's military support for the MPLA government in Angola in the late 1970s and 1980s culminated in the deployment of a much larger force of 50,000 Cuban troops, who played a significant role in defeating a combined UNITA/South African force at Cuito Cuanavale in 1988. This successful exercise of the right of collective self-defence by Cuba and Angola changed the balance of power in southern Africa, leading to South African withdrawal from Namibia as well as Angola, in exchange for a Cuban withdrawal from Angola. Apartheid ended in South Africa soon afterwards and, in 1991, Nelson Mandela praised Cuba for the 'decisive defeat of the aggressive apartheid forces' at Cuito Cuanavale, which 'served as an inspiration to the struggling people of South Africa'.[12] The revolution in Cuba of 1959 brought effective external self-determination (independence) to Cuba for the first time, and the Cubans were hugely influential in bringing about such emancipatory self-determination to southern Africa in the 1970s, 80s and 90s. However, as shall be seen later in this chapter, the Cuban revolution's fiercely fought and held independence meant that it felt it could ill-afford to relax its grip on power and allow for greater internal self-determination at home in case this would allow pro-American supporters to push Cuba back towards the US.

## 4.3  Cuba's later interventions under international law

Cuba's later interventions in Nicaragua and Grenada in support of newly installed revolutionary governments brought it into more direct confrontation with the United States. In 1979 Castro sent advisers and arms (as did the Soviet Union) to support the Sandinista government in Nicaragua in its fight against the CIA-backed Contra rebels (consisting, in the main, of soldiers from the former military regime).[13] In a case brought against the United States by Nicaragua alleging, inter alia, that the US support for the rebels breached the prohibition on the use of force in the UN Charter and in customary international law, the Court found for Nicaragua, dismissing the US argument that its support for the Contras was justified counter-intervention and collective self-defence since the Nicaraguan government had only supplied arms to FMLN (Farabundo Martí National Liberation Movement) rebels in

12  Ibid., 277–9.
13  Ibid., 270–1.

US-backed El-Salvador.[14] The Court, in effect, condemned arming rebels in independent states as a form of illegal use of force by those states supplying arms, while recognising the right of established governments to receive arms.[15] Although the sending of arms by Nicaragua to the rebels in El Salvador from 1979 to 1981 amounted to an illegal use of force by Nicaragua against El Salvador, it did not give rise to a right of individual or collective self-defence against Nicaragua since the use of force did not amount to an armed attack by Nicaragua. For an armed attack to have occurred, the supporting state must have sent the armed rebels or be substantially involved in their sending.[16] Furthermore, the Court did not see the US support for the Contras in Nicaragua between 1981 and 1984 as amounting to an armed attack, although it did constitute an illegal use of force.[17]

Although objected to by the US,[18] the judgment of the International Court of Justice in the *Nicaragua Case* of 1986 developed the *jus ad bellum* (the law governing resort to force) in order for it to be applicable to modern 'mixed' conflicts, where internal wars are externally fuelled. Applying the rationale of the *Nicaragua Case* retrospectively, it can be argued that the US had sent (or was at least substantially involved in the sending of) the Cuban exile force to the Bay of Pigs in Cuba in 1961. This involvement, therefore, constituted an armed attack on Cuba by the US, entitling Cuba to defend itself not only against the exile force but also, in principle, against the United States. Although Cuba successfully defended itself from the Bay of Pigs attack it did not rely on Soviet support to do so, although the subsequent receipt of Soviet missiles and military aid can be seen as part of a wider defensive response. Besides which, any form of economic, political or other form of intervention undertaken to subordinate the target state's sovereign rights is prohibited under international law.[19] Furthermore, any direct or indirect forcible action, which aims at denying a people its right to self-determination is a violation of the UN Charter.[20]

In examining the relationship between Cuban interventions in Latin America and Africa and US interventions in Cuba both forcible and non-forcible, it would be stretching history to suggest that in general one policy

---

14  *Nicaragua Case* (n.7), paras 228–38.
15  Ibid., paras 206, 246. This reflects the position in international law – see H.A. Wilson, *International Law and the Use of Force by National Liberation Movements* (Oxford: Clarendon, 1988) 29.
16  *Nicaragua Case* (n.7), para 195; relying on UNGA Res 3314 (1974), 'Definition of Aggression', Article 3(g).
17  *Nicaragua Case* (n.7), para 247.
18  See dissenting opinion of US Judge Schwebel in the *Nicaragua Case* (n.7), 249.
19  UNGA Res 2131 (1965), 'Declaration on the Inadmissibility of Intervention in the Domestic Affairs of States and the Protection of their Independence and Sovereignty'.
20  UNGA Res 2160 (1966), 'Strict Observance of the Prohibition of the Threat or Use of Force in International Relations, and the Right of Peoples to Self-Determination'.

of intervention was taken in response to another, although in individual conflicts it is possible to do so. Cuban arms found their way into El Salvador (via Nicaragua) in the late 1970s, but this could not legally justify US counter-intervention in Nicaragua in the early 1980s, nor indeed justify its measures against Cuba. The Court addressed this issue in the *Nicaragua Case* when answering the question: 'if one state acts towards another state in breach of the principle of non-intervention, may a third state lawfully take such action by way of counter-measure against the first state as would otherwise constitute intervention in its internal affairs?'.[21] The Court confined third states' responses involving the use of armed force to those taken 'when the wrongful act provoking the response was an armed attack', otherwise the responses themselves would constitute an unlawful intervention and use of force.[22] Since Nicaragua had not attacked El Salvador, although Nicaragua had committed a wrongful act by arming the FMLN, the US (as a third state) was not entitled to intervene in Nicaragua by arming and advising the Contra rebels. But then the further question inevitably arises as to how then could Cuba have been brought to account for its behaviour in ways that accord with international law? Can the US have a role in this, or does this make it a self-appointed sheriff with no authority to act as such? These questions are returned to in Chapters 5 and 7.

The sending of regular troops to aid a rebel movement's fight against an established government constitutes an armed attack by the sending state against the target state, and Cuba appeared guilty of this when sending forces to undermine independent Latin American countries in the period 1962–7, although the involvement was small scale. The larger Cuban contingent sent to Angola in 1975 can be justified as support for self-determination struggles against colonisation and, later, as collective self-defence against external attacks from South Africa. The former argument for using force in support of national liberation movements is controversial and would not have been accepted as lawful by Western states, but would have been supported by newly independent states in Africa and Asia.[23]

Heather Wilson defines a war of national liberation as a 'conflict waged by a non-state community against an established government to secure the right

---

21  *Nicaragua Case* (n.7), para 210.
22  Ibid., paras 205, 211.
23  In voting for the 1970 Declaration on Friendly Relations (n.1) Western states cast their votes in favour on the understanding that the paragraph permitting 'support' for self-determination struggles did not diminish the UN principle prohibiting the use of force: see, for example, New Zealand UNGA 6th Committee, 1181st meeting (1970); Portugal UNGA 6th Committee, 1182nd meeting (1970). Socialist and Non-Aligned states had a more ambivalent attitude: see, for example, Poland UNGA 6th Committee, 1178th meeting (1970); Senegal UNGA 6th Committee, 1180th meeting (1970).

of the people of that community for self-determination'.[24] Wilson analyses the orthodox position of international law as follows:

> Despite . . . disagreements in specific cases and the tendency to make exceptions to the general rules, one theme remains clear: international law has favoured the established government in an internal war by prohibiting assistance to rebels and allowing assistance to the government except in cases of recognized belligerency when outside states must remain neutral. Traditional international law favoured repression over revolution. This predisposition has been seriously challenged in the last forty years.[25]

General Assembly resolutions supported by the vast majority of nations and adopted over the middle and later parts of the Cold War during the period of decolonisation have lent ambiguous support to the creation of an exception to the rule prohibiting armed support for rebels in the instance of national liberation movements. The 1970 Declaration on Friendly Relations, adopted by consensus, included the statement that:

> Every state has the duty to refrain from any forcible action which deprives peoples . . . of their right to self-determination and freedom and independence. In their action against, and resistance to, such forcible action in pursuit of the exercise of their right to self-determination, such peoples are entitled to seek and to receive support in accordance with the purposes and principles of the Charter.[26]

The Declaration does not unequivocally recognise the right of a people using force to receive arms or other forms of military assistance from outside states; but the deliberate ambiguity of the word 'support' allowed Western states to argue it only meant political and moral support, while developing and socialist states argued that this entitled national liberation movements to receive arms and other military support.[27] Cuba was not only an advocate of such an approach in its voting at the General Assembly, it put it into practice by exporting its revolutionary fervour.

The coming to power of a Marxist government led by Maurice Bishop in Grenada in 1979 led to more direct US–Cuban confrontation. Bishop explicitly adopted Castro's 1959 rejection of US imperialism, by declaring that 'we are not in anybody's backyard, and we are definitely not for sale'.[28] Cuba offered

---

24  Wilson, (n.15), 2.
25  Ibid., 33.
26  UNGA Res 2625 (n.1). See also UNGA Res 3314 (n.16), Article 7.
27  Wilson (n.15), 127, 187.
28  In Gott (n.2), 271.

medical help to the new government as well as university scholarships and some military equipment and advisers. Cuban construction of an airport on Grenada provoked US plans for intervention as the US saw it as a Soviet–Cuban military base in the Caribbean. An internal power struggle in Grenada in 1983 proved the trigger for US military intervention to restore order, remove the government, and hold elections. The US invasion was met with some resistance by troops loyal to the Revolutionary Military Council assisted by what William Gilmore ambiguously describes as Cuban 'construction workers'.[29] Gott depicts the effects of US intervention in the following terms: a 'promising attempt to seek an alternative path to development in the Caribbean was utterly destroyed'.[30]

During the Cold War self-determination in the Caribbean without US intervention seemed difficult to achieve, at least when the resulting government was left-wing. The US justifications for using force in Grenada in 1983, namely that it was protecting US nationals, that it had received authorisation from a hitherto dormant sub-regional body (the Organisation of Eastern Caribbean States – OECS), and that it had been invited to intervene by the Governor General of Grenada, were both singularly and collectively flimsy justifications for what was an illegal use of force.[31] The Governor General did not have any constitutional authority under domestic law to issue such an invitation, his office being a vestige of British colonialism, and OECS did not have constitutional authority under international law under Chapter VII or VIII of the UN Charter.[32] Finally, although there is some support in state practice for limited military intervention to protect nationals, this does not support the full-scale invasion and occupation of the island leading to elections and the installation of a friendly government.

The Cuban presence on the island was not overtly military, besides which a sovereign government is entitled to invite in outside military assistance. The weight of world opinion was against the US action, evidenced not only by overwhelming condemnation by the UN General Assembly,[33] but by the fact that the US was alone in using its veto to protect itself from condemnation in the Security Council.[34]

The Cold War battle lines between the US and Cuba had been drawn whereby the chances of direct confrontation between US troops and Cuban

---

29  W.C. Gilmore, *The Grenada Intervention: Analysis and Documentation* (London: Mansell, 1984) 36.
30  Gott (n.2), 272.
31  Gilmore (n.29), 37.
32  Article 53 UN Charter states that: 'The Security Council shall, where appropriate, utilize such regional arrangements or agencies for enforcement action under its authority. But no enforcement action shall be taken under regional arrangements or by regional agencies without the authorization of the Security Council . . .'.
33  UNGA Res 38/7 (1983).
34  UNSC 2491st meeting (1983).

troops (which might drag in the Soviet Union) were limited; instead, Cuba supported ideologically compatible rebel movements and governments in Latin America and Africa; while the US supported rebels and governments that opposed such ideology (whether democratic or not). While support of established governments is generally permissible in international law, support for rebel movements is illegal. However, Cuba's support for independence struggles in Africa had greater legitimacy, although it cannot be said to be in line with customary international law.[35]

## 4.4 From external to internal self-determination

The Cuban revolution achieved independence and supported other national liberation movements in achieving theirs but, ironically, its reliance on Soviet support may have undermined its continued respect for the Cuban people's right to self-determination. Cuba's struggles were very much part of the debates over the changing nature of international law, but those only came to a head when the Soviet Union collapsed and Soviet support for Cuba ended. The end of the Cold War saw the collapse of Socialist states in the Soviet Union and Yugoslavia, resulting in a further round of external self-determination in the form of newly independent states emerging from the former republics of the USSR and the SFRY (Socialist Federal Republic of Yugoslavia). As with the decolonisation of Africa and Asia in the post-Second World War period, the post-Cold War period marked the end of empires of a different kind.

External self-determination seems to be a once and for all event for those peoples living within colonised or similar territories, with three exceptions. First, further secession by distinct peoples within an existing state may occur by agreement between the state and the people wanting secession; second, forceful secession may be justified in extreme circumstances as a remedial right when a distinct people's rights within a state have been consistently and brutally denied;[36] and third, secession from an existing state may occur as a fact when a state breaks up or is broken up – new states may emerge and be recognised even though they are not created through the exercise of any *right* to self-determination.[37] Putting aside these limited exceptions, self-determination, as a continuing right, only makes sense if it also has an internal aspect.[38]

---

35  Wilson (n.15), 127, 187.
36  *Reference Re Secession of Quebec* [1998] 2 SCR 217, paras 112 and 126.
37  *Accordance with International Law of the Unilateral Declaration of Independence in Respect of Kosovo* (2010) ICJ Rep 403, paras 56, 78, 84.
38  D.J. Harris, *Cases and Materials on International Law* (7th edn, London: Sweet and Maxwell, 2010) 104; Human Rights Committee General Comment No. 12, 'The right to self-determination of peoples (Art.1)', 13 March 1984, para 3.

The growth of minority rights,[39] the rights of indigenous peoples,[40] and greater emphasis on democratic rights (including freedoms of expression, thought, opinion, association, assembly, and the right to participate in elections),[41] are arguably the internal aspects of the right to self-determination (to be exercised within established states). More accurately, as has been stated, the right to internal self-determination is fulfilled by a state having a government representative of the 'whole people . . . without distinction as to race, creed, or colour'.[42] Moreover, a neat change in perspective from external to internal self-determination, with the latter focusing on civil and political rights, fails to take account of the economic aspect of self-determination, which is supported by core economic and social rights. Political rhetoric from Western states and writers about the 'right' to democracy within developing states promotes civil and political rights to the detriment of economic and social rights.[43] According to the Committee on Economic, Social and Cultural Rights, the violation of core economic and social rights would occur if 'any significant number of individuals' within a state 'is deprived of essential foodstuffs, of essential primary health care, of basic shelter and housing, or the most basic forms of education'.[44] Self-determination, as a continuing right, is dependent upon both political and economic elements of self-determination being protected by a government which is representative of the whole people, accepting its obligations under human rights law by protecting and respecting basic civil and political, and economic and social, rights.

Despite the lack of commitment until recently to human rights treaties by Cuba and the United States, in a wider sense, the nature of the conflict between the two countries is a conflict over human rights, since the United States accuses Cuba of denying its citizens basic civil, political and democratic rights; while the embargo seems to violate the fundamental economic, social and cultural rights of the Cuban people. More profoundly the dispute is about self-determination as a principle upon which human rights can be built. The US vision is one of democracy based on a democratically elected government, while the Cuban vision is on a revolutionary government fiercely protecting the nation's hard fought independence from unwanted external interference in its economic, as well as political choices. Both sides claim that the right of self-determination of the Cuban people is being violated by the other. In

---

39  Article 27 International Covenant on Civil and Political Rights 1966.

40  UNGA Res 61/295 (2007), 'United Nations Declaration on the Rights of Indigenous Peoples'.

41  Articles 18, 19, 21, 22, 25 International Covenant on Civil and Political Rights 1966.

42  UNGA Res 2625 (n.1).

43  T.M. Franck, 'The Emerging Right to Democratic Governance', (1992) 86 *AJIL* 46.

44  Committee on Economic, Social and Cultural Rights, 'The Nature of States Parties Obligations: Article 2(1) of the Covenant', General Comment 3, UN Doc E/1991/23, para 10.

essence the conflict reflects profound differences in understanding of modern international law, and goes to the heart of human rights law and its claims to universality.[45]

## 4.5  The continuing right to self-determination of the Cuban people

The history of Cuba reviewed in Chapter 2 shows that the Cuban people's right to self-determination was denied during the period of Spanish colonisation from the sixteenth century to the end of the nineteenth century. The period of US occupation (1898–1902) that ended Spanish rule did not lead to the Cuban people exercising either their political or economic right to self-determination. Elections that followed were either fraudulent, unopposed or disputed. Direct US military interventions were designed to stop unfriendly regimes from being established and to protect US economic interests. American domination of the economy and Cuba's dependence on exports of sugar to the US meant that by 1959 the Cuban people had not achieved self-determination. Indeed, the governments of the period 1902–59 were not only flawed democratically, they were unrepresentative of the different sections of Cuban society. Most infamously this was revealed in the massacre of 3,000 blacks in 1912 ordered by President Gómez, described by Richard Gott as a 'race war, crushed by white Cubans'.[46]

Self-determination was first achieved by securing the full independence of Cuba as a sovereign state in 1959; it then continued to be protected externally by the principle of non-intervention and internally if there was in place a government that included or represented all sections and groups in society. This can be achieved by the development of a representative democracy but this is not a pre-requisite for self-determination, as detailed in Chapter 7. The post-1959 revolutionary regime in Cuba could be seen, for a period, as representative even though unelected. Gott's historical exposition of the build-up to, and the immediate aftermath of, the revolution of 1959 strongly suggests that the motivations of the revolutionary movement and the government that emerged from the revolution did respect, indeed embody, the principle of self-determination. Under Castro's leadership the 'Cuban people "stood up" in the vivid expression of Mao Tse-tung – and understood for the first time who they really were'.[47] Fraudulent democracy had run its course in Cuba by 1959 and many Cubans supported the overthrow of the

45  T. Evans, 'Power, Hegemony and the Universality of Human Rights' in T. Evans (ed.), *Human Rights Fifty Years on: A Reappraisal* (Manchester: Manchester University Press, 1998) 2.
46  Gott (n.2), 124.
47  Ibid., 148.

corrupt US-backed regime.[48] The revolution was based on a rejection of imperial domination of Cuba by the US. In his first speech on 2 January 1959 Castro declared that 'this time it will not be like 1898, when the North Americans came and made themselves masters of our country. This time, fortunately, the Revolution will truly come to power'.[49]

Castro's speech to the UN's General Assembly in September 1960 included language that amounted to a claim that the revolution embodied both political and economic aspects of self-determination, in particular the claims: to be representative of the people, to be free from colonial or other imperial political domination, not to be dependent economically upon other countries, and to have ownership over natural resources, and, if necessary, to be able to reclaim those from foreign concerns.

> We are not, as we have been pictured, a mere group of men governing the country. We are a whole people governing a country – a whole people firmly united, with a great revolutionary consciousness, defending its rights.
>     . . . we are on the side of those peoples that wish to be free, not only politically – for it is very easy to acquire a flag, a coat of arms, an anthem, and a colour on the map – but also economically free, for there is one truth which we should all recognize as being of primary importance, namely, that there can be no political independence unless there is economic independence, that political independence without economic independence is a lie; we therefore support the aspirations of all countries to be free politically and economically. Freedom does not consist in the possession of a flag, a coat of arms, and representation in the United Nations.
>     We should like to draw attention here to another right: a right which was proclaimed by the Cuban people at a mass meeting quite recently, the right of the underdeveloped countries to nationalize their natural resources and the investments of the monopolies in their respective countries without compensation; in other words, we advocate the nationalization of natural resources and foreign investments in the underdeveloped countries.[50]

The coming to power of the revolution brought a government that united the people by combining nationalism and socialism; indeed nationalism was arguably the more significant element, given that the 'legend of Martí proved more influential than the philosophy of Marx'.[51] Castro embodied that

---

48  Ibid., 149.
49  Ibid., 165.
50  UNGA 864th meeting (1960).
51  Gott (n.2), 148–9.

combination and it seemed for a period after the revolution that he and his government did represent the Cuban people, black, white and mixed.[52] Furthermore, the new regime set about reclaiming the nation's natural resources from foreign ownership, redistributing land and property among the people. Foreign assets were not seized for the benefit of the new regime but for the people so again this is strong evidence of economic self-determination being a driving force behind the revolution. However, as well as driving away those supporters of the former regime and the US, the revolutionary regime's seizure of US assets in the immediate post-revolutionary period, was followed, in 1968, by President Castro's crushing of any form of counter-revolution by removing small private commercial enterprises – affecting not just small companies but bars, groceries, garages, small stores and other independent workers such as plumbers.[53] This effectively disenfranchised another section of Cuban society, rendering the revolution less representative.

Ironically, however, it was the United States – by its imposition of the embargo in October 1960, in response to the new regime and its policy of expropriation and nationalisation of US assets, companies and properties – that undermined the continuing self-determination of Cuba under the revolutionary regime. US antipathy towards Cuba forced the latter towards the Communist bloc and the Soviet Union, who stepped in to buy Cuban sugar and to provide the new regime with the means to defend itself. The alliance with the Soviet Union brought Cuba into global as well as local confrontation with the US. Soviet leader Khrushchev made this clear in 1960 when he provocatively declared the Monroe Doctrine to be dead.[54] Revolutionary self-determination turned into state control. As Richard Gott relates:

> Getting rid of imperialism meant abolishing the economic power of the American companies that owned the commanding heights of the Cuban economy – the sugar mills, the oil refineries, the cattle ranches and most of the manufacturing industry. These enterprises deemed 'imperialist' would in the future be run by the state.[55]

Economic state control, which was asserted almost immediately, was combined eventually with political state control, as the confrontation with the US afforded no dissent and required both iron will and military discipline. The representative nature of the Cuban government was in doubt, as was its accountability to the Cuban people. Self-determination as a continuing right

---

52  Ibid., 174.
53  Ibid., 236.
54  Ibid., 184.
55  Ibid., 186.

of a people within an established state is respected and protected by a government that is both representative and accountable; there came a point in time when the Cuban government lost these attributes.

Pérez-Stable argues that 1970 was the point in time when the revolution ended:

> The social bases of political power had been transformed, and the institutionalization that was about to begin would impart a settled dynamic on Cuban society. Charismatic authority, vanguard politics, and mass mobilizations would subsequently acquire a new context. The reality of socialism would slowly gain ascendance over the effervescence of the revolution.[56]

Whereas Pérez-Stable focuses on the internal changes in Cuba to mark the end of revolution and, arguably, representation and self-determination, Gott concentrates on its external relationship with the Soviet Union. On this basis Gott identifies the critical date as slightly earlier by arguing that Cuba showed it had fully joined the Soviet camp by politically supporting the Soviet intervention in Czechoslovakia in 1968. From this point and for the next twenty years there would be a 'close alliance with the Soviet Union – in foreign affairs, economic policy, cultural matters and the very structure of government'. Tellingly, 'Cuba was to subject itself to a make-over in the Soviet image'.[57] In 1979, Cuba gave similar support for the Soviet invasion of Afghanistan.[58] By 1975 Cuba had without doubt achieved the 'status of a recognisably orthodox Soviet satellite',[59] a 'well-established, well-organised and well-armed Communist state',[60] with Soviet advisers having huge influence on the running of the economy and on building political institutions and structures of government, in which the Communist Party (hitherto of limited influence) became pivotal.[61] In economic terms, Cuba joined Comecon, the Soviet dominated organisation that governed trading relationships between countries in the Soviet bloc; sugar was reinstalled as the sole significant export and, given the high price paid for it, the economy boomed from 1975 to 1985, so that it was not until the collapse of the Soviet Union in 1991 that Cuba turned to alternative economic development, principally tourism, as a major source of revenue.[62]

---

56  M. Pérez-Stable, *The Cuban Revolution: Origins, Course and Legacy* (2nd edn, Oxford University Press, 1999) 120.
57  Gott (n.2), 235.
58  Ibid., 237.
59  Ibid., 238.
60  Ibid., 245.
61  Ibid., 239, 244.
62  Ibid., 242–4.

It was somewhat ironic that at about the same time that Cuba became a Soviet satellite state, the potential it had (especially in the period 1959–68) for treading a path between the superpowers and providing leadership to developing states, was belatedly recognised in 1976 by Fidel Castro being appointed as chairman of the Non-Aligned Movement (NAM), following Cuba's decisive intervention in Angola in 1975 and its defeat of apartheid South African forces in battle there.[63] The sixth regular summit of the NAM was held in Havana in 1979, when the Havana Declaration was adopted to clarify the purpose of NAM as ensuring 'the national independence, sovereignty, territorial integrity and security of non-aligned countries' in their 'struggle against *imperialism, colonialism, neo-colonialism, racism*, and all forms of foreign aggression, *occupation*, domination, interference or *hegemony* as well as against *great power* and bloc politics'. Whereas Cuba would have embodied these sentiments in 1959, by 1979 its support for Soviet imperialism and domination of Czechoslovakia and Afghanistan undermined its claims to non alignment. More significantly, in terms of self-determination, the revolution's claim to embody the will of the Cuban people was undermined, as the Soviet way had become the only way for Cuba, at least until the collapse of the USSR in 1991.

The end of the Soviet Union and of Soviet support for Cuba did not see the opening of the Cuban economy or the liberalisation of politics. In fact, initially the state took firmer control of the economy in order to steer it through the withdrawal of Soviet trade. In addition, there was no indication that Soviet premier Gorbachev's ideas of 'glasnost' and 'perestroika' – 'the promotion of political openness and economic restructuring' – were going to be adopted by the Cuban government.[64]

In terms of economic self-determination the dependence of Cuba on the Soviet Union, even by 1989, was significant – 63 per cent of Cuba's food imports and 80 per cent of its imported machinery came from the Soviet Union, while 63 per cent of its sugar exports went to the Soviet Union.[65] From 1989 to 1993 the Cuban economy went into freefall, shrinking year on year. Starvation was not found in Cuba but malnutrition became widespread.[66] Cuba switched emphasis from sugar to tourism, allowing foreign enterprises to own up to 49 per cent of joint ventures.[67] The US dollar was recognised by Decree-Law 140 in August 1993, becoming the currency for trade, and leading to an erosion of the 'egalitarian ethic' central to revolutionary Cuba.[68] Decree-Law 141 of September 1993 allowed self-employment for certain

---

63  Ibid., 256.
64  Ibid., 274–5.
65  Ibid., 287.
66  Ibid., 288.
67  Ibid., 290.
68  Ibid., 291.

activities, and allowed for private bars and restaurants. Decree-Law 142 established agricultural cooperatives to replace the state-run farms, and private farmers' markets were allowed. These major reforms were discussed in every workplace.[69] In terms of political self-determination, there was not only widespread discussion of the economic reforms, there was direct election of deputies to the National Assembly but only from an approved list of candidates. Furthermore, Marxism–Leninism was dropped from the constitution.[70]

Cuba, and its form of government, survived transition from Soviet dependence and GDP began to rise again in 1994.[71] Cuba eschewed its former policy of foreign intervention and looked instead towards ensuring its survival, looking for new partners, so that by 1994 China had become Cuba's third largest trading partner.[72] Despite the legalisation of the dollar, the US 'tightened the economic screw', assuming that Cuba would fall just as the countries in the eastern bloc had done once Soviet support was withdrawn.[73] The US made the mistake of comparing Cuba to countries in eastern Europe when the Cuban revolution was indigenous and, largely remained fuelled by the continuous assertion of independence, made stronger in a sense after the demise of the Soviet Union.[74] In a sense, the Cuban desire to resist unwanted external intervention, to reassert its external self-determination, particularly towards the US, enabled it to survive the collapse of the socialist ideal. Nevertheless, the survival of the revolution led to a third exodus of thousands of Cubans over the period 1990–92, many in small boats, to the United States.[75] An analysis of whether post-Soviet Cuba has returned to a path of internal self-determination and towards greater internal freedoms and human rights from 1990 onwards is returned to in Chapter 7.

## 4.6 Conclusion

The Cuban revolution of 1959 fulfilled the destiny of the Cuban people to live in a sovereign, independent state. The revolutionary movement not only liberated Cuba from US domination, thereby achieving external self-determination, the revolutionary government that followed from it embodied that self-determination – effectively internalising it. The revolution's confidence in its own self-determination credentials led to the export of that revolutionary ideology to Latin American countries where right-wing

---

69  Ibid., 292–3.
70  Ibid., 294.
71  Ibid., 295.
72  Ibid., 297.
73  Ibid.
74  Ibid.
75  Ibid., 299.

dictatorships prevailed and, more successfully (and with greater commitment in terms of blood and treasure), to African colonies where national liberation movements struggled for self-determination against their colonial and neo-colonial masters.

Strong on external self-determination, the revolutionary government of Fidel Castro could, for a decade at least, claim to be sufficiently representative and accountable to the Cuban people to be fulfilling the continuing obligation to protect and respect the right to self-determination, though it remained unelected. The experience of fraudulent, externally engineered, elections in the period 1902–59 in part explains this, but this should not have prevented a move towards greater democratic accountability in time. Instead, the need to protect both Cuba and the revolution forced the revolutionary government in the opposite direction; one in which the Cuban Communist party, heavily influenced by the Soviet Union, asserted an iron grip on the people. Allegiance to Fidel Castro remained strong, however, as was the desire for independence free from the US, so much so that the collapse of the Soviet Union did not lead to the collapse of the government, but it left the direction of political and economic development of Cuba in the balance.

This chapter, covering the period from the revolution in 1959 to the collapse of the Soviet Union in 1991, sets up the discussions in subsequent chapters not only in relation to the continuation of the embargo (in Chapter 6), but also in relation to changes in Cuba and the prospects for normalisation of relations between the US and Cuba (in Chapters 7 and 8). Before that we return to the question raised in the heart of this chapter of whether international law permits the US to take on the role of world police force and take measures (principally the embargo) against Cuba for its interventions in Latin America and Africa, as well as punish Cuba for its seizures of US-owned property in the early years of the revolution.

# 5  Self-help and international law

## 5.1 Introduction

This chapter builds on the previous ones by contrasting the apparent equality of sovereign states before the law, and the inequality in the world outside the Peace Palace in The Hague, where the International Court of Justice has its seat. It considers the role of power in international law and confronts the pragmatic argument that many rules of international law are 'paper rules', which do not act as real constraints on the behaviour of powerful states. In this regard, the restriction of self-help in modern international law, embodied in the doctrine of countermeasures, is contrasted with the real world of economic coercion by powerful states against weaker ones. Although the Cuban embargo does not appear to accord with the doctrine of countermeasures and, therefore, is a *prima facie* breach of international law, there is a considerable amount of state practice where punitive economic coercion has been applied on a regular basis as a means of enforcing perceived rights. Although a detailed analysis of the Cuban embargo and its compatibility, or otherwise, with international law, is left to Chapter 6, this chapter sets the scene by considering the pragmatic challenge to the restricted legal framework that has been constructed around self-help in the post-1945 world order.

## 5.2 Equality before the law

The principle of sovereign equality means that each sovereign state has the same rights and duties under international law. The principle is seen at its most prominent before international courts and tribunals. For example, in the *Admissions* opinion of 1948, the Court advised that members of the UN Security Council were not legally entitled to make membership conditional upon issues of ideology, additional to the requirement contained in Article 4 of the UN Charter (that member states basically had to be peace-loving). The Court was not prepared to recognise considerations of power that had prevented the admission of many new states. It asserted that, although membership decisions allowed for much discretion on the part of the Security

Council, they were nevertheless still bound by the law of the UN Charter.[1] However, the assertion of what amounts to an international rule of law by the Court was pushed to one side by two permanent members (the US and USSR). These states simply carried on their practice of asserting the supremacy of political considerations over issues of admission of new members to the UN.[2]

The judicial protection of the equality of states is even more evident in the *Nicaragua Case* of 1986, in which the International Court's judgment was premised on the idea of universal international law where the norms of the UN Charter embody fundamental rules that bind great powers and weaker states alike. This, in part, explained how the Court was able to find that both Nicaragua and the United States were in breach of the prohibitions on the use of force and intervention in international law: Nicaragua by arming the left-wing rebels in El Salvador, and the US by counter-intervening and supporting (by arming, advising and training) the right-wing Contras in Nicaragua.[3] In this way the judgment embodied that fundamental notion of justice – equality before the law. The Court rejected any notion that ideological differences could justify an intervention by the US in Nicaragua stating that 'adherence by any state to any particular doctrine does not constitute a violation of international law', to argue otherwise would be contrary to a 'fundamental principle of international law, state sovereignty, and violates the freedom of choice of the political, economic, social and cultural system of states'.[4] The US rejected the judgment of the Court – in fact it had pulled out of the case at an earlier stage. Interestingly, the Court did not address a range of non-forcible measures imposed by the US upon Nicaragua starting in 1982 (discussed below), which were remarkably similar to those imposed upon Cuba, raising the issue of whether such measures are acceptable forms of self-help in contrast to forcible reprisals.

The re-assertion by the International Court in the *Nicaragua Case* of what Simpson labels the 'existential equality' of states,[5] in other words the right of states to take whatever internal form they like within a pluralist system that is underpinned by a strong norm of non-intervention, echoed the prescient statement of the Cuban delegate at the San Francisco Conference on the UN in 1945, when he declared that 'every state has the right to exist . . . to organise

---

1  *Conditions of Admission of a State to the United Nations (Article 4 of the Charter)* (1948) ICJ Rep 63–5.
2  H.G. Schermers and N.M. Blokker, *International Institutional Law* (5th edn, Leiden: Nijhoff, 2011) 85.
3  *Case Concerning Military and Paramilitary Activities in and Against Nicaragua* (1986) ICJ Rep 14 at paras 228–30.
4  Ibid., para 263.
5  G. Simpson, *Great Powers and Outlaw States: Unequal Sovereigns in the International Legal Order* (Cambridge: Cambridge University Press, 2004) 54.

itself as it sees fit . . .'.[6] In fact, Latin American states, most of which had achieved independence from European powers in the nineteenth century much earlier than African and Asian colonies, advocated a stronger form of sovereign equality. As Simpson states: 'the rising power of the United States was the single most important phenomenon in the Western hemisphere in the nineteenth century and the development of legal equality within the Americas can only be understood in the light of this fact'.[7]

The Monroe Doctrine, propounded by US President Monroe in 1823, was a warning to European states not to (re)intervene in the Americas,[8] facilitating the move towards independence of American states (for example Mexico gained independence from Spain in 1821, Brazil from Portugal in 1822). Indeed, the Pan-American system, one of the oldest regional systems, which was to become the OAS in 1948, was inaugurated in 1899 on the basis of sovereign equality. At the time, the US Secretary of State, James G. Blaine, said of the forerunner to the OAS, that it was an 'honorable, peaceful conference of seventeen independent American powers, in which all states meet together on terms of absolute equality'.[9]

Cuba, even in the period of US domination (1898–1959), played a significant role in the Pan-American project on the basis of being a sovereign equal state, reflected in its hosting of the Sixth Pan-American Conference in 1928. Indeed, at that Conference a number of treaties were adopted including the Convention on the Status of Aliens in the Respective Territories of the Contracting Parties. Interestingly, the Convention did not put forward an international minimum standard for the treatment of foreigners; instead it stated that they were to be treated the same as nationals and subject to local jurisdiction and law. Furthermore, the Convention prohibited foreigners from interfering in the political affairs of host states, recognising that the host state had the right to punish any individual that so interfered.[10] This signified that at least in formal treaty law, US citizens possessed no special privileges in Cuba, but as we have seen in Chapter 2, their influence and interests in Cuba were predominant in the period 1902–59.

By 1965, when President Johnson issued his doctrine that the US could not tolerate any further left-wing regimes within its hemisphere, the Monroe-inspired principle of non-intervention had been replaced by one of US intervention, including in Cuba. In a more general sense, Simpson questions whether existential equality persists for a handful of outlaw states, which are

---

6 UNCIO III, 496.
7 Simpson (n.5), 129.
8 Ibid., 130.
9 In Simpson (n.5), 130. See also Simpson's account of the negotiations at the Hague Conferences of 1899 and 1907, in particular the arguments of the Brazilian delegate Rui Barbosa – at 136–47.
10 Articles 2 and 7, (1928) 22 *AJIL* 136.

subject to great power intervention.[11] Such intervention may be justified as self-help, reprisals, self-defence or counter-intervention, but essentially it is based on the premise that the target state has somehow lost its right to sovereign equality and, moreover, to have its sovereignty respected, either because of its international actions or because of its political system, or both.

Although sovereign equality is respected by the International Court, as Simpson points out, most international legal disputes are not resolved before the Court in that 'International Law departs from its domestic counterpart most obviously in the fact that its enforcement regime envisages a large element of self-help'.[12] Further, 'rights will often be vindicated via mechanisms of self-help rather than through court procedures'.[13] Self-help inevitably favours stronger states. It could be argued that despite such inequalities, sovereign equality is preserved because the right to self-help is available to both strong and weak states, or we can accept Simpson's challenge and recognise that what we in fact have is a legal system that is tainted with inequality, one where although self-help is a legal process 'its operation seems wholly dependent upon political power'.[14]

## 5.3  Unequal states

Returning to Gerry Simpson's thesis, his analysis compounds state inequality by concluding that major powers have special rights that are not universally granted to all states, not only those rights found in the UN Charter such as the right of veto, but also, special prerogatives such as an expanded notion of self-defence, developed outside the Charter, and exercised primarily in relation to pariah states. Pariah states are:

> Not simply states that fail to comply with international law. They are delinquent states deprived of the full benefits of international legal personhood on account of their moral traits or associability.[15]

Simpson makes a distinction between two forms of 'outsider' or 'pariah' states, the first of which is the criminal state which seems to cover those states, or their leaders, responsible for international crimes such as aggression, genocide, crimes against humanity or systematic war crimes, to which can be added terrorist crimes, and so would comfortably cover states such as Libya and Sudan (both for crimes against humanity and support for terrorism), Iraq, Serbia and Syria (for aggression and crimes against humanity), and Afghanistan

11  Simpson (n.5), 55.
12  Ibid., 46.
13  Ibid.
14  Ibid., 47.
15  Ibid., 337, 342.

(for support for terrorism). Simpson argues that there are new rules of intervention for these states.[16] The second group of 'outsider' or 'pariah' states are 'undemocratic or illiberal or uncivilised states'. Such a state 'fails to offer its citizens a typical range of civil and political rights (including market rights), lacks a system of government in which authority is dispersed and does not hold free periodic elections in which the government is elected by the citizens of that state'. This 'brings them into conflict with the democratic governance norm'.[17] Although the rules of intervention in relation to this second type of state are less clear, the line between the two types of 'pariah' state has been blurred with the end of the Cold War and the liberal triumphalism of Fukuyama *et al.*[18] Certainly, some US writers had already argued for pro-democratic intervention in illiberal states during the Cold War, for example, in relation to the US invasion of Grenada.[19]

In the recent past the United States has included Cuba as a pariah state, although it is clearly not core to this group. In his State of the Union address, in 2002, President Bush described an 'axis of evil' of North Korea, Iran and Iraq:

> States like these, and their terrorist allies, constitute an axis of evil, arming to threaten the peace of the world. By seeking weapons of mass destruction, these regimes pose a grave and growing danger. They could provide these arms to terrorists, giving them the means to match their hatred. They could attack our allies or attempt to blackmail the United States. In any of these cases, the price of indifference would be catastrophic.[20]

Later in 2002, US ambassador to the UN, John Bolton, added Syria, Cuba and Libya to this list as countries that sponsor terror and pursue the development of WMD. He said that Cuba 'has at least a limited offensive biological warfare research and development effort', and has 'provided dual-use technology to other rogue states'.[21] This post-9/11 US view of Cuba contrasts with its position taken in 1997 when it had concluded that, with the end of Soviet support, Cuba did not represent a military threat to the

16  Ibid., 280.
17  Ibid., 282–3.
18  F. Fukuyama, *The End of History and the Last Man* (London: Penguin, 1992).
19  W.M. Reisman, 'Coercion and Self-Determination: Construing Charter Article 2(4)' (1984) 78 *AJIL* 642. In contrast see O. Schachter, 'The Legality of Pro-Democratic Invasion', (1984) 78 *AJIL* 645.
20  State of the Union Address, 29 January 2002 (available at www.washingtonpost.com/wp-srv/onpolitics/transcripts/sou012902.htm (accessed 15 May 2014)).
21  'Beyond the Axis of Evil' speech, 6 May 2002 (available at www.heritage.org/research/lecture/beyond-the-axis-of-evil?ac=1 (accessed 15 May 2014)).

US.[22] The evidence against Cuba is not strong, although Cuba has links with North Korea. This was shown in July 2013 when Cuban arms were found during a search conducted at the Panama Canal on a North Korean ship, the *Chong Chon Gang*, heading for North Korea.[23] Cuba claimed that the weapons (some of which were from the Soviet era) were being sent to North Korea for refurbishment. A UN Panel of Experts investigated whether this breached the UN Security Council arms embargo imposed against North Korea,[24] and concluded in its report of March 2014, which covered a range of North Korean transgressions, that 'both the shipment itself and the transactions between Cuba and the Democratic People's Republic of Korea were sanctions violations'.[25] No action against Cuba has been taken as a result, although the Security Council, in accepting the report, urged all states to cooperate with the sanctions committee established by the Security Council as well as the Panel of Experts 'in particular by supplying any information at their disposal on the implementation' of the sanctions imposed on North Korea. The mandate of the Panel of Experts was extended for another year, raising the possibility of it uncovering any further breaches of the embargo by Cuba, as well as the possibility that such transgressions might result in action being taken.[26]

## 5.4 Law as power

The contention that Cuba has placed itself outside the protection of the doctrine of sovereign equality, which guarantees it the same rights as other states, thereby justifying US measures against it, requires further investigation. While we may believe that law is something that can restrain power, law – international law especially – may be better explained as power. The argument that we have to focus on the 'real' rules governing state behaviour (ones reflecting the self-interest of states) and not those formal, 'paper' rules of the UN Charter and other foundational treaties, was articulated by Hans Morgenthau during the Second World War.[27] A modern exposition, one that follows the legal realist traditions of the great American judge, Oliver Wendell Holmes, whose exposition on the law coincided with the Treaty of Paris 1898,[28] is given by Michael Glennon. Glennon's pragmatic approach goes a long way to

---

22  P.J. Haney and W. Vanderbush, *The Cuban Embargo* (Pittsburgh, PA: University of Pittsburgh Press, 2005) 6.

23  BBC News, 'Panama: UN probes North Korean arms shipment', 14 August 2013 (www.bbc.co.uk/news/world-latin-america-23690639 (accessed 15 May 2014)).

24  UNSC Res 1718 (2006), 1874 (2009), 2087 (2013), and 2094 (2013).

25  UN Doc S/2014/147 (2014), Report of the Panel of Experts established pursuant to Resolution 1874 (2009), para 70; dismissing Cuba's arguments at para 78.

26  UNSC Res 2141 (2014).

27  H.J. Morgenthau, 'Positivism, Functionalism and International Law', (1940) 34 *AJIL* 260.

28  O.W. Holmes, 'The Path of the Law', (1897) 10 *Harvard Law Review* 457.

helping to explain the American government's approach to international law, and more particularly its use of self-help. Although Glennon's focus is on the rules and institutions on the use of force in international relations, his analysis can readily be applied to non-forcible measures such as the embargo imposed against Cuba. It must not be forgotten as well that the US has engaged in forcible measures against Cuba, first by sponsoring the failed Bay of Pigs invasion in 1961, and by the more successful imposition of a military quarantine around Cuba during the Missile Crisis of 1962.

It is too easy to dismiss pragmatic approaches such as Glennon's as an apology or justification for 'might equals right',[29] but this does a disservice to realists who put forward strong arguments that should be countered with care and precision. Furthermore, such arguments present a clear explanation of American actions, and thus help develop a deeper understanding of decisions to invade countries, or to submit them to embargoes. The pragmatic approach is not just about considerations of power; it is more sophisticated than the classical realist approach. Classical realism treats states as uniform, not in the sense of legal equality, but in the sense of self-interest and, further, is not prepared to delve deeply into the internal politics that explain external action.[30] Our analysis of the Cuban embargo, in the next chapter, shows that the measures were very much a product of domestic politics and law, and that international law was often peripheral to the decisions to impose, maintain and strengthen the embargo.

According to Glennon, pragmatism shares a great deal with other theoretical positions: with positivism's scepticism of natural law, with the policy school's 'reaction against formalism', with realism's recognition that 'law is shaped by power', with liberal cosmopolitanism's view that 'domestic variables also drive state behaviour'; and even postmodernism's scepticism of grand narratives and truths, although 'pragmatism does not value toleration of "otherness" (or anything else) as an all-trumping ideal'. Pragmatists not only eschew grand theories and question the formal application of rules, they emphasise a more empirical approach that considers the behaviour of states; and they are sceptical about formalism's claim that assumes that rules actually shape or cause state behaviour, and are deeply sceptical of the natural-law inspired notion of *jus cogens*.[31] For example, the fact that most states appear to observe the ban on the use of force because they have not used force in international relations is pointed to by formalists, including the International

---

29　N. Chomsky, 'Commentary: Moral Truisms, Empirical Evidence, and Foreign Policy', (2003) 29(4) *Review of International Studies* 605 at 619.

30　K. Waltz, *Man, the State, and War: A Theoretical Analysis* (New York: Columbia University Press, 1959) 121.

31　M. Glennon, *The Fog of Law: Pragmatism, Security, and International Law* (Chicago, IL: Stanford University Press, 2010) 1–12, 68–74.

Court of Justice,[32] as evidence of the rule being complied with, but there is no attempt to prove this. For example, it may be the case that most states are too weak militarily to attempt aggression against another state, at least an aggression that has 'scale and effects',[33] or that their priorities are understandably elsewhere. When it comes to non-forcible measures, as we shall see later in this chapter, the formal rules are less clear than those governing the use of force, arguably increasing their irrelevance in the face of power.

Glennon argues that international rules governing the use of force (those contained in Article 2(4) and 51 of the UN Charter) are mere paper rules and do not work to constrain state behaviour. This, he argues, can be demonstrated empirically.[34] There is no doubt that Glennon would apply the same reasoning to non-forcible measures of self-help. In general terms, he states that an 'international rule ought not to be considered law if its behavioural effects fall significantly short of what is ostensibly intended'; indeed it should be recognised that such rules fall into desuetude – 'a rule's abandonment through non enforcement or non compliance'.[35]

The persistent violation of the rule prohibiting intervention in the case of the Cuban embargo and other instances of economic coercion in the practice of states, the pragmatists would argue, signifies that the rule is not only a paper one (as opposed to a real rule of international law that explains how 'states seek to preserve and enhance their security'),[36] but also arguably one that has fallen into desuetude. For Glennon rules are not binding because of some 'mystical, transcendental obligation to obey law', not because 'states have somehow consented to be obliged'; rather a norm is obligatory 'because the costs of violation outweigh the benefits for nearly all states nearly all the time'.[37] Applying Justice Holmes' 'bad man' approach to international law, Glennon argues that just as law in a domestic legal system is a prediction of what will happen to a bad man, so in 'the international legal order, the prediction is that states will make transgressions costly enough to prevent bad states from being bad'.[38] While domestic legal rules may be more resistant to claims of desuetude since they may still be enforced, albeit sporadically, by state apparatus, international rules are more open to falling into disuse because state actors that have made the rules are, by not observing them, in effect remaking the rules.[39] In domestic legal systems there is a separation of lawmakers and subjects, while there is no such separation in the international

32  *Nicaragua Case* (n.3), paras 186–8.
33  Ibid., para 195.
34  Glennon (n.31), 21.
35  Ibid., 22–3.
36  Ibid., 29.
37  Ibid., 54.
38  Ibid., 55, 226.
39  Ibid., 84.

legal order – 'the system has no Leviathan of the sort that dominates a domestic legal system, no people in uniform with guns and handcuffs who show up when a violation occurs'.[40]

Thus, for the pragmatist, 'no rules will work that do not reflect underlying geopolitical realities', so that states will continue to judge for themselves what is required to defend their essential interests.[41] 'Pragmatism focuses on what experience tells us will work, not on what doctrine, dogma, or morality tells us must work'. For the pragmatist the 'question is always, what are the probable costs and benefits – the long- and short-term consequences – of the proposed action?'[42] The consequence of this approach is that the real rules that govern state behaviour may vary from region to region,[43] which could be extrapolated to argue that in the American hemisphere, in the 'backyard' of the United States, different rules will apply between the United States and countries like Cuba that challenge its dominance.

Glennon applies these principles to the role of self-help in the international legal system. He questions the consensual basis of international law, pointing out that analogies with the law of contract in domestic systems are unhelpful, since in the domestic system the voluntary contract is ultimately enforced by state machinery, while the international system 'lacks a similar framework of coercion'.[44] This leads to self-help, something which is clearly not voluntary on the part of the target state. Glennon makes the point that 'states that deviate from expected patterns of practice face recriminations'; 'sometimes those responses take the form of immediate diplomatic, economic, or military sanctions', or they may be longer term and reputational. In 'either event, violations incur costs, even though those costs are imposed horizontally, by other actors within the system, rather than vertically, by some supranational institution'.[45] Glennon ignores the competence of the UN and other institutions to impose non-forcible measures, but his point is that the international system still permits plenty of self-help within it. Despite increased post-Cold War action taken by the UN Security Council, Glennon still argues that a 'vigilant and muscular Security Council' has not materialised, rendering self-help as the only 'realistic alternative'.[46]

This chapter turns to consider the role of self-help as recognised in post-1945 international legal doctrine, and considers whether these rules are of the 'paper' variety only, or whether they play a more profound role in terms of judging and regulating the behaviour of states, no matter how powerful they are.

40  Ibid., 102.
41  Ibid., 122–3.
42  Ibid., 124.
43  Ibid., 128.
44  Ibid., 34.
45  Ibid., 37.
46  Ibid., 119.

## 5.5 Self-help in international law

Traditionally, states co-exist in a legal system that is essentially consensual.[47] States, no matter their disparities in size or strength, are sovereign and equal. Obligations are accepted by states either in treaty or custom by consent; they are not imposed by any higher authority. In its purest form such a legal condition arguably existed for European states in the eighteenth and nineteenth centuries. Obviously there was no equality between European states and colonised territories and peoples and so international law was not universal. This period was one of self-help between European states, in that if a state breached one of its obligations, the victim state(s) of such a breach could take both non-forcible and forcible measures to remedy or to punish that breach. Forcible measures could range from measures short of war, such as armed reprisals, or could take the form of war. War itself could be a relatively minor exchange of fire, even mere confrontation without hostilities, or it could be a full-scale bloody conflict, the causes of which could be relatively minor. Self-interest was the norm.

One of the principal methods of enforcing perceived rights or, more realistically, punishing perceived wrongs, in this period was by armed reprisal. Such reprisals were clearly lawful in the period up to the First World War, and were only prohibited when states finally agreed upon a norm prohibiting all types of armed force in the UN Charter in 1945. The seminal example given in legal texts is the *Naulilaa Case*, one of the rare instances when the legality of an armed reprisal was adjudicated upon.[48] Reprisals were the normal method of law enforcement while judicial settlement was the exception. In the *Naulilaa Case* the two were brought together. In the case, Germany had carried out an armed reprisal from its colony in South-West Africa (now Namibia) against the Portuguese colony of Angola in October 1914. These hostilities were not formally part of the First World War because Portugal was, at the time, a neutral power. The initial injury to Germany arose out of an incident on the Angolan–Namibian border, one that resulted in the deaths of three German soldiers. The German army responded by mounting a military expedition deep into Angola causing significant damage and loss of life. Both states agreed to arbitration after the end of the First World War, and while the arbitral tribunal accepted that reprisals were lawful under international law when taken in response to a violation of international law, they were subject to certain limitations that Germany had not complied with: first, Germany had not first made an unsatisfied demand that Portugal remedy its unlawful actions and, second, Germany's reprisal was out of all

---

47 This section draws from the author's analysis in N.D. White and A. Abass, 'Countermeasures and Sanctions' in M. Evans (ed.), *International Law* (4th edn, Oxford University Press, 2014) ch.18.
48 *Naulilaa Case* (1928) 2 RIAA 1052.

proportion to the wrong that had provoked it. It is interesting that this move towards limiting reprisals occurred, in effect, between the Wars, establishing a trend that ended in the prohibition of the use of force in the UN Charter,[49] and in a clear statement in 1970 by the General Assembly that this meant that armed reprisals were contrary to international law.[50]

With the advent of the League of Nations in 1919, created in the aftermath of the failure of the system of self-help, there emerged structures as well as norms that were again suggestive of a more hierarchical approach. The Covenant of the League of Nations purported to regulate, if not prohibit, war, and the organisation it established potentially had weak authority over states. Brierly argued that the League remained based on the principles of consensuality and voluntarism,[51] a view that would suggest that the organisation did not upset the pre-existing order. McNair, on the other hand, thought that the League marked a move away from a system of purely 'private' law between consenting states towards a system of 'public' law,[52] indicating a more vertical system of regulation.

The idea of an international organisation, with some measure of authority over states, took an even firmer grip on the imagination of states during the Second World War. The United Nations was created in 1945, its Charter containing, in Article 2(4), a rule prohibiting the threat or use of force in international relations, and creating machinery to promote and restore international peace and security. The prohibition of force, which itself formed a core norm in an emerging corpus of peremptory norms of international law (*jus cogens*) from which states could not derogate, immediately cut back on the type of measures a state could take in response to a breach of international law. Self-help was reduced to half its former size by the UN Charter. Although states were still permitted to take forcible action in self-defence in response to an armed attack against them (under Article 51 of the Charter), forcible measures beyond that were prohibited by the new legal regime initiated by the Charter. Some states and writers have repeatedly tried to resurrect the concept of armed reprisals.[53] A modern example of what appears to be a reprisal is the US attacks on targets in the Libyan cities of Tripoli and Benghazi in 1986, which were taken in response to a terrorist bombing of a Berlin Disco allegedly by Libyan agents in which a US serviceman was killed and about

---

49  Article 2(4) UN Charter 1945.
50  UNGA Res 2625 (1970), 'Declaration on Principles of International Law Concerning Friendly Relations and Co-operation among States in Accordance with the Charter of the United Nations' – 'States have a duty to refrain from acts of reprisal involving the use of force'.
51  J.L. Brierly, 'The Covenant and the Charter', (1946) 23 *BYBIL* 83 at 92.
52  A.D. McNair, 'The Functions and Different Character of Treaties', (1930) 11 *BYBIL* 100 at 112.
53  D.W. Bowett, 'Reprisals Involving Recourse to Armed Force', (1972) 66 *AJIL* 1.

200 civilians were injured. Although the facts were disturbingly similar to the *Naulilaa Case*, in that the US bombing led to hundreds of deaths, the justification put forward by US President Reagan and his administration was an argument of preventive self-defence – that the action was taken to prevent further Libyan-inspired terrorist activities rather than as punishment.[54] In other words, although the incident looked like a punitive reprisal undertaken by the US, it was justified as an action in self-defence, indicating a lack of *opinio juris* in the legality of reprisals *per se*. A majority of states in the General Assembly condemned the armed attack by the US.[55]

The prohibition in the UN Charter of forcible measures of self-help left the position of non-forcible measures untouched but, at the same time, unclear. Clarity was lacking because the doctrines that had emerged over the centuries were inevitably subject to many interpretations. In addition, the UN itself was given significant power to impose obligations on member states to impose non-forcible measures against miscreant member states by virtue of Article 41 of the UN Charter.[56] The developing Inter-American (OAS) system of collective security also provided for the application of such measures,[57] a trend that was to be followed by some other regional organisations. After 1945 a self-help system of non-forcible measures, deriving from an earlier period of international relations, had to co-exist with a system of centralised 'sanctions' based on notions of hierarchy and governance.

The concept of lawful non-forcible measures survived the new world order of the post-1945 period. Article 2(4) of the Charter prohibited the 'threat or use of force', 'force' being clearly understood as military force.[58] State practice in the immediate post-1945 period provided evidence of a continuation of the concept of non-forcible measures. As Elagab states '[r]egardless of whether the conditions of legality had been complied with in each case, the crucial feature was the very fact of such claims being staked at all. This provides a presumption of continuity of counter-measures as a viable mode of redress'.[59] In the first decade after the UN Charter the US adopted, *inter alia*, measures freezing the assets of China, Bulgaria, Romania, and Hungary, in response to perceived illegalities committed by those states. The coinage of the term

---

54   UNSC 2674th meeting (1986) 41.
55   UNGA Res 41/38 (1986).
56   Article 41 provides: 'The Security Council may decide what measures not involving the use of armed force are to be employed to give effect to its decisions . . . These may include complete or partial interruption of economic relations and of rail, sea, air, postal, telegraphic, radio, and other means of communication, and the severance of diplomatic relations'.
57   Articles 8, 17, 20 Rio Treaty, 1947, 21 UNTS 77.
58   But see J. Paust and A.P. Blaustein, 'The Arab Oil Weapon – A Threat to International Peace', (1974) 68 *AJIL* 410 at 417.
59   O.Y. Elagab, *The Legality of Non-Forcible Counter-Measures in International Law* (Oxford: Oxford University Press, 1988) 38.

'countermeasures' in the *Air Services Agreement Case* of 1978,[60] and the codification of countermeasures by the International Law Commission (ILC) culminating in Chapter III of the Articles on State Responsibility of 2001, represent the consolidation of countermeasures as a legitimate form of self-help in the structures of international law.

## 5.6 Countermeasures

Countermeasures have been equated to the biblical eye for an eye, tooth for a tooth writ on to the international stage.[61] However, this punitive depiction seems a long way from countermeasures as codified by the International Law Commission in 2001. Despite the proliferation of international institutions since 1945, the ILC was confident in asserting in 2001 that countermeasures remained inherent in a decentralised system where 'injured states may seek to vindicate their rights and to restore the legal relationship with the responsible state which has been ruptured by' an unlawful act.[62] As noted by Alland – 'countermeasures are a mechanism of private justice', which can result in 'contradictions inherent in a self-assessed (i.e., auto-interpreted or auto-appreciated) decentralised policing of an international *ordre public*'.[63] Provost is even more explicit in depicting the weaknesses of such a system, when he writes that 'the right of states unilaterally to assess a breach by another state and to validate what would otherwise be an illegal act has the potential of significantly destabilising international relations'.[64]

Nevertheless, as has been stated above, a totally decentralised system no longer exists. While injured states are entitled to take certain non-forcible actions within a bilateral context against states responsible for a breach of international law, sanctions imposed by the UN and other international organisations, create a vertical relationship between the institutions and the implementing states. Essentially, the horizontal system of self-help has been supplemented by the empowerment of organisations with the competence to create vertical relationships. After 1945 there no longer exists a pure system of self-help, and this has affected practice as shall be seen. States wanting to take measures against a state in violation of international law may go to international bodies for authority/legitimacy, indeed it could be argued that they ought to do this when they are not the direct victims of the unlawful act.

---

60  *Air Services Agreement Case* (1978) 54 ILR 303.
61  T.M. Franck, 'On Proportionality of Countermeasures in International Law', (2008) 102 *AJIL* 715 at 763.
62  J. Crawford, *The International Law Commission's Articles on State Responsibility* (Cambridge: Cambridge University Press, 2002) 281.
63  D. Alland, 'Countermeasures of General Interest', (2002) 13 *EJIL* 1221 at 1235.
64  R. Provost, *State Responsibility in International Law* (Aldershot: Ashgate, 2002) xv.

After the adoption of the Articles on State Responsibility of 2001, the concept of countermeasures has taken on a narrow form, situating them at one end of a spectrum of non-forcible measures that are taken by states in international relations. At the other end of the spectrum are sanctions imposed by international organisations. In between, there is a grey area where regulation is rudimentary, indeed, arguably, non-existent, and it is in this area that the Cuban embargo sits. As Bederman suggests 'the central conceptual mission' of the ILC's articles on countermeasures, is 'the search for a polite international society'.[65] Further, he contends that the countermeasures articles represent a 'profound impulse toward social engineering for international relations . . . imagining a time in international life when unilateral and horizontal means of enforcement through robust self-help will be a thing of the past'.[66] Indeed, while the ILC does purport to define and constrain countermeasures, in so doing it leaves question marks hanging over the legality of a large segment of state practice on wider non-forcible measures.

Countermeasures 'are intrinsically unlawful, but are justified by the alleged failing to which they were a response'.[67] In its final Articles on State Responsibility of 2001, the ILC defined countermeasures as non-forcible measures taken by an injured state in response to a breach of international law in order to secure the end of the breach and, if necessary, reparation. Non-forcible countermeasures may only be taken in response to an internationally wrongful act and then only against the state responsible for that act.[68] If such measures are taken without fulfilling these conditions, they themselves will constitute internationally wrongful acts, giving rise to state responsibility and possible countermeasures. According to the ILC, countermeasures are limited to the temporary non-performance of one or some of the international obligations that the injured state owes to the responsible state.[69] Cassese's summation is perhaps stronger than that of the ILC, but useful nonetheless. He states that 'in the event of a breach of international law, the injured state is legally entitled to disregard an international obligation owed to the delinquent state'.[70] Countermeasures are not intended to be punishment for illegal acts but as 'an instrument for achieving compliance with the obligations of the responsible state'. Countermeasures are taken 'as a form of inducement, not punishment'. The ILC's definition does not restrict states taking countermeasures to the suspension of performance of the same or very similar obligation. Countermeasures, however, are more likely to accord with the conditions of proportionality and necessity if they are so taken. Such measures

65  D.J. Bederman, 'Counterintuiting Countermeasures', (2002) 96 *AJIL* 817 at 819.
66  Ibid., 831.
67  Alland (n.63), 1221.
68  Article 49 Articles on Responsibility of States for Internationally Wrongful Acts 2001.
69  Ibid.
70  A. Cassese, *International Law* (2nd edn, Oxford University Press, 2005) 302.

which correspond to the obligation breached by the responsible state are sometimes called 'reciprocal countermeasures'.[71]

The suspension or temporary non-performance of a treaty obligation, quite often the suspension of a trade agreement, and the freezing of the assets of a state, are primary examples of countermeasures.[72] The paradigmatic case of countermeasures is the *US-French Air Services Arbitration* of 1978. This case concerned the application of the bilateral air services agreement that existed between the two countries – France and the US. France had objected, as being incompatible with the treaty, to a change of type of aircraft by PanAm on its flight from the US to Paris. French authorities prevented PanAm passengers from disembarking in Paris. By the time of arbitration, the US had initiated (but had not implemented) measures that would have prohibited certain French flights to the US. The arbitral tribunal found that the change of aircraft-type by PanAm was permitted under the treaty and that US retaliatory measures were permissible countermeasures, which were not disproportionate to the treaty violation committed by France. The arbitral tribunal stated:

> If a situation arises, which in one state's view, results in the violation of an international obligation by another state, the first state is entitled, within the limits set by general rules of international law pertaining to the use of armed force, to affirm its rights through 'countermeasures'.[73]

Of course, the case reveals the inherent problem with countermeasures, indeed with measures of self-help more generally, in that the crucial element, the determination of the initial wrongful act, is a subjective one. As Alland makes clear it is this 'self-assessed' aspect of countermeasures which 'manifests the danger they represent in the international legal order: they open the possibility to all states to take prejudicial measures contrary to the obligations incumbent on them on the basis of subjective unilateral claims'.[74]

Countermeasures are a limited form of self-help and, for that reason, are unlikely to satisfy a powerful state that wants to use its economic power to enforce compliance by another state. Countermeasures must not be forcible.[75] Furthermore, 'anticipatory non-forcible counter-measures are unlawful; since by definition they precede actual occurrence of breach'.[76] Countermeasures should be directed against the responsible state and not third states.

---

71 Crawford (n.62), 282–6.
72 Ibid., 286.
73 *Air Services Agreement Case* (n.60), 337.
74 D. Alland, 'The Definition of Countermeasures' in J. Crawford, A. Pellet and S. Olleson (eds), *The Law of International Responsibility* (Oxford: Oxford University Press, 2010) 1127 at 1129.
75 Article 50(1)(a) Articles on Responsibility of States for Internationally Wrongful Acts 2001.
76 Elagab (n.59), 63.

Countermeasures are temporary and should, whenever possible, be reversible so the future legal relations between victim state and responsible state can be restored.[77] If the measures taken punish the responsible state by inflicting irreparable damage on it then they are not countermeasures.[78] Such punitive measures would appear to be non-forcible reprisals, the legality of which is not discussed by the ILC, but that body's movement away from the notion of punishment as the rationale for countermeasures indicates uncertainty about the legality of non-forcible reprisals. This is supported by the International Court's statement in the *Gabčíkovo Case* that the purpose of countermeasures is to 'induce the wrongdoing State to comply with its obligations under international law, and that the measures must therefore be reversible'.[79] It is also noteworthy that James Crawford, the ILC Rapporteur on this topic, stated that the 'international community has moved away from the classical terminology of reprisals and towards the notion of countermeasures as temporary, reversible steps'.[80] As with many changes in international law it is not possible to draw a clear line between the demise of one concept or principle and the emergence of another; the transition is gradual.

Furthermore, countermeasures must be proportionate. According to the ILC, they 'must be commensurate with the injury suffered, taking account of the gravity of the internationally wrongful act and the rights in question'.[81] Disproportionate countermeasures give rise to the responsibility of the state taking them. Taking a different approach Franck asserts that the response must be proportionate to the initial unlawful act, equivalent to the biblical eye for an eye, tooth for a tooth approach.[82] However, there appears to be difficulties in both the approaches of the ILC and Franck. The issue ought not to be one of proportionality to the unlawful act or the injury it causes, because this would suggest that countermeasures are taken to punish the responsible state, thus confusing countermeasures with reprisals. As Cassese states 'in current international law the purpose of countermeasures must be seen . . . in impelling the offender to discontinue its wrongful conduct or to make reparation for it. If this is so, the proportionality must be appraised by establishing whether the countermeasure is such as to obtain this purpose'.[83] This would mean that in certain cases a weak state may be subject to countermeasures that are quantitatively less than the injury suffered by a

---

77  Article 49 Articles on Responsibility of States for Internationally Wrongful Acts 2001.
78  Crawford (n.62), 287.
79  *Gabčíkovo-Nagymaros Project (Hungary/Slovakia)* (1997) ICJ Rep 7, paras 56–7.
80  J. Crawford, 'The Relationship Between Countermeasures and Sanctions' in V. Gowlland-Debbas (ed.), *United Nations Sanctions and International Law* (The Hague: Kluwer, 2001) 57 at 66.
81  Article 51 Articles on the Responsibility of States for Internationally Wrongful Acts 2001.
82  Franck (n.61), 763.
83  Cassese (n.70), 306.

powerful state, if the measures are sufficient to bring an end to the illegal act.

According to the ILC's Articles of 2001, countermeasures must not violate basic obligations under international law (namely those prohibiting the threat or use of force, protecting fundamental human rights, and concerning obligations of a humanitarian character), and those arising under *jus cogens*. Countermeasures must follow an unsatisfied demand by the injured state that the responsible state comply with its international obligation(s). The injured state must also notify the responsible state that it intends to take counter-measures and offer to negotiate, except in the case of urgent countermeasures necessary to preserve the injured state's rights (for example temporary staying orders or the temporary freezing of assets).[84] Furthermore, countermeasures must be suspended if the wrongful act has ceased and the dispute has been submitted to a tribunal with binding authority.[85]

As can be seen, countermeasures is a limited doctrine and, as such, it appears to have limited traction in the case of the Cuban embargo. Further analysis is undertaken in Chapter 7 but, while the initial US embargo imposed in 1960 in response to Cuban expropriation of US-owned property might be viewed as a countermeasure, its continuation, disproportionality and punitive nature would not meet the limitations placed upon countermeasures. However, if the embargo is seen as a response to wider Cuban violations of international law (in the form of its interventions into Latin American and African countries reviewed in Chapter 4), then we have to consider whether international law permits the US to enforce international laws on behalf of victim states other than itself. We also need to consider whether the formal rules on countermeasures codified by the ILC do not capture the range of coercive economic measures undertaken by states.

## 5.7 Collective countermeasures

According to the 2001 Articles, countermeasures are normally taken by a state injured by an internationally wrongful act committed by another state. However, the Articles recognise that responsibility may be invoked by states other than the injured state acting in the collective interest.[86] Responsibility is not invoked by these third states as a result of injury to themselves but as a result of breach of an obligation owed to a group of states of which it is a member – obligations *erga omnes partes* (for example regional human rights regimes), or to the international community as a whole – obligations *erga*

---

84  Ibid., 299.
85  Article 52 Articles on Responsibility of States for Internationally Wrongful Acts 2001.
86  Crawford (n.62), 276.

*omnes* (for example, laws prohibiting genocide, aggression, slavery, racial discrimination, self-determination).[87]

However, the Articles distinguish between third states invoking responsibility and such states taking countermeasures. The latter issue is left open. Third states can demand cessation and performance in the interests of the injured states or the beneficiaries of the obligation breached,[88] but the question remains as 'to what extent these states may legitimately assert a right to react against unremedied breaches' by taking countermeasures against the responsible state. [89] One problem in taking collective countermeasures is that of proportionality, although it is difficult to prove a violation of this principle if the aim is to stop a breach of an obligation owed *erga omnes*. In the absence of institutional sanctions imposed by the UN Security Council under Chapter VII of the Charter, for example, the legality of such measures is in doubt, although there seems to be some practice to support the proposition that such measures are allowed. However, practice is inconsistent, making the drawing of any conclusions as to *opinio juris* extremely difficult if not impossible.

Further, it is inaccurate to portray such 'collective' countermeasures as a replacement for centralised collective action through an international organisation. The term 'collective countermeasures' gives the 'illusion of concerted action when in reality such collective countermeasures are really individual initiatives – even though there is more than one such initiative at the same time'.[90] In addition, the subjective assessments by states as to whether to impose such countermeasures undermine the enforcement of these crucial norms.[91] However, it is true to say that to expect international institutions such as the UN Security Council to replace this subjective assessment with something more objective when considering whether to impose non-forcible measures under Chapter VII of the UN Charter would, in reality, 'be replacing one subjectivity (of states) by another (of the Security Council)'.[92] It is therefore premature to argue that the UN Security Council's sanctioning machinery has, or indeed should, replace a system of collective countermeasures even though that system is very weak. In reality there currently exist two weak systems of non-forcible sanctions, one decentralised and one (partly) centralised, for the enforcement of community norms.

Indeed, state practice under the decentralised system as analysed by the ILC leads it to conclude that:

---

87  Article 48 Articles on the Responsibility of States for Internationally Wrongful Acts 2001.
88  Ibid.
89  Crawford (n.62), 302.
90  Alland (n.63), 1222.
91  Ibid., 1237.
92  P. Klein, 'Responsibility for Serious Breaches of Obligations Deriving from Peremptory Norms of International Law and United Nations Law', (2002) 13 *EJIL* 1241 at 1249.

The current state of international law on countermeasures taken in the general or collective interest is uncertain. State practice is sparse and involves a limited number of states. At present there appears to be no clearly recognized entitlement of [third] states . . . to take countermeasures in the collective interest.[93]

Hence Article 54 of the ILC Articles states that a third state's right to take 'lawful' measures is not prejudiced by any of its other provisions on countermeasures. What are lawful measures in this context is an issue that is, in effect, left open. Bederman's summary of the ILC's position on collective countermeasures characterises it as the 'only possible political solution', which was 'to defer debate to another day and to allow customary international lawmaking processes to elaborate any conditions on the use of collective countermeasures'.[94]

In its commentary the ILC mentions the US prohibition in 1978 of export of goods and technology to Uganda and all imports from that country in response to alleged genocide by the government of Uganda.[95] This certainly appears to be a response to a breach of an obligation owed *erga omnes*, but it did not only concern the suspension of existing US–Ugandan treaty obligations and, therefore, went beyond the concept of countermeasures as defined by the ILC. The US response appears to consist of unilateral non-forcible measures, in effect sanctions, imposed to enforce community norms. The ILC also refers to measures taken by Western states against Poland and the Soviet Union in 1981 in response to internal repression by the Polish government. Measures included suspension of treaty landing rights for scheduled civilian aircraft. These actions seemed to take the form of countermeasures but were they a response to a breach of an obligation owed *erga omnes*? It is still difficult, though not impossible, to argue for a right to democracy in the twenty-first century, but in 1981 such an argument was mainly a political, not a legal, one. The US countermeasures in the form of the suspension of treaty landing rights against South African airlines in 1986 seem to be a clearer example given the odium attached to the system of apartheid, and its categorisation as a crime against humanity.

Crawford casts further doubts on the role in international law of obligations *erga omnes*.[96] The ICJ inspired the concept in the *Barcelona Traction Case*,[97] but in a dictum wholly inapplicable to the case. When the Court was faced, in the *Second South West Africa* and the *East Timor Cases*, with concrete arguments

---

93  Crawford (n.62), 305. But see L.-A. Sicilianos, 'Countermeasures in Response to Grave Violations of Obligations Owed to the International Community' in Crawford, Pellet and Olleson (n.74), 1137 at 1148.
94  Bederman (n.65), 828.
95  Crawford (n.62), 302–4.
96  Ibid.
97  *Barcelona Traction, Light and Power Company* (1970) ICJ Rep 3, paras 33–4.

based on *erga omnes*, it shied away from the application of the concept. This may indicate doubts about whether collective measures, taken outside the UN or other organisations by third states, can constitute lawful countermeasures. In reality, they are a modern form of non-forcible measure or sanction that operates outside the narrowly defined countermeasures regime. They are in essence, in the grey area between the doctrine of countermeasures as defined by the ILC, and the imposition of centralised sanctions by the UN and other legitimate international organisations.

Cassese suggests that in the case of countermeasures taken by third states in response to 'aggravated responsibility' (i.e., breach of fundamental rules), then a precondition is that they have sought to bring the matter before an international organisation. This can be the UN or a regional organisation, with a view to settlement or the adoption of sanctions. This precondition is 'dictated by the inherent nature of this class of responsibility'. This responsibility 'arises out of a gross attack on community or "public" values'. The response 'to the wrongdoing must therefore be as much as possible public and collective'. However, according to Cassese, 'if those bodies take no action, or their action has not brought about cessation of the wrong or adequate reparation . . . all states are empowered to take peaceful countermeasures on an individual basis'.[98]

The reality is that economic measures taken by a third state will often be motivated by the desire to enforce community norms, but only when these coincide with the national interest of the sanctioning state. It is worthwhile highlighting the economic measures taken by the US against Nicaragua in the 1980s. In addition to US support for the Contras against the left-wing Sandinista government in Nicaragua, support that was condemned as unlawful intervention and illegal use of force by the International Court of Justice,[99] the US government also imposed economic measures against Nicaragua. In 1982, the US imposed a strict sugar quota on imports from Nicaragua in response to Nicaragua's subversive acts in the neighbouring states of Honduras and Costa Rica. In 1985, the US increased countermeasures by prohibiting the import of goods and services from Nicaragua as well as exports to that country. It also suspended in-coming flights by Nicaraguan airlines and prohibited Nicaraguan vessels from entering US ports. This was justified by the US by the 'unusual and extraordinary threats to its national security and foreign policy resulting from Nicaragua's aggressive policies in Central America caused by the subversion of its neighbouring countries and the enhancement of its military and security ties with the USSR and Cuba'.[100]

---

98    Cassese (n.70), 274.

99    *Nicaragua Case* (n.3).

100   E. Katselli, 'Countermeasures: Concept and Substance in the Protection of Collective Interests' in K.H. Kaikobad and M. Bohlander (eds), *International Law and Power: Perspectives on Legal Order and Justice* (Leiden: Nijhoff, 2009) 401 at 426.

These actions were not judged upon by the International Court of Justice,[101] but that does not mean they were lawful. Rather they embody Glennon's depiction of pragmatism based on national self-interest. Furthermore, they bear a strong resemblance to the measures taken against Cuba, reviewed in Chapter 6.

## 5.8 Economic coercion

While the 2001 Articles limit lawful countermeasures to quite a specific and 'civilised' or 'polite' form of self-help, thereby implicitly excluding reprisals and unilateral or collective sanctions taken outside of international organisations, the reality of international relations seems to be very different. Powerful states do not always appear to be constrained by the niceties of the requirements of countermeasures; they do not simply suspend obligations; they do not simply seek to remedy the illegality; what they seek is coercion and punishment by the application of coercive, but non-forcible sanctions. While preferring a collective umbrella for these actions if possible, the United States, for example, is prepared to go it alone if necessary. Its sanctions against Iran first imposed in 1979 and those against the Soviet Union in 1980 are cases in point. Neither could be authorised by the Security Council, and so the US imposed them unilaterally. This has led one leading US commentator to state that 'the suggestion that economic sanctions are unlawful unless approved by the Security Council (or by a regional organisation such as the OAS) is obsolete'. Furthermore, he states that 'sanctions have become sufficiently common – and often better than the alternatives – to have become tolerated (not to say accepted) as a tool of foreign relations'.[102] Furthermore, as we shall see in Chapter 6, US practice (especially on Cuba) includes the imposition of extraterritorial measures to enforce sanctions.[103] Even when the Security Council does agree on sanctions, for instance against North Korea for WMD proliferation,[104] the United States' own non-forcible measures, although largely similar, make no reference to them.[105]

The US approach reflects an older version of international law. Writing in 1933 Lauterpacht stated that 'in the absence of explicit conventional obligations, particularly those laid down in commercial treaties, a state is entitled to prevent altogether goods from a foreign state from coming into its territory'. The prevention of trade going the other way from the victim

101 *Nicaragua Case* (n.3), para 87.
102 A.F. Lowenfeld, 'Unilateral versus Collective Sanctions: An American Perspective' in Gowlland-Debbas (n. 80), 95 at 96.
103 See US Helms-Burton Act 1996.
104 UNSC Res 1874 (2009).
105 Executive Order 13466, promulgated by President Bush on 26 June 2008, renewed by President Obama on 24 June 2009.

state to the responsible state seemed equally permissible in the pre-Charter period. Further, this is justified on the basis that 'in a community from which war in its technical sense has been eliminated and which has not reached the stage of moral perfection, pacific means of pressure are unavoidable. To prohibit them would mean to court the more radical remedy of war'.[106] In a modern sense, this still appears to be the case, subject to the requirements of the multilateral trade regime of the World Trade Organisation (WTO). Non-forcible measures, ranging from countermeasures in the ILC sense to punitive economic sanctions, can be justified under the view that 'restrictions upon the independence of States, cannot be presumed',[107] in other words on the basis of a state's freedom to trade. However, this basic tenet of sovereignty has to be balanced against another tenet – that of non-intervention. The sovereign freedom of a state must always be balanced against the infringement of the sovereignty of other states.

To take two obvious instances – the Arab oil embargo of 1973–74, and the US embargo against Cuba in place since 1960. These appear much more coercive, hurtful, and intrusive than the regime of countermeasures suggested by the ILC. Their motivations were political – to support the Palestinians and to undermine a communist regime respectively – they were not solely about the suspension of obligations in response to an illegal act in order to try and remedy that act. Such embargoes appear to breach the law as stated in several General Assembly resolutions that prohibit coercive economic intervention that is intended to undermine the territorial integrity or political independence (and arguably other sovereign rights) of the target states.[108] It is interesting to note too that the General Assembly has, in recent years, regularly called for the ending of the US economic, commercial, and financial embargo against Cuba and in so doing, it recalls the principle of non-intervention.[109] In its most recent resolution on the topic adopted on 29 October 2013 by 188 votes to 2 (Israel and US) with 3 abstentions (Marshall Islands, Micronesia, and Palau) the UN General Assembly again called for an end to the decades-long US economic, commercial and financial embargo against Cuba. The Assembly also expressed concern about the continued application by the US of laws such as the Helms-Burton Act of 1996, the extraterritorial reach of which affected the sovereignty of other states as well as the legitimate interests of foreign entities and persons.[110]

This debate is revisited in more detail in the next chapter, but there is a clear gap between the normative prescriptions of the General Assembly and

---

106  H. Lauterpacht, 'Boycott in International Relations', (1933) 14 *BYBIL* 125 at 130, 140.
107  *'Lotus', Judgment No. 9*, 1927, PCIJ, Ser A, No. 10 at 18.
108  UNGA Res 2131 (1965) on Non-intervention; UNGA Res 2625 (1970) on Friendly Relations; UNGA Res 3171 (1973) on Permanent Sovereignty over Natural Resources; UNGA Res 3281 (1974), Charter of Economic Rights and Duties of States.
109  Starting with UNGA Res 47/19 (1992).
110  UNGA Res 68/8 (2013).

the consistent practice of powerful states. As a form of compromise Lillich suggests a 'general principle that serious and sustained economic coercion should be accepted as a form of permissible self-help only when it is also compatible with the overall interests of the world community, as manifested in the principles of the UN Charter or in decisions taken or documents promulgated thereunder'.[111] However, this again favours the subjective interpretations of the powerful states. Furthermore, the approach advocated by Lillich is that non-forcible, principally economic activity and measures must be presumed to be lawful unless there is evidence of intent by the sanctioning state – 'measures not illegal *per se* may become illegal only upon proof of an improper motive or purpose'.[112] Given the unclear state of international law, that presumption could equally be replaced by the opposite proposition that such measures that interfere with the sovereign rights of another state are unlawful.

Elagab considers state practice and Assembly resolutions and concludes rather ambivalently (but perhaps accurately) that 'there are no rules of international law which categorically pronounce either on the *prima facie* legality or *prima facie* illegality of economic coercion'. However, he is of the opinion that this does not leave economic coercion unregulated by international law, rather that 'individual rules of international law may be applied to determine the legality of economic conduct on a given occasion'. He seems to suggest that while non-forcible measures may involve some element of coercion, their regulation is not subject to the narrow doctrine of countermeasures but to general principles of international law.[113] Thus, the sanctions against Cuba by the US appear to go far beyond countermeasures and amount to economic coercion. This is then subject to applicable rules of international law, such as *jus cogens*, fundamental human rights standards and the principle of non-intervention, which (despite significant erosion over the years) has a core element, prohibiting coercion of political independence.[114]

## 5.9  Conclusion

It is true that pragmatism comes close at times to dismissing the formal rules of international law as irrelevant, but Glennon does not contend that international law has no relevance in decision-making; rules such as the ban on the use of force and non-intervention do play a role in decision-making alongside issues of self-interest, policy and politics. His point is that 'orthodox

---

111  R.B. Lillich, 'Economic Coercion and the International Legal Order', (1975) 51 *International Affairs* 358 at 366.
112  D.W. Bowett, 'Economic Coercion and Reprisals by States', (1972) 13 *Virginia Journal of International Law* 1 at 3–7.
113  Elagab (n.59), 212–13.
114  L. Boisson de Chazournes, 'Other Non-Derogable Rights' in Crawford, Pellet and Olleson (n.74), 1205 at 1209–11.

international lawyers typically overestimate the role that international law plays in maintaining the international system'.[115] Even pragmatic international lawyers are reluctant to embrace an approach that starts each dispute with a clean slate, to evaluate what the 'real rules' are between states X and Y. For to do so would be to admit that what international lawyers should engage with is not international law in the sense of treaty and customary commitments, but an assessment of what state X can do to state Y and get away with without consequence.

In contrast to the pragmatic and other power-focused theories, the universal approach portrays international law as being legitimately universally applicable to all states on the basis of sovereign equality, an approach that recognises the weaknesses of international law but still sees its rules and principles as embodying the values of the international community of states and other actors (values of equality, peace, humanity and justice), producing a system of law that can be held up against even the most powerful of actors. However, in evaluating the claim to universality of international law, the essential message of the pragmatist must not be forgotten. The ease with which international law is brushed aside by powerful states, with very little by way of sanction, needs to be taken seriously and requires a critical re-evaluation of the universal approach to international law.

We must also bear in mind the powerful critiques of sovereignty and sovereign equality relayed in this book in the writings of Antony Anghie and Gerry Simpson, whereby the sovereignty of developing states is viewed as more permeable and less robust than that of the major powers, so that equality before the law only truly exists before a court of law. In the face of real inequality found in the very essence of statehood how can we insist on the universality of international laws, laws that are very much founded on the notions of sovereign equality? Can a relatively thin veneer of sovereign equality support a strong set of universal rules that protect weak states from the strong? More specifically can a state whose sovereignty has been defined by its relationship to a powerful neighbour have rights of non-intervention and non-coercion in relation to that state? These questions are returned to in considering the Cuban embargo in the next chapter.

---

115  Glennon (n.31), 80, 125.

# 6  The Cuban embargo

## 6.1 Introduction

This chapter examines the US domestic political and legal framework for the embargo from the Presidential Executive Order that initiated it. The obstacles in the way of trying to end the embargo, both political and legal, are examined. This chapter considers the extent to which the US authorities have enforced the letter of the law and finds that, despite some lack of political will when faced with European objections to the extra-territorial effects of the Helms-Burton Act, the embargo has been applied and enforced against Cuba resulting in considerable suffering of the Cuban people, especially when Soviet economic relations with Cuba ended with the demise of the USSR in 1991.

Following from this chapter, Chapter 7 considers the legality of the embargo under the law of nations governing relations between governments, and in terms of more recent forms of international law including human rights law, bearing in mind that a solution will not entail the straightforward application of international law to the dispute, but will require the adjustment of both US and Cuban policy and law in the light of that international legal framework. This necessitates a consideration of wider claims to illegality by both parties to the dispute, bearing in mind that both countries point to violations of international law, including human rights law, by the other. From the US perspective Cuba has illegally expropriated US property and concerns (thereby violating the property rights of its citizens), intervened in other countries and has denied individual rights and democratic freedoms, ultimately the Cuban people's right to self-determination. From the Cuban point of view the US has illegally intervened in Cuba and has violated its people's economic and social rights, as well as its right to self-determination, in the sense of being left to decide its political and economic future.

Chapter 8 then considers what might follow from a determination of responsibility for breaches of international law uncovered in Chapter 7. It will illustrate that although it is possible to determine state responsibility under international law, legal accountability does not automatically follow in the absence of judicial mechanisms that might have jurisdiction or be given jurisdiction. It is further argued in Chapter 8 that the theory of responsibility must give way to the practicalities of dispute settlement, which uses law as a framework within which to settle the dispute rather than in a determinant manner under which one side loses and the other wins. Adapting Koskenniemi's idea of law being a 'gentle civiliser of nations' to the context of a bilateral dispute, Chapter 8 shows that when a political regime (such as that governing the US and Cuba since 1960) collapses, law plays a crucial role in establishing a new political regime. Furthermore, the chapter argues that, alongside formal rules of applicable law, underpinning values of peace, reconciliation, mutual respect and justice provide a complex and supple framework within which to resolve seemingly intractable problems. Although armed conflict between the US and Cuba has been limited, primarily to the Bay of Pigs confrontation in 1961, the level of hostility between the two countries has been such that before normal relations between the two states can be established, a post-conflict or rather post-confrontation transitional phase has to be passed through. It is by recognising both the limitations as well as the value of international law that it can be said to have a promising future, a future explored in the conclusion to the book in Chapter 9.

## 6.2 The politics of the embargo

The US embargo placed on Cuba began in October 1960 under President Eisenhower, when he revoked Cuba's sugar quota and invoked the Trading with the Enemy Act of 1917, which effectively prohibited all exports from the US to Cuba excluding food and medicine. In the period between the US recognising the revolutionary Cuban government in January 1959 and its severing of diplomatic relations in January 1961, and in response to the Cuban government's expropriation of US-owned farmlands greater than 1,000 acres, President Eisenhower prohibited US refineries in Cuba from refining crude oil from the Soviet Union, significantly cut the Cuban sugar quota, and imposed an economic embargo on all trade with Cuba except for food and medicine. In response, President Castro confiscated US oil refineries in Cuba, nationalised US and foreign owned properties, and expelled a significant number of US embassy staff. This period of 'back and forth' measures and countermeasures ended with the severance of diplomatic relations by the US. It also left in place the embargo, which has significantly evolved as the following recent description shows:

> The embargo is not a monolith; rather it is made up of several components: restrictions on travel to and from the island and on the sale of goods and services there, bans on investment in business ventures, constraints on immigration, limits on journalists and scholars going to Cuba, caps on how much money can be sent to family members in Cuba, and the like.[1]

---

1   P.J. Haney and W. Vanderbush, *The Cuban Embargo: The Domestic Politics of an American Foreign Policy* (Pittsburgh, PA: University of Pittsburgh Press, 2005) 2.

In its initial period, the embargo was in effect a weapon wielded by the US President. Haney and Vanderbush describe the US President in the Cold War period as an 'imperial' leader:

> From the imposition of the embargo by Executive Order, to the failed invasion at the Bay of Pigs, through failed attempts at restoring more normal relations during the détente of the 1970s, the president largely called the shots on Cuban policy during this period.[2]

Following the unsuccessful CIA-backed Bay of Pigs invasion in April 1961, President Kennedy signed the Foreign Assistance Act of 1961 authorising the President to impose a total embargo on trade with Cuba, which he invoked in February 1962 in Executive Order 3447.[3] After securing the withdrawal of Soviet missiles from Cuba in 1962, President Kennedy prohibited financial transactions by US citizens with Cuba and any travel to Cuba, and later ordered the freezing of all Cuban assets in the US.

Following President Kennedy's assassination in November 1963, his successor President Johnson persuaded OAS Foreign Ministers, acting as Organ of Consultation, to impose economic sanctions on Cuba as well as break off diplomatic relations with the Cuban government under Articles 6 and 8 of the Rio Treaty.[4] This was achieved by a 15–4 vote, purportedly as an act of collective self-defence in response to acts of subversion committed by Cuba against Latin American countries, particularly Venezuela.[5] President Nixon drew on the accusations levelled against Cuba regarding its interventions in Latin America, as well as intelligence about the construction (subsequently abandoned) of a Soviet submarine base in Cuba at Cienfuegos, to justify the continuation of the embargo.[6] Nixon's resignation in 1974, following the Watergate scandal, opened up the prospect of normalising US–Cuba relations and was followed by the OAS vote to lift its sanctions against Cuba in 1975. By 1975, a majority of OAS states no longer supported sanctions against Cuba but could not obtain the two-thirds vote necessary in the Organ of Consultation. However, by amending the Rio Treaty to permit the withdrawal of sanctions by a simple majority vote,[7] a majority of OAS states then adopted a resolution enabling each member state the 'freedom to normalize or conduct

---

2  Ibid., 1–12.
3  S. Lamrani, *The Economic War Against Cuba: A Historical and Legal Perspective on the US Blockade* (New York: Monthly Review Press, 2013) ch. 2.
4  OAS Doc OEA/Ser. C/II.9, Doc 48, Rev. 2 (1964).
5  M. Krinsky and D. Golove (eds), *United States Economic Measures Against Cuba: Proceedings in the United Nations and International Law Issues* (Northampton, MA: Aletheia Press, 1993) 301–2.
6  Haney and Vanderbush (n.1), 22–3.
7  OAS Doc AG/RES 178 (V-0/75).

their relations with the Republic of Cuba in accordance with their own national policy and interests'.[8] Cuba's military intervention in the Angolan conflict in support of the Marxist MPLA ended the prospect of the US normalising its relations with Cuba.[9]

It was under President Carter that the US came closest to ending the embargo. By amending the Treasury Department's Cuban Assets Control Regulation in 1977 he lifted travel restrictions to Cuba and allowed US citizens to spend up to $100 while there. The Carter Administration also oversaw an agreement on fishing rights and maritime boundaries between the two countries and both countries opened an 'interests' section in Washington and Havana performing some diplomatic functions. The prospect arose of the embargo coming to an end, although again it was Cuban involvement in Africa, this time in Ethiopia, which threatened this development. However, it was the 'discovery' of the presence of a Soviet military brigade in Cuba in 1979, which effectively ended such a prospect.[10] By 1980, Congress 'was becoming more assertive on issues of foreign policy', and the Cuban exile community 'began to emerge as a political force as parts of the exile community recognised that they needed to rethink their strategy from covert forceful acts against Castro . . . towards Washington lobbying'.[11]

In 1980, a newly formed interest group – the Cuban American National Foundation (CANF) – consisting of a group of 'Cuban American businessmen and ideologues', became a 'strategic partner' with the Administration of President Reagan,[12] modelling itself on the Israeli lobby,[13] and enabling the President to exert some control over Congress, which was becoming increasingly active in foreign affairs.[14] Although CANF did not fully represent the 1.5 million Cuban Americans (militant groups such as Alpha 66 and Omega 7 still advocated armed attacks against Cuba), CANF became the most effective organisation politically, enjoying a 'unique and privileged relationship with the federal government during the 1980s'.[15] CANF did not simply lobby Congress in support of a tightening of the embargo; in 1985 it also successfully lobbied for the establishment of the US Information Agency's Radio Martí, followed by TV Martí in 1990, with funding from Congress and described by one critic as 'virtually a Cuban exile propaganda organ'.[16]

CANF's declared objectives were initially to 'challenge the myths propagated by the Cuban government, through the objective analysis and

---

8 OAS Doc OEA/Ser. F/II. Doc 9/75 Rev. 2 (1975).
9 Haney and Vanderbush (n.1), 26.
10 Ibid., 27–8. US officials had known about this back in 1963.
11 Haney and Vanderbush (n.1), 29.
12 Ibid., 31.
13 The American Israel Public Affairs Committee, Haney and Vanderbush (n.1), 32, 35.
14 Haney and Vanderbush (n.1), 33.
15 Ibid., 38.
16 Ibid., 41–2.

reporting of conditions in Cuba, of Cuba's repressive dictatorship and destructive international policies, while promoting the ideals of respect for human rights and self-determination for the Cuban people'.[17] This aligned with the Reagan Administration's concern in the 1980s to push back the growing Cuban/Soviet involvement in Central America, for example by virtue of arms supplied to left-wing FMLN rebels in El Salvador, and with US support for anti-Marxist armed groups such as the Contras in Nicaragua. As related by Haney and Vanderbush, the Reagan Administration made a direct link from Moscow to Managua through Havana, a link that legitimated assistance to the Contras fighting the Sandinista government in Nicaragua, the invasion of Grenada, and substantial military support for the Salvadoran government, all in the early 1980s.

According to Haney and Vanderbush, cracking 'down on communism in Cuba, and attacking leftist governments or movements elsewhere in the hemisphere, were intertwined in the Reagan administration's policy of bringing the Cold War to the region in a more assertive way'.[18]

President Reagan stated:

> If we do not act promptly and decisively in the defense of freedom, new Cubas will arise from the ruins of today's conflicts. We will face more totalitarian regimes, tied militarily to the Soviet Union; more regimes exporting subversion.[19]

The policy of not allowing 'another Cuba' drove and justified the 1983 invasion of Grenada to replace a left-wing regime, military support to the right-wing government of El Salvador fighting the left-wing FMLN, and military support given to the right-wing Contra insurgents fighting the left-wing Sandinista regime in Nicaragua,[20] echoing, indeed, amplifying the doctrine of President Johnson when he justified the invasion of the Dominican Republic in 1965. The right–left/right–wrong polarity justified a strengthening of the embargo against Cuba by the reinstatement of travel constraints and the lapse of existing agreements arrived at in the Carter years. More importantly it facilitated the entrenchment of the embargo in US foreign policy after the loosening that occurred during the term in office of President Reagan's predecessor.

'Through much of the cold war period, the president and his advisers made Cuba policy, like most foreign policy, largely out of public view and away from domestic pressures', but control started to move away from the executive towards Congress as well as interest groups.[21] This meant that the

17  Ibid., 36, reporting that this statement remained on CANF's website until 1997.
18  Haney and Vanderbush (n.1), 53–4.
19  Ibid., 66.
20  Ibid., 56.
21  Ibid., 3.

underpinnings of Cuban foreign policy, including the embargo, spread from a relatively narrow focus on national security to include issues of trade, economics and human rights.[22] The partnership between President Reagan and CANF helped move US foreign policy on Cuba and Central America to the right 'but this would end up as a short-term win for President Reagan, and perhaps a longer term loss for the presidency, in terms of it being able to exercise control over Cuba policy'.[23]

## 6.3  The move to legislation

The administration of George Bush, who was elected in 1989, represented a pivotal point in the evolution of the embargo – from an executive policy tool aimed at isolating Cuba, continuing to punish it for its confiscation of US properties, removing it from Africa and stopping its interventions in Central America – towards a legislative tool aimed at promoting democracy and human rights in Cuba. It was the demise of the Soviet Union that served to end Cuban foreign interventions due to the effect of the sudden removal of Cuban–Soviet trade, which in 1989 accounted for nearly 75 per cent of all Cuba's trade.[24] Rather than end the embargo in 1991 on the basis that the threat from Cuba was minimal, the US maintained its measures as Cuba and Castro were seen as vulnerable. The Bush Administration argued for free, fair and internationally supervised elections, as were being held in former eastern-bloc socialist states, and demanded respect for human rights.[25]

The influence of CANF in Congress began to show through in legislative proposals regarding the embargo. After several unsuccessful proposals, the Cuban Democracy (Torricelli) Act was adopted in 1992, containing both carrots and sticks. The latter took the form of shutting off trade between foreign subsidiaries of US multinationals and Cuba, and by making it difficult for any ships that had stopped at a Cuban port to enter US ports. These measures were aimed at closing the '*de facto* loosening of the embargo' that followed the demise of the Soviet Union and the opening of the Cuban economy to the rest of the world.[26] The carrot took the form of reaching 'out to the Cuban people by making communication and family visits to Cuba easier'.[27] The Act passed into law in the last few days of Bush's presidency but only after his challenger, Bill Clinton, had accepted it, forcing the incumbent to endorse the Act as they both vied for the Cuban exile vote.[28]

22  Ibid., 4.
23  Ibid., 51.
24  Ibid., 79.
25  Ibid.
26  Ibid., 87.
27  Ibid.
28  Ibid., 91.

In effect both candidates signalled that control of the embargo was to pass to Congress.

Haney and Vanderbush report that control of the embargo finally fully shifted from the President to Congress 'when the embargo policy was codified into law in 1996 in the controversial Helms-Burton legislation'.[29] Before 1992, the embargo was an executive (Presidential) policy but, after 1996, it was fully a product of the US legislature. Helms-Burton effectively consolidated the move initially made in 1992, showing that the shift to Congress was not simply a politically expedient move explicable as one of the last throws of the 1992 Presidential election campaign. This constituted a significant pivotal point in the life of the embargo by making it subject to US democratic decision-making in Congress and, thereby, rendering its demise less likely. Helms-Burton 'codified all standards, regulations, and presidential orders passed since 1962, thereby elevating to the rank of law the whole arsenal of measures against Cuba that had been approved in the past'.[30] President Clinton felt he could no longer resist the demands of the pro-embargo members of Congress for codification after the Cuban air force had shot down two planes flown by 'Brothers to the Rescue' early in 1996. 'Brothers to the Rescue' is an organisation of Cuban exiles whose aims include searching for people fleeing Cuba by boat across the Florida Straits, following a growing exodus of Cubans that had begun in 1994.[31]

## 6.4 Helms-Burton Act 1996

The embargo was codified into US law during President Clinton's term in office by means of the Cuban Liberty and Democratic Solidarity Act (LIBERTAD) 1996,[32] known by its sponsors' names (both Republican senators) as the Helms-Burton Act 1996. Whereas before 1996 most aspects of the embargo could be lifted by the President, after 1996 the President would have to appeal to Congress to repeal legislation on the embargo.[33]

The 'lobbying capacity' of Cuban exiles was 'formidable', 'influencing legislation through control of the relevant committees' in Congress.[34] Legislation took the form of two new pieces of legislation. The Cuba Democracy Act of 1992 (the Torricelli Act) was aimed at 'frustrating Cuban trade' by, for example, prohibiting trading by subsidiaries of US corporations, as well as inducing change in Cuba by stating that sanctions would only be lifted if 'free, fair and internationally supervised elections' were to take place.

29  Ibid., vii.
30  Lamrani (n.3), ch. 2.
31  Haney and Vanderbush (n.1), 4, 98–9.
32  Public Law 104–114, H.R. 927; in (1996) 35 ILM 357.
33  Haney and Vanderbush (n.1), 1.
34  R. Gott, *Cuba: A New History* (New Haven, CT: Yale University Press, 2004) 301.

The Cuban Liberty and Democratic Solidarity (Helms-Burton) Act of 1996 was aimed at undermining investment in Cuba by European countries, Canada and Japan. In addition, the Helms-Burton Act extended the pressure for democracy by stating that no democratic Cuban government could include Fidel or Raúl Castro and no new government would be recognised by the US unless compensation was paid to US citizens or Cuban Americans whose property had been nationalised in the immediate post-1959 period. The 1996 Act took the issue of the expropriation of US property further by empowering the victims of such expropriations to sue before US courts any individual or corporation 'trafficking in property' that had belonged to US citizens (or to Cubans who had become US citizens).[35]

The Act was divided into four Titles: 'I. Strengthening international sanctions against the Castro government'; 'II. Assistance to a free and independent Cuba'; 'III. Protection of the property rights of United States nationals'; and 'IV. Exclusion of certain aliens'. Its purposes were stated broadly and reflected the historical position of the US as regards Cuba under Fidel Castro:

1   to assist the Cuban people in regaining their freedom and prosperity, as well as joining the community of nations that are flourishing in the Western hemisphere;
2   to strengthen international sanctions against the Castro government;
3   to provide for the continued national security of the United States in the face of continuing threats from the Castro government of terrorism, theft of property from United States nationals by the Castro government, and the political manipulation by the Castro government of the desire of Cubans to escape that results in mass migration to the United States;
4   to encourage the holding of free and fair elections in Cuba, conducted under the supervision of internationally recognised observers;
5   to provide a policy framework for United States support to the Cuban people in response to the formation of a transitional government or a democratically elected government in Cuba; and
6   to protect United States nationals against confiscatory takings and the wrongful trafficking in property confiscated by the Castro regime.[36]

Title I of the Helms-Burton Act aimed to strengthen sanctions against the Castro government. It opened with a statement that 'the acts of the Castro government, including its massive, systematic, and extraordinary violations of human rights, are a threat to international peace', and called upon the Security Council to adopt a mandatory economic embargo against the

35  Ibid., 303–4.
36  Helms-Burton Act 1996 (n.32), section 3.

totalitarian regime in Cuba under Chapter VII of the UN Charter.[37] Title I also entrenched US opposition to Cuban membership of the IMF and World Bank,[38] which, given US domination of the world's financial institutions, effectively blocked Cuba seeking loans to cover balance of payments difficulties or for development projects. Title I provided for a vast range of measures for the enforcement of the embargo, including penalties against individuals for violation, and confiscation of property and funds. It also reiterated the prohibition of importation, or dealings outside the United States in merchandise of Cuban origin, or merchandise that has been located in or transported through Cuba, or the export of merchandise that consisted of any article grown, produced or manufactured in the United States.[39] In effect Title I represented the codification of the existing Cuban embargo into US law.[40]

Title II detailed the assistance that the US will provide in the event of a free and independent Cuba, in effect it constituted an enticement to the Cuban people to overthrow the Castro government. The policy was outlined in terms of supporting the self-determination of the Cuban people and encouraging the 'Cuban people to empower themselves with a government which reflects the self-determination of the Cuban people'. In effect, the US declares itself to be ready to provide the Cuban people with assistance to facilitate transition to 'representative democracy and a market economy', which would be the trigger for the lifting of the embargo.[41]

Many US allies protested against the Act as a violation of international law.[42] However, from the US perspective, the Act was a continuation of its response to violations of international law by Cuba when it expropriated US-owned property in the first years of the revolution without the payment of prompt, adequate and effective compensation. While the US maintained that it was 'defending property rights of its citizens that had been infringed in violation of an international "treatment of aliens" standard', Europeans and NAFTA trade partners regarded 'US action as a violation of the international rules of "jurisdiction to prescribe", which delimit each sovereign's legislative sphere'.[43]

Title III was based on determinations that 'individuals enjoy a fundamental right to own and enjoy property which is enshrined in the United States

---

37 Ibid., section 101.
38 Ibid., section 104.
39 Ibid., sections 102–10.
40 Ibid., section 102(h).
41 Ibid., section 201.
42 See, for example, EU: 'Demarches Protesting the Cuban Liberty and Democratic Solidarity Act', (1996) 35 ILM 397.
43 A. Reinisch, 'A Few Public International Law Comments on the Cuban Liberty and Democratic Solidarity (LIBERTAD) Act of 1996', (1996) 7 *EJIL* 545 at 546.

Constitution'; that there had been a 'wrongful confiscation or taking of property belonging to United States nationals by the Cuban government, and the subsequent exploitation of this property at the expense of the rightful owners'; that since Fidel Castro seized power in 1959 he had not only confiscated the property of thousands of US nationals, thousands of Cubans had fled Cuba and become US citizens and also millions of his own citizens had suffered. The Act continued by stating that the Cuban government was 'offering foreign investors the opportunity' to invest in ventures 'using property and assets some of which were confiscated from' US nationals. According to the Act, 'trafficking' in confiscated property provided badly needed financial support for the Cuban government and, thereby, undermined the foreign policy of the US. Furthermore, it declared that since the 'international judicial system, as currently structured, lacks fully effective remedies for the wrongful confiscation of property and for unjust enrichment from the use of wrongfully confiscated property by governments and private entities at the expense of the rightful owners of the property', alternative access to justice was necessary. It invoked the 'effects' doctrine, found in international jurisprudence and finding some support in state practice, namely that 'international law recognises that a nation has the ability to provide for rules of law with respect to conduct outside its territory that has or intended to have substantial effect within its territory'. All of this, it was contended, meant that the US government had an 'obligation to its citizens to provide protection against wrongful confiscations . . . including the provision of private remedies'. Thus, in order to 'deter trafficking in wrongfully confiscated property', US nationals 'who were the victims of these confiscations' were 'endowed with a judicial remedy' in US courts that would 'deny traffickers any profits from economically exploiting Castro's wrongful seizures'.[44] The Title then stated that any person who 'traffics in property which was confiscated by the Cuban government on or after 1 January 1959, shall be liable to any United States national who owns the claim to such property for money damages in an amount equal to the sum of', which is calculated as the 'fair market value of that property . . . as being either the current value of the property, or the value of the property when confiscated plus interest, whichever is the greater'.[45]

The main effect of Title III was to allow for foreign companies that do business in Cuba, involving property which had been confiscated by the Cuban government in 1959 or thereafter, to be sued in a private law action before US courts.[46] There are serious issues of international law raised by this aspect of the Helms-Burton Act of 1996, operating at two levels. First, the Act raises a jurisdictional issue or, more simply put, it raises issues as to the extent of

44  Helms-Burton Act 1996 (n.32), section 301.
45  Ibid., section 302.
46  Haney and Vanderbush (n.1), 101.

the geographical limits on a state's ability to legislate; and, second, it has a particular conception of self-determination that it is trying to ensure is realised by the Cuban people. On the first question, the 'classical' view of jurisdiction is given in the *Lotus* judgment delivered by the Permanent Court of International Justice in 1927, which in reality is an extreme vision of unlimited freedom for states to legislate unless they are prohibited by a positive rule of international law from so doing.[47] The depiction of a state-colossus standing astride the earth may match a caricature of the US (especially in 1991 at the end of the Cold War), but in the *Lotus* version of international law all states were seen as omnicompetent *de jure*, since they recognised no authority above them, although they may be restricted *de facto* by limitations of power. A second, and more convincing, version of state jurisdiction to legislate sees jurisdiction being based upon a state's territory and also upon the nationality of the perpetrator of any wrongful act. After jurisdiction based on territoriality and nationality there are lesser, more controversial (in that they are neither universally accepted nor applied universally) grounds for jurisdiction: the passive personality principle (based on the nationality of the victim), and the protective principle for purposes of national security or, more exceptionally still, upon the universality of the offence committed.[48] The latter is asserted over international crimes such as genocide or crimes against humanity wherever they are committed irrespective of the nationality of the perpetrators or victims. Successful attempts have been made to extend the notion of territory to include wrongful acts, which might start from outside the territory but are completed within the territory of the state asserting jurisdiction, or which start inside that state and extend outwards. An extension of the former is the controversial effects doctrine which allows a state to legislate against acts which have substantial effects within a country (for example, on the economy of that country).

It can be seen from the language used in Title III of the Helms-Burton Act that the US was alluding to the 'effects' doctrine, but it also used language that is appropriately attributable to the passive personality principle (that the victims of the wrongful acts of expropriation were US citizens), or the protective principle – that the essential security interests of the US were at stake.[49] Significantly it used the word 'trafficking' in relation to expropriated Cuban property, a term governments often use when justifying the assertion of extraterritorial jurisdiction in order to protect themselves from drug 'trafficking'.[50] The 'effects' doctrine and the 'passive personality principle' are both contentious grounds for jurisdiction in international law. Indeed, even

---

47  *The Case of the S.S. Lotus (France v Turkey)*, PCIJ Reports Ser. A, No. 10 (1927).
48  V. Lowe, *International Law* (Oxford: Clarendon, 2007) 170–80.
49  An argument made elsewhere – see *Attorney-General of the Government of Israel v Eichmann*, (1961) 36 ILR 5 at para 30 (District Court of Jerusalem).
50  Lowe (n.48), 176.

if the 'effects' doctrine were to be accepted by states, 'it would be difficult to argue that . . . foreign investment activities' in Cuba have harmful effects within the US.[51] Furthermore, the US extension of the protective principle to cover 'trafficking' in expropriated US property is unconvincing, as the taking of property by a government for a public purpose is, *prima facie*, lawful.[52] On balance, these justifications would probably not be accepted by an international court of law, unless the principle enunciated in the *Lotus* judgment is still seen as good law. Even at the time of the Permanent Court's judgment, its premises were rejected by mainstream international lawyers. Brierly wrote, in 1928, that the Court's 'reasoning was based on the highly contentious metaphysical proposition of the extreme positivist school that the law emanates from the free will of sovereign independent states, and from this premise [it] argued that restrictions on the independence of states cannot be presumed'.[53] Rather than a historical process whereby a state's unlimited competence has gradually been restricted, it would be far more accurate to describe the process as one whereby a state first asserted jurisdiction narrowly over its nationals and then extended it to anyone found in its territory.[54] However, the lack of a legitimate jurisdictional basis for Helms-Burton does not mean to say that the underlying allegation – that the confiscation carried out by the Cuban government was in breach of an international legal principle to provide 'prompt, adequate and effective' compensation – should not be adjudicated upon, it simply means that the methods employed by the US to assert jurisdiction are not justifiable under international law. Although Title III of the Act has been suspended since 1996 due to international pressure and threats by the EU to take the case to the WTO,[55] it will have deterred foreign investment in Cuba. However, its legitimacy is undermined by its incompatibility with international law. An alternative method would be to agree with Cuba on a mechanism for settlement of the underlying dispute, perhaps akin to the Iran–US Claims Tribunal, which has been operating successfully for a number of years – something we will return to in Chapter 8. This could be a step towards normalising relations between the two states.

Nonetheless, the Helms-Burton Act is not a full-blown illegitimate exercise in the assertion of extra-territorial jurisdiction, despite EU protestations to that effect.[56] Claimants are confined to US citizens or corporate entities and enforcement only takes place before US courts, but the defendants can be from anywhere – 'any person or entity, including any agency or instrumentality of

---

51  Reinisch (n.43), 553.
52  See discussion in Chapter 7.
53  J.L. Brierly, 'The Lotus Case', (1928) 44 *Law Quarterly Review* 154 at 155.
54  Ibid., 156.
55  Lamrani (n.3), ch. 2.
56  EU, 'Demarches Protesting the Cuban Liberty and Democratic Solidarity Act' (n.42) at 398.

a foreign state', who 'trafficks' in formerly US-owned property that has been expropriated by the Cuban government.[57] In a narrow sense all that the Helms-Burton Act does is create a 'private law liability claim enforceable in US courts'.[58] However, Reinisch argues that 'in substance the provisions of Title III are an exercise of extraterritorial jurisdiction to prescribe', in that the 'choice of a private law tool (including the threat of treble damages)' should be seen as equivalent, or as an effective alternative to, a criminal law prohibition against investing in Cuba.[59] Furthermore, the defendant in any private law action – for example a Canadian corporation with a US presence that has trafficked in such property – is not the perpetrator of the allegedly wrongful expropriation. Indeed, under international law governing expropriation, even if the seizure is undertaken unlawfully, it still effectively vests title in the property in the expropriating state (i.e. Cuba), who can then dispose of it. This does not remove the Cuban government's responsibility to compensate but it does mean that those who subsequently acquire title to the property are not acting unlawfully.[60] Another objection raised by European states was that Helms-Burton's purported restrictions on the right of companies to engage with Cuba was a restriction on freedom of trade, a freedom which had recently been embodied in the World Trade Organisation (WTO) created in 1995. The US government responded by arguing that the WTO Constitution allowed for security exceptions.[61] The issue remained unresolved due to the suspension of Title III by the US, suggesting that it lacked confidence in its arguments. But disputes about free trade are in reality a side issue that distracts from the coercive nature of the embargo, which is not only a violation of the public international law principle of non-intervention, but the effects of which result in violations of basic human rights. Whether these violations are wrongful acts which can be attributed to the US is an issue returned to in the next chapter.

Debates about jurisdiction and free trade tend to obscure the deeper international legal dispute between the US and Cuba – one concerning the self-determination of the Cuban people. Although Helms-Burton was narrowly about granting US citizens a form of access to justice before US courts for acts of expropriation by the Cuban government, it was more broadly about offering the Cuban people assistance if they rejected Communism in favour of democracy and free markets.

By trying to frighten off foreign investment in Cuba the US seemed not to have shaken off the vestiges of the Monroe Doctrine. Pressure from European governments, and corporations who had invested in Cuba especially in the

---

57  Helms-Burton Act 1996 (n.32), section 4(13)(A).
58  Reinisch (n.43), 550.
59  Ibid., 550.
60  Ibid., 558.
61  Haney and Vanderbush (n.1), 115.

tourist industry, led to President Clinton suspending the enforcement of this part of the Act, which has been the position since.[62] Although suspension reduced some of the extra measures added by Helms-Burton, it could not disguise the seismic shift in the embargo: away from the President to Congress, away from a tool of foreign policy towards being part of domestic politics and, even more profoundly, part of domestic US legislation. In return for the suspension of Title III, the EU adopted a Common Position on Cuba, which expressed the organisation's desire for democratic freedom and respect for human rights in Cuba. Future economic aid from the EU to Cuba was tied to progress towards political change in Cuba.[63]

The impact of Helms-Burton was not what the US hoped for, which was to push Cuba away from Communism after the end of the Soviet-era:

> Cubans might wish for greater political freedom, and might hope for economic improvement. Some might wish to ditch socialism and take the capitalist road. Yet few were ready to abandon the Revolution at the behest of the United States, or to give up the first genuine attempt in their history to establish an independent republic.[64]

Maintaining Cuba's independence and external self-determination were more important to Cubans than the form of internal self-determination in terms of government. However, dissent has grown. In the 1990s the 'government faced a new phenomenon: citizens who did not care for the Revolution but who remained on the island to try and change things from within'.[65] These were members of the professional middle class who did not have access to the US dollar, and a number ended up behind bars. A petition of 11,000 signatures called for political change, but was eclipsed by a government-organised referendum which confirmed the socialist character of the constitution.[66] Fidel Castro, who had embodied much of the Cuban people's desire for independence, stepped down in 2008 due to ill-health, to be succeeded by his brother Raúl.

## 6.5  After Helms-Burton

The end of the Cold War, the reduction of Cuba as a strategic threat to the US, and the move to legislation as the legal basis of the embargo, have all meant that the US policy towards Cuba has become very much a matter of domestic politics and law rather than international policy and law.[67] The effect

---

62  Gott (n.34), 305.
63  Ibid., 306.
64  Ibid., 306.
65  Ibid., 314.
66  Ibid., 314–16.
67  Haney and Vanderbush (n.1), 111.

of Helms-Burton 1996 was to entrench the embargo in that it could not be suspended or terminated without the consent of Congress. This could only come about if the President proposed an end to the embargo, which according to the Act could only occur following the election of a democratic government in Cuba that did not include Raúl or Fidel Castro.

President Clinton interpreted his now constrained powers within the Act liberally in order to exercise an enforcement waiver over Title III, thereby suspending or preventing law suits being brought against foreign companies, although he argued that this put them on notice that they may be sued in the future if the waiver was lifted.[68] Title IV of Helms-Burton, which purported to prevent foreign nationals from entering the US if that person had 'trafficked' in property in Cuba to which a US national had a claim, was also only sporadically enforced under President Clinton (a number of Canadian, Mexican and Italian executives of companies were excluded from entry into the US under Title IV).[69] Finally, President Clinton used the limited discretion given to him under Helms-Burton to reinstitute licences to allow US residents to send money to their families in Cuba and allow them to travel to Cuba to visit their families.[70] In 1998 Clinton also allowed Canadian airliners heading for Cuba to pass through US airspace. This was done in the face of imminent defeat before the International Civil Aviation Organisation (ICAO), a UN specialised agency, which was about to rule on the dispute and was unlikely to accept US arguments that restriction was necessary for its national security.[71]

The introduction of free trade arguments after Helms-Burton, combined with falling international commodity markets served to embolden the US farm lobby, which was looking for new markets and argued strongly for the ending of the embargo.[72] However, the importance of Florida in US Presidential elections from 2000 onwards meant that the Cuban American community would continue to exercise a disproportionate influence over US policy towards Cuba including, at its heart, the embargo.[73]

After 2001, the administration of President G.W. Bush created expectations that the embargo would be hardened as a political reward to Cuban American voters in Florida for their support, a hardening which would include the lifting of the waiver on Title III and the enforcement of Title IV of Helms-Burton. However, while there was some tightening of travel restrictions and increased funding of dissidents, the President continued the waiver of Title III in the face of continued European hostility, and only allowed limited enforcement of Title IV against non-European countries. The Bush rhetoric hardened after 9/11 by including Cuba among terrorism-supporting countries (with Iran,

68  Ibid., 113.
69  Ibid., 114.
70  Ibid., 115.
71  Ibid., 116.
72  Ibid., 124.
73  Ibid., 130.

Iraq, Libya, North Korea, Sudan and Syria), also accusing Cuba in 2003 of producing biological weapons.[74] According to the Arms Control Association, an NGO based in Washington, there is no credible evidence against Cuba for production or possession of either chemical or biological weapons.[75] Cuba has ratified arms control treaties outlawing the production and possession of such weapons: the Biological Weapons Convention in 1976 and the Chemical Weapons Convention in 1997.

In response to US support for dissidents, in the so-called 'Black Spring' of 2003 Cuban courts sentenced dozens of activists to long jail sentences (up to twenty-six years), after short trials. In secret trials three men who had hijacked a ferry to take them to the US were sentenced to death and four who used weapons to help the hijackers were given life sentences.[76] Again, although the anti-embargo lobby was growing in the US, leaders of both countries seemed to take actions that ensured that it would continue: Bush by further demonising Castro, and Castro by dealing harshly with dissent. Neither leader seemed to want to break the Cold War political relationship between them which included, by default, the embargo. It was increasingly being recognised that the US would have more influence over Cuba if US citizens and companies were allowed unimpeded access into Cuba, and maybe this explains why Castro acted to ensure that it would be difficult, if not impossible, for Congress and the President to make that decision.[77] However, pressure was mounting to loosen the embargo leading to decisions to ease travel restrictions and allow for the sale of food and agricultural products by US companies, which, by the end of 2002, amounted to 20 per cent of Cuba's food imports.[78] Even Senator Helms did not try to block the Senate Foreign Relations Committee's authorisation to sell food and medicine to Cuba in 2000, following approval of the sale of food and medicine in the House of Representatives (in the form of the Trade Sanctions Reform and Enhancement Act).[79] At first, the Cuban government declined to buy, arguing for normal two-way trade.[80] However, in November 2001 the US exported food to Cuba for the first time in forty years following a request by the Cuban government in the aftermath of Hurricane Michelle. The embargo was increasingly being seen as an issue of international trade rather than 'ethnic

---

74  Ibid., 131–7. But see J.P. Zanders, E.M. French and N. Pauwels, 'Chemical and Biological Weapon Developments and Arms Control', (1998) *SIPRI Yearbook* 586 for an unsubstantiated allegation of US use of an insect pest against Cuba.

75  www.armscontrol.org/factsheets/cbwprolif (accessed 21 March 2014).

76  Haney and Vanderbush (n.1), 143.

77  Ibid., 143–5.

78  Ibid., 149.

79  Ibid., 159; Lamrani (n.3), ch. 2.

80  L. Schoultz, 'Benevolent Domination: The Ideology of US Policy Toward Cuba', (2010) 41 *Cuban Studies* 1 at 3. See further at 4 where he reports that by 2008 US farmers had become Cuba's largest supplier of food and agricultural products.

politics'.[81] The human rights underpinnings of Helms-Burton were also undermined by the establishment by the US of normal trading relations with China in 2000, a 'communist country whose human rights record is worse than Cuba's'.[82] Despite the rhetoric coming from the Bush Administration, simply 'holding the line' on the Cuban embargo was all that even a hard-line President could do.[83] Although Helms-Burton appeared to be airtight it turned out to be fairly porous. Nonetheless, Congress retained its authority over the embargo by not only keeping it in place, but also by permitting the financing of some goods and medicine sales to Cuba.[84] Ultimately, it will take a decision of Congress to lift the embargo.

By 2004 trade was increasing between the US and Cuba. Cuban Americans visited the country and sent large remittances.[85] This, along with tourism, enabled the Castro government to have access to sufficient hard currency to ride out the embargo. However, the path towards increased trade was not a smooth one, especially during President GW Bush's second term. In May 2004, a report by Secretary of State Colin Powell (Report of the Commission for Assistance to a Free Cuba), outlined how the US would 'assist' Cuba in transition to democracy. Lisandro Pérez writes that: 'it is not far-fetched to suggest that' the Report 'is a plan for a [US] protectorate'.[86] Following this report the US again restricted family visits and the level of cash remittances allowed from Cuban Americans. There was further evidence of a crackdown on dissidents by the Cuban government in April 2007 when a lawyer and a journalist were both given lengthy jail sentences after secret trials. The Cuban government expressed anger at the US decision, in 2007, to drop charges against Luis Posada Carriles, a former CIA operative, and Cuban 'Public Enemy No. 1' accused of being responsible for the destruction of a Cuban airliner in 1976. The antipathy between the government of Fidel Castro and the US government was evidenced earlier in the so-called propaganda war in 2006, when in February of that year President Castro unveiled a monument which was deliberately constructed to block a view of messages, some concerning human rights, illuminated on the US mission building. In 2008 Lisandro Pérez provided the following sober evaluation of US–Cuba relations:

> For nearly half a century little has changed in the basic outlines of the Cuban situation. A government that includes Fidel Castro stubbornly defends a socialist order that has been defiantly erected in the backyard

---

81  Haney and Vanderbush (n.1), 159.
82  Ibid., 159.
83  Ibid., 153.
84  Ibid., 161.
85  Ibid., 167.
86  L. Pérez, 'Reflections on the Future of Cuba', (2008) 39 *Cuban Studies* 85 at 87. See further at 90 where she writes that the 'last time the United States intervened, presumably to help Cuba, Cubans lost their sovereignty and self-determination'.

of the United States despite the equally stubborn and persistent efforts of Washington and an exile community to do away with it. Some details, characters and nuances have changed over the years, but that basic confrontational scenario has not changed since 1961.[87]

The political framework governing relations between the US and Cuba has essentially remained unchanged in the period 1961–2014. The possibility of the 'tit-for-tat' cycle of responses and counter-responses of both governments coming to an end arose in 2008, when an ailing Fidel Castro gave way to his brother and fellow revolutionary Raúl Castro. This was quickly followed by a number of far-reaching economic reforms by the Cuban government.[88] In May 2008 the prohibitions on mobile phones and computers were removed; plans to abandon salary equality were announced in June 2008; restrictions on the amount of land available to private farmers were relaxed in July 2008; fifty-two dissidents were freed in a deal brokered by the Catholic Church and Spain in July 2010; a massive reduction in public sector jobs was announced in September 2010; the last two political prisoners detained during 'Black Spring' were released in March 2011, followed by the release of 2,500 prisoners in December 2011 prior to a Papal visit; and the National Assembly approved of economic reforms reducing state bureaucracy and encouraging private enterprise in August 2011, followed by the introduction of a law that permitted individuals to buy and sell private property for the first time in fifty years. In October 2012 Cubans wishing to travel abroad were no longer required to purchase expensive exit visas, although, in order to prevent a brain-drain, highly qualified professionals such as doctors, scientists and engineers still had to gain permission to travel. In February 2013, the National Assembly re-elected Raúl Castro as President of Cuba, and he announced that he would stand down in 2018. 2014 saw new reforms with restrictions on Cuban baseball players' salaries being lifted in January 2014 along with opportunities for them to sign to foreign (but not US) teams after a number of high profile defections of Cuban players to the US.[89] The prohibition on the purchase of new cars was lifted in January 2014, presaging the beginning of the end of the omnipresent American cars from the 1950s and Soviet Ladas from the 1980s.[90]

In addition to these far-reaching changes within Cuba wrought by Raúl Castro,[91] at the international level changes started to occur: in June 2008 the

---

87  Ibid., 85.
88  'Cuba Profile', BBC News, 4 July 2013, available at www.bbc.co.uk/news/world-latin-america-19576144 (accessed 10 January 2014).
89  'Cuba Grants its Baseball Stars Licence to be Big Hitters on the World Stage', *Guardian Weekly*, 3 January 2014.
90  'Cuba's Classic Cars Near the End of the Road', *Guardian Weekly*, 10 January 2014.
91  'Paintballing, gay bars, cash machines: Cuba looks forward to a post-Castro age', *Guardian Weekly*, 24 January 2014.

EU lifted diplomatic sanctions imposed on Cuba in 2003 over the 'Black Spring' clampdown on dissidents; both China and Russia signed trade and investment accords with Cuba in 2008; oil production was increased by the state oil company and Cuba signed an agreement with Russia allowing for oil exploration in Cuban waters in the Gulf of Mexico in July 2009. In June 2009 the OAS lifted its suspension of Cuban membership first imposed in 1962.[92] Cuba welcomed this development but indicated that it would not rejoin the OAS. In January 2014 the Netherlands broke ranks with other EU states and signed an agreement with Cuba to engage in political consultations, building on the back of trade worth $791 million between the two countries in 2012.[93]

The election of Democratic President Barack Obama in January 2009 also brought hope that there would be sufficient willingness on the US side to engage with a changing Cuba, despite the continuation in force of the Helms-Burton Act and, with it, a ban on making a deal with any Cuban government that included either of the Castro brothers. In March 2009, US Congress voted to lift restrictions on Cuban Americans visiting Cuba and sending remittances imposed during the previous administration, and further relaxed travel restrictions to Cuba in January 2011; and in April 2009 President Obama announced at the Summit of the Americas that the US was seeking 'a new beginning with Cuba'.[94] Nevertheless, despite his re-election in 2012, President Obama remained hidebound by a hostile Congress' control over the embargo. The surprising handshake between the US President and Raúl Castro at the funeral of Nelson Mandela in December 2013 raised hopes of a normalisation in relations but it appears that the political pieces are not yet in place, particularly in the US. If a cooperative Congress had been in place during President Obama's second term then a fundamental change in relations might have been possible. Incremental changes will occur as with the resumption of migration between the US and Cuba in January 2014, which looked to revive a 1994 agreement between the two countries under which the US granted immigration visas for up to 20,000 Cubans each year in order to stem the flow of those trying to travel illegally by boat to the US. Nevertheless, it may well remain true to say that the 'forces for continuity

---

92  On 3 June 2009, the Ministers of Foreign Affairs of the Americas adopted resolution AG/Res 2438 (XXXIX-O/09), which resolved that the 1962 exclusion of Cuba from participation from the OAS ceased to have effect. The 2009 resolution stated that the participation of Cuba will be the result of a process of dialogue initiated at the request of the government of Cuba, and will be in accordance with the practice, purposes and principles of the OAS.

93  'Dutch urge EU thaw towards Cuba', *Guardian Weekly*, 17 January 2014.

94  'Obama Says US will Pursue Thaw with Cuba', *New York Times*, 17 April 2009. But in his campaign speech to CANF in May 2008 he said the US 'must be a relentless advocate for democracy' – Schoultz (n.80), 5.

may prove more powerful than the forces for change'.[95] Lisandro Pérez accurately assesses the reasons for the longevity of the Cuban revolution:

> The Cuban revolution's ability to consolidate its power in the early 1960s was in large measure because of its success in capitalising on political values that were part of the process of nation building in the nineteenth century and have therefore long been part of Cuban national identity. They were values most clearly ... articulated by José Martí ... They were values that the Cuban Republic, from 1902 to 1958, largely failed to realise: sovereignty, social justice, the dignity of all its people, and a national purpose guided by a history of exceptionalism that gave Cubans a particular sense of destiny as an independent nation in this hemisphere. The Cuban revolutionary government played very successfully on those themes. Its redistribution efforts, a real attempt to address the serious socioeconomic inequalities of the past, were a success, in terms of both actual accomplishment and political symbolism, vesting the bulk of the population in the revolution's longevity.[96]

The embargo was sustained by the US during the Cold War for security reasons – a 'Soviet-friendly government in Cuba was an unacceptable challenge to the primordial US interest in security'.[97] The nationalisation of US-owned assets in the first years of the revolution also 'attacked substantial economic interests', which has not been forgotten or forgiven.[98] Nonetheless, with the end of the Cold War, the embargo remained out of a combination of: inertia, the Florida vote, the control Congress has had since 1996 but, above all, because US policy has remained effectively the same since 1898. This policy has been depicted as one of 'benevolent domination', embodying the idea that Cuba needs steering towards democracy and freedom, despite the strong argument that 'if history tells us anything, it is that the Cubans do not want to be uplifted by the United States of America'.[99]

## 6.6 The impact of the embargo

In the case of a unilateral embargo, albeit one that has extraterritorial effects, it is normally difficult to assess whether the cut-off in trade has directly caused suffering in the target country. Nevertheless, living conditions, education, economic infrastructure, and development will all be affected by a unilateral embargo imposed by the target country's largest potential trading partner,

95  Pérez (n.86), 88.
96  Ibid., 89.
97  Schoultz (n.80), 3.
98  Ibid., 3.
99  Ibid., 16.

especially one with huge economic power. Indeed, the history of Cuba from 1902 to 1959 shows that the US was Cuba's major trading partner to the extent that Cuba was largely dependent upon the US for the export of sugar and, while the Soviet Union largely filled that role until 1991, its demise has left a trading gap that Cuba has struggled to fill. While the embargo must have had a major impact on the Cuban economy, possibly to the extent alleged by the Cuban government, this section aims to identify specific impact and damage in one of the core elements of a state – the provision of health care. Nonetheless, it is worth noting that in 2012 the Inter-American Commission on Human Rights (IACHR) repeated its general determination that human rights were being impacted by the embargo; stating that:

> As regards the economic and trade embargo imposed by the United States on Cuba since 1961 and which continues in force, the IACHR reiterates its position in terms of the impact of such economic sanctions on the human rights of the Cuban population; accordingly, reiterates [its position] that the embargo should end.

However, the IACHR made it clear that the impact of the embargo did not excuse Cuba from its international human rights obligations, nor for the violations of civil and political rights by the Cuban government found by the IACHR (and analysed in Chapter 7).[100]

In a 2007 report submitted to the UN's Human Rights Council on the 'Situation of Human Rights in Cuba', the Personal Representative of the UN's High Commissioner for Human Rights also pointed out that:

> The restrictions imposed by the embargo help to deprive Cuba of vital access to medicines, new scientific and medical technology, food, chemical water treatment and electricity. The disastrous effects of the embargo in terms of the economic, social and cultural rights of the Cuban people have been denounced by the United Nations Food and Agriculture Organization, the United Nations Children's Fund, the United Nations Educational, Scientific and Cultural Organization (UNESCO) and the World Health Organization (see all the reports issued by these specialized agencies in 2002).[101]

During the debates over the 2013 General Assembly Resolution condemning the US embargo against Cuba, which was adopted by 188 votes in favour to 2 against (US and Israel) with three abstentions (Marshall Islands,

---

100 Inter-American Commission on Human Rights, Annual Report, 2012, para 17 (www.oas. org/en/iachr/docs/annual/2012/TOC.asp (accessed 10 February 2014)).
101 UN Doc A/HRC/4/12, 'The Situation of Human Rights in Cuba', 26 January 2007, para 7.

Federated States of Micronesia and Palau),[102] Bruno Rodríguez Parrilla, Cuban Minister for Foreign Affairs, spoke about the human damage caused by the embargo. In general he stated that the embargo's impact was incalculable with 76 per cent of Cubans living under its effects since birth. However, he did put the economic damage to Cuba since the embargo was first imposed at more than $1 trillion. He stated that although Cuba had made progress on improving health, education, gender equality and on other social indicators, it could have done so much more without this 'colossal obstacle to our development and the enormous human and financial costs' imposed on Cuba. He cited the example of health, stating that the embargo had prevented patients getting the treatment they needed. He claimed that the embargo was both an act of genocide and a form of economic warfare.[103]

Of major significance in assessing the impact on health in Cuba is the Report of the American Association for World Health (AAWH) of March 1997.[104] This NGO was established in 1953 and serves as the US Committee for the World Health Organization and the Pan American Health Organization. The report is critical of the very nature of the embargo, as well as its impact on Cuba. It is critical of the nature of the embargo as it is one of the few such regimes that 'explicitly includes foods and medicines in its virtual ban on bilateral commercial ties'. This is not completely accurate, as the Report clarifies at a later point, for although the effect of banning subsidiaries of US multinationals from dealing with Cuba largely prevents medicines reaching Cuba, the embargo legislation does allow for humanitarian exceptions. As Lamrani explains:

> Economic sanctions have had a dramatic impact in the field of health. Indeed, nearly 80 percent of the patents granted in the medical sector are issued to U.S. pharmaceutical multinationals and their subsidiaries, which gives them a virtual monopoly. Cuba cannot get access to these medications due to restrictions imposed by the government of the United States.[105]

Nonetheless, the AAWH's empirical assessment of the *de facto* impact of the embargo on health remains instructive. The impact was assessed by a team of AAWH's experts operating in 1995–6 by: examining US regulations and

102  UNGA Res 68/8 (2013).

103  UNGA A/68/PV.38 (2013).

104  American Association for World Health, 'Denial of Food and Medicine: The Impact of the US Embargo on Health and Nutrition in Cuba', March 1997 (available at www.medicc.org/resources/documents/embargo/An%20Executive%20Summary.pdf (accessed 15 May 2014)).

105  Lamrani (n.3), ch. 3. He gives a number of specific examples of drugs, medical equipment and treatments that are unavailable in Cuba due to the effects of the embargo.

their implementation, surveying twelve American medical and pharmaceutical companies, assessing the experience of Cuban import firms, and assessing the impact on health by visiting forty-six treatment centres in Cuba, and by conducting interviews with experts. The report was one of fact finding 'for informed decision making on Cuba'. In its summary of findings the report stated that the:

> U.S. embargo of Cuba has dramatically harmed the health and nutrition of large numbers of ordinary Cuba citizens. . . . It is our expert medical opinion that the U.S. embargo has caused a significant rise in suffering and even deaths in Cuba. For several decades the U.S. embargo has imposed significant financial burdens on the Cuban health care system. But since 1992 the number of unmet medical needs patients going without essential drugs or doctors performing medical procedures without adequate equipment has sharply accelerated. This trend is directly linked to the fact that in 1992 the US trade embargo, one of the most stringent embargoes of its kind, prohibiting the sale of food and sharply restricting the sale of medicines and medical equipment, was further tightened by the 1992 Cuban Democracy Act.[106]

Eschewing the focus in the legal literature on the extra-territorial effects of the Helms-Burton Act 1996, the Report points to the more devastating impact of the 1992 Act, especially its ban on subsidiary trade, severely limiting Cuba's ability to import medical supplies from third (non-US) countries, given the US dominance of the world-wide pharmaceutical industry. Although the licensing of sales of medicines and medical supplies to Cuba was clearly permitted for the first time under the 1992 Act, thereby creating a humanitarian exception on paper, the system of licence application has deterred US companies from applying given the rejection of numerous applications on the grounds that the proposed exports would be 'detrimental to U.S. foreign policy interests'. The 1992 Act prohibited ships from loading or unloading in US ports for 180 days after delivering cargo to Cuba. This has led to a severe reduction in the delivery of medical equipment to Cuba.[107] The medical exemption to the embargo was effectively undermined by the other provisions of the 1992 Act and the subsequent Helms-Burton Act 1996, so that many medicines became virtually unattainable.[108] More broadly the AAWH team of medical experts identified that the embargo was causing malnutrition in newborn babies (due to the outright ban on American foodstuffs); that water quality had deteriorated due to severe limitations on

---

106  AAWH Report (n.104).
107  Ibid.
108  A.F. Kirkpatrick, 'Role of the USA in Shortage of Food and Medicine in Cuba', (1996) 348 *The Lancet* 1489.

gaining access to water treatment chemicals; and that, by 1995, there had been a reduction of 32 per cent in medicines that were available to Cuban doctors in 1991.

The Report recognises that the 1992 Cuban Democracy Act was adopted in the context of the end of the Soviet Union and the consequent withdrawal of Soviet trade and support for Cuba and admits that this had the severest impact on the Cuban economy, but that could have been overcome if Cuba could have turned to its 'closest and most obvious trading partner, the United States'.[109] This raises the difficult issue of causation in international law, whether the US embargo caused this period of severest hardship in Cuba or whether this was caused by the collapse of the Soviet Union. The rudimentary development of a doctrine of causation in international law is considered in Chapter 7. However, the reality is that the period of greatest hardship in Cuba was due to both the collapse of the Soviet Union and the continuation and tightening of the US embargo. The US could not escape responsibility by pointing to the collapse of Cuba's socialist ally as the sole cause given that it adopted the Cuban Democracy Act and the Helms-Burton Act to increase the impact of the embargo on Cuba after the collapse of Soviet trade and support. While the collapse of the Soviet Union was an unfortunate geopolitical development for Cuba,[110] the continuation and tightening of the embargo was a deliberate act aimed at the removal of the Cuban government by deepening the suffering of the Cuban people thereby provoking change from within. The 1997 AAWH Report, produced at this critical time, established that this was not only the intent behind the US legislation of the 1990s, it was also the effect of those measures – they did cause significant harm in Cuba, especially as regards the health of Cuban citizens.[111]

## 6.7 The current debate

The debates over the 2013 General Assembly Resolution, condemning the US embargo against Cuba,[112] show how far apart the two states remain. After describing the impact of the embargo Bruno Rodríguez Parrilla, Cuban Minister for Foreign Affairs, accused the US of using espionage surveillance to monitor Cuban financial transactions, which resulted in the imposition of fines of more than $2.4 billion on thirty US and foreign entities in the period

---

109  AAWH Report (n.104), 19.
110  The evidence is that the Cuban health system survived the shock of the collapse of the USSR better than the Russian health system – see I. Borowy, 'Similar but Different: Health and Economic Crisis in 1990s Cuba and Russia', (2011) 72 *Social Science and Medicine* 1489.
111  AAWH Report (n.104), 21.
112  UNGA Res 68/8 (2013).

2009–2013, including HSBC, Mitsubishi and Reuters.[113] He declared that 'our small island poses no threat to the national security of the superpower' and asked why American businesses could not have access to the Cuban market. The blockade was the main obstacle to broader access to the internet, the free circulation of persons, the exchange of ideas, and the development of cultural, sporting and scientific relations.[114]

The Cuban Foreign Minister urged President Obama to use his constitutional powers without the support of Congress, if necessary, to move US policy out of its Cold War approach to Cuba. Although the differences between both governments were significant, he argued that the only way forward would be to find a civilised way to relate to each other – by cooperation, dialogue and negotiation. The recent resumption of talks on migration, the re-establishment of direct postal relations, and growing cooperation in combating oil spills and air search and rescue missions, all serve to illustrate that dialogue can work. It was clear from this speech that Cuba wished to establish a broader constructive dialogue with the US based on equality and respect for Cuban independence.[115]

The US representative to the UN, Ronald Godard, stated in the 2013 debate in the General Assembly that the US strongly supported the Cuban people's desire to design their own future, but that aspiration had been obstructed by the Cuban government. US policy had been to strengthen connections between American and Cuban citizens and since the start of the Obama Administration hundreds of thousands of Americans had travelled to Cuba and had sent remittances, which, in 2012, amounted to $2 billion.[116] The US was the largest supplier of food and agricultural products to Cuba as well as its principal trade partner. US companies were among the leading providers of humanitarian assistance to Cuba. He said that the Assembly should not ignore Cuba's various human rights problems, and accused Cuba of using the US as an 'external scapegoat' for its economic problems, which were actually caused by its own policies over the past half century. According to the US, Cuba could only thrive if it radically changed its policies, opened itself up for competition, respected international property rights, and allowed unfettered access to the internet.[117] There was no taking up of the Cuban offer for wider dialogue.

---

113  UNGA A/68/PV.38 (2013). See further Lamrani (n.3), ch. 5, for many instances of the impact of sanctions on companies and individuals for trading with Cuba.

114  UNGA A/68/PV.38 (2013).

115  Ibid.

116  Ibid. Haney and Vanderbush (n.1), 3, who indicate that in 2002 135,000 US citizens travelled to Cuba, and in that year remittances amounted to $1 billion, and that US companies sold over £150 million worth of food and medicine to the island.

117  UNGA A/68/PV.38 (2013).

The UN General Assembly debate in 2013 is a clear indication of how far apart both countries remain. Variations of that debate have been held in the General Assembly since 1992.[118] Cuba blames the US for its economic problems and for violations of the rights of its peoples to the extent of accusing the US of genocide; while the US blames the policies of the Cuban government for denying its own people not only basic freedoms but also for the failures of the Cuban economy. On specific issues, the arguments of both sides mirror each other; for example the US accuses Cuba of not allowing its citizens full access to the internet, while Cuba argues that the blockade has prevented the technological development of Cuba. In a broader context the US claims Cuba is denying to its own people the right to self-determination, while Cuba sees US intervention as a violation of Cuba's right to self-determination. No doubt the truth, if it exists in an absolute sense, is to be found somewhere between these two positions. The next two chapters explore whether international law has a role to play, not simply as a tool in the hands of each state, but in providing a framework for a process of dispute settlement enabling common ground and agreement to be found.

---

118 The majorities in favour of the resolution condemning the embargo have increased since 1992 when the vote on UNGA Res 47/19 (1992) was fifty-nine in favour, three against (US, Israel Romania) and seventy-one abstentions. See, in contrast, UNGA Res 47/139 (1992) on the situation of human rights in Cuba, adopted by sixty-nine votes to eighteen, with sixty-four abstentions. In this the Assembly condemned the violations by Cuba of basic human rights and freedoms including freedom of expression, due process, and freedom to leave the country – see further Chapter 7.

# 7 Violations, responsibility and remedies

## 7.1 Introduction

This chapter considers the legality of the embargo and other acts of the US, as well as Cuba, under international law (both the law on nations governing relations between governments and under more recent forms of international law including human rights law). This is not the end point of our thesis, rather it enables us to identify the issues which need to be addressed, bearing in mind that a solution to the dispute will not entail the straightforward application of international law to the dispute, but will entail the adjustment of both Cuban and US policy and law in the light of the international legal framework. This is considered in Chapter 8. It must be borne in mind that both countries point to violations of international law, including human rights law, by the other. From the US perspective, Cuba has: illegally expropriated US property and concerns, intervened in other countries, denied individual rights and democratic freedoms of its citizens and, ultimately, the Cuban people's right to self-determination. From the Cuban point of view the US has: illegally intervened in Cuba, violated its people's economic and social rights, and its right to self-determination in the sense of being left to decide its political and economic future. The legality of the embargo *per se* is discussed alongside the norms surrounding it such as the principle of non-intervention and customary human rights norms. This chapter catalogues the wrongful acts committed by both states, and re-introduces the concept of responsibility for those breaches,[1] as well as the possibilities for remedies and access to justice. The implementation of that responsibility and the availability of possible remedies are discussed in Chapter 8.

---

1 See Chapter 5 for how self-help plays a role in international law and sits uneasily within the law of state responsibility.

## 7.2 Responsibility in international law

'In any legal system there must be liability for failure to observe obligations imposed by its rules'.[2] In international law, the secondary rules that determine such liability are called the rules on state responsibility. Thus, there is responsibility for breaches of the primary rules of international law committed by a state.[3] For instance, an act of aggression by one state against another is a wrongful act under international law and gives rise to the responsibility of the aggressor state, both to the victim state and, for such a serious breach of international law, to the international community. These secondary rules determine a range of issues concerning responsibility: whether or not a wrongful act is imputable to a particular state or states; whether other states are complicit in the commission of a wrongful act; and whether a state has any defence excusing it from responsibility. It also includes norms prescribing: the level and types of reparation or remedies for the victim state or states (which may be exercised on behalf of individuals, corporations or other non-state actors); the enforcement of the responsibility by the victim state itself by, for example, adopting countermeasures against the responsible state (reviewed in Chapter 5 above); and the settlement of the issue by dispute resolution or by resort to international organisations.

In 2001 the International Law Commission finalised its Articles on the Responsibility of States for Internationally Wrongful Acts,[4] Article 1 of which states that 'every internationally wrongful act of a state entails the international responsibility of that state'. According to Article 2, an internationally wrongful act is conduct which is attributable to a state and which constitutes a breach of an international obligation of that state. This seems very straightforward but it must be remembered that states are abstract entities so that attributing wrongful acts or omissions to a state requires establishing that it was indeed the conduct of that state, acting through its organs (for example its military or police forces), or through individuals or entities exercising governmental authority (for example private companies running prisons), or through private individuals who act under the 'instructions of, or under the direction or control of, that state in carrying out that conduct' (for example the acts of insurgents whose conduct is under the effective control of a state supporting them).[5]

As can be seen from this brief description of some of the Articles, they are of an abstract nature but they do enable a legal analysis of state conduct not

---

2  D.J. Harris, *Cases and Materials on International Law* (7th edn, London: Sweet and Maxwell, 2010) 421.

3  J. Crawford, *The International Law Commission's Articles on State Responsibility* (Cambridge: Cambridge University Press, 2002) 14.

4  Noted by the UNGA in Res 56/83 (2001).

5  Articles 4, 5 and 8 Articles on Responsibility of States for Internationally Wrongful Acts 2001.

in terms of legality but in terms of responsibility. Whether this responsibility is actually determined by a court, or by a quasi-judicial body or, indeed, a political organ is not the concern of the Articles, nor are there specified modalities for gaining access to justice or reparation (an issue returned to towards the end of this chapter). In this way the secondary rules of responsibility fit the notion that international law simply provides a framework within which states settle their international disputes. In the practical world of dispute settlement the 'applicable rules come about through a complex diplomatic play that aims at freedom and constraint simultaneously'.[6]

In determining whether or not a primary rule has been breached there has been a continuing controversy over the years as to whether there has to be an element of intent or negligence on behalf of the state for it to be deemed liable. This approach is known as the 'fault' theory or, alternatively, as 'subjective responsibility'. There are authorities that appear to support this approach, for example, the *Home Missionary Society Claim* of 1920.[7] In this case British authorities imposed a 'hut tax' in the colony of Sierra Leone, which led to an uprising during which the Society's property was damaged and some of its missionaries killed. The US exercised diplomatic protection to bring a claim on behalf of the Society. The US and the UK agreed to arbitration. The arbitral body dismissed the claim in the following terms:

> It is a well-established principle of international law that no government can be held responsible for the act of rebellious bodies of men committed in violation of its authority, when it is itself guilty of no breach of good faith, or of no negligence in suppressing insurrection.[8]

On the other hand in the *Caire Claim* of 1929, the claims commission set up by France and Mexico to arbitrate in the dispute appeared to apply a 'risk' theory or 'objective' responsibility, where liability is attached to a state in the absence of intent or fault. In that case France was bringing a claim on behalf of its citizen who was shot by Mexican soldiers for failing to give them $5,000. The Commission upheld the Presiding Commissioner declaring that:

> I am interpreting the said principles in accordance with the doctrine of 'objective responsibility' of the state, that is the responsibility for the acts of the official or organs of a state, which may devolve upon it even in the absence of any 'fault' of its own.[9]

---

6  M. Koskenniemi, 'Doctrines of State Responsibility' in J. Crawford, A. Pellet and S. Olleson (eds), *The Law of International Responsibility* (Oxford: Oxford University Press, 2010) 45 at 51.

7  (1920) 6 RIAA 42.

8  Ibid.

9  (1929) 5 RIAA 516.

How these cases are currently interpreted is to consider whether intent or fault is required, not as a secondary and general issue of responsibility, but as a specific question of the content of the primary rule of international law.[10] In national law there is a subjective element in some primary rules, for example, those prohibiting murder, while there is not in others, for example for minor traffic offences. In international law we have the same variety so that for genocide, for example, there is a requirement of intent:

> In the present Convention, genocide means any of the following acts committed with intent to destroy, in whole or in part, a national, ethnical, racial or religious group.[11]

However, for most norms of international law, there is no specification of intent or fault, which is partly explained by the difficulty of proving that a state has 'intent' or 'fault'. In reality, individuals commit genocide (which requires proof of their intent), and such wrongful acts can be imputed to the state if they are state agents, exercise elements of governmental authority, or act under the instructions or control of the state. Furthermore, if a state, while not carrying out genocide through any of the modes mentioned, fails to prevent genocide occurring in its territory then it may have failed to fulfil its 'due diligence' obligations under international law, something that does not require a finding of 'fault' but rather a determination that the state failed to take 'all reasonable or necessary measures' to prevent genocide.[12]

While the idea of a state committing 'crimes' has not entirely disappeared from the lexicon of international law, the ILC's final articles were premised on there being only one form of state responsibility, there being no division into civil and criminal responsibility.[13] This approach was supported by the International Court of Justice in the *Bosnia Genocide* case, where the question of a violation of the Genocide Convention by Serbia was treated as a breach of treaty not to be confused with the individual criminal responsibility of Bosnian Serb and Serb leaders for crimes of genocide, which were tried before the International Criminal Tribunal for the Former Yugoslavia (ICTY).[14]

Before determining the possible consequences of any breach of international law in the dispute between Cuba and the United States, it is worth reviewing and analysing in a little more detail the potentially wrongful acts of both

---

10  A. Pellet, 'The Definition of Responsibility in International Law' in Crawford, Pellet and Olleson (n.6), 3 at 6.

11  Art II Convention on the Prevention and Punishment of the Crime of Genocide 1948.

12  J. Crawford, *State Responsibility: The General Part* (Cambridge: Cambridge University Press, 2013) 227.

13  Pellet (n.10), 13.

14  *Case Concerning the Application of the Convention on the Prevention and Punishment of the Crime of Genocide*, (2007) ICJ Rep para 167, 170.

countries. It should be borne in mind that the secondary rules on state responsibility as found in the ILC's Articles should not be seen as a form of international legislation, to be applied by courts and other bodies without regard to practice and context. They are abstract principles that require shaping by states to provide them with a tool of international law with which they can normalise their international relations when there is a rupture due to a violation of international law. To view the articles on state responsibility as an inflexible set of rules would be a mistake. They are not constructed in such a way. For instance, there is no pure division into primary and secondary rules reflected in the inclusion in the Articles of self-defence and counter-measures as circumstances precluding wrongfulness. These could be seen equally as primary rules to guide state conduct as well as being responses to breaches of primary rules.[15] In addition the very fact that the ILC's Articles did not take the form of a treaty, but are left as soft laws to be developed by states interpreting and applying them to their disputes, implies that they are meant to be adapted and shaped by state practice.

## 7.3  Cuba's conduct under international law

The change in government in Cuba in 1959, even by armed revolution, was not a breach of international law, even though it resulted in a government that was ideologically opposed to the US. In the *Nicaragua Case* in 1986 when, faced with US opposition to the left-wing Sandinista government, the International Court of Justice made it clear that ideological differences were not a sufficient justification for US intervention in Nicaragua.[16] While there has been a trend towards democracy, manifest in controversial post-Cold War claims that there is a right to democracy,[17] there was no requirement in 1959 that a new government had to be 'democratic'. However, since 1990 the UN General Assembly has supported democratisation within states including the holding of free and fair elections;[18] but this has not been imposed or required of states as an international legal obligation. Nonetheless, we will return to the issue of whether a continuing right to self-determination, as it has evolved since the 1960s, now requires a particular form of government. While the

---

15  E. David, 'Primary and Secondary Rules' in Crawford, Pellet and Olleson (n.6), 27 at 31; S. Szurek, 'The Notion of Circumstances Precluding Wrongfulness' in Crawford, Pellet and Olleson (n.6), 427; J.-M. Thouvenin, 'Circumstances Precluding Wrongfulness in the ILC Articles on State Responsibility: Self-Defence' in Crawford, Pellet and Olleson (n.6), 455.

16  *Case Concerning Military and Paramilitary Activities in and Against Nicaragua*, (1986) ICJ Rep 14, at paras 207–8.

17  T.M. Franck, 'The Emerging Right to Democratic Governance', (1992) 86 *AJIL* 46 at 52.

18  N.D. White, 'The United Nations and Democracy Assistance: Developing Practice Within a Constitutional Framework' in P. Burnell (ed.), *Democracy Assistance: International Cooperation for Democratization* (London: Frank Cass, 2000) 74–6.

revolutionary government that came to power in Cuba in 1959 was not, in itself, a violation of international law, indeed it embodied the form of external self-determination that was being forged at the time by countries emerging from colonialism and forms of imperialism, that does not mean that self-determination was completed in 1959 and in the immediate post-revolutionary years. It has been gradually recognised that there is an on-going internal aspect to self-determination, building on the statement in the General Assembly's Declaration on Friendly Relations of 1970 – that a country in compliance with the principle of self-determination of peoples should be 'possessed of a government representing the whole people belonging to the territory without distinction as to race, creed or colour'.[19]

The new Cuban government expropriated US property and assets in 1959–60, offering limited compensation based on the value of the assets as declared on the individuals' and companies' own tax returns. Such state actions can be lawful if they are undertaken for a public purpose and are not discriminatory. A process of nationalisation of natural or national resources for the internal needs of a state is viewed as a public purpose,[20] while non-discrimination signifies that the measures should not target one particular state.[21] The Cuba expropriations were part of a policy of general nationalisations directed at the internal needs of Cuba and were, therefore, for a public purpose and were not targeted at the US alone but included Mexican, British, Canadian, Swiss and French companies. Indeed, in 1964 the US Supreme Court accepted the legality of the Cuban nationalisation of the sugar industry in *Banco Nacional de Cuba v Sabbatino*,[22] when it accepted that the act of state doctrine applied to it.

However, compensation has to be offered even for expropriations that are *prima facie* lawful. It is at this point that there is a disagreement between the Western standard of full (prompt, adequate and effective) compensation, and the national standard advocated by developing countries including Cuba. Whereas the former would include loss of profits, the latter would (probably) not. There is evidence of the emergence of a compromise standard termed 'appropriate' (sometimes 'reasonable') compensation,[23] but there is still

---

19  UNGA Res 2625 (1970), 'Declaration on Principles of International Law Concerning Friendly Relations and Co-operation Among States in Accordance with the Charter of the United Nations'.

20  *Amoco International Finance Corp v Iran*, (1987) Iran-USCTR 189, para 145.

21  *BP v Libya*, (1974) 53 ILR 297 at 317.

22  (1964) 376 US 398. Overturned by the Hickenlooper Amendment of October 1964.

23  *Aminoil Case (Kuwait v American Independent Oil Co)*, (1982) 21 ILM 976 para 143. Barker argues that practice under investment treaties suggests that consensus is forming around a modern version of the 'prompt, adequate and effective' formula, although his analysis shows that this has come a long way towards the 'appropriate' standard – J. Barker, 'The Different Forms of Reparation: Compensation' in Crawford, Pellet and Olleson (n.6), 599 at 599.

disagreement on the precise content of this standard, particularly as to whether it includes loss of profits.[24] In essence the contention is about valuation techniques, which are aimed at identifying a fair market value for which compensation should be paid.[25] For instance, if compensation includes the capital assets of the business it provides a 'basis for restoring the income stream in a different form', therefore making a parallel claim for lost future income a 'form of double-counting'.[26]

While the US Supreme Court accepted the legality of the Cuban nationalisation, it is clear that the Cuban offer of compensation was neither full nor, indeed, appropriate. On the other hand it is difficult to accept the US position that the failure to pay compensation itself makes the expropriation unlawful, a position which seems to have been rejected in international practice and law.[27] What remains is an unsettled dispute over the levels of compensation to be paid by Cuba to the US acting on behalf of US companies and citizens whose property and assets were lawfully seized in 1959–60.

Cuba was involved militarily in certain Latin American and African countries in the 1960s and 1970s. Some of these interventions violated fundamental principles of international law, including the use of force. Just as the US could not intervene on the grounds of the ideological incompatibility of the state or government being intervened in, so Cuba could not justify its interventions in Latin America in the 1960s to undermine right-wing regimes. Such interventions, in violation of peremptory norms of international law, can give rise to responsibility that can be invoked by third states (i.e. not just those subject to the wrongful act), if the intervention amounted to an illegal use of force (which can consist of the supply of weapons to rebels, which took place in El Salvador in the late 1970s, although via Nicaragua). On this basis the US could invoke Cuba's responsibility but the law is unclear, beyond the prohibition of forcible measures, on how it can enforce that – even collective countermeasures are not fully accepted,[28] never mind an embargo that goes beyond the limits of countermeasures. In any case, once the interventions ceased in the 1980s then so did the justification to continue with economic coercion. However, Cuba's interventions in the 1970s and 80s in Africa were not so clearly unlawful uses of force or interventions since they were in support of an established (or emerging) government (as in Angola), as was its support for left-wing regimes in Nicaragua and Grenada in the 1980s. Military support under the agreement of the legitimate government is accepted in international law.[29] If Cuban support is not seen as support for a government

---

24  Harris (n.2), 490.
25  Barker (n.23), 601.
26  Ibid., 609.
27  Ibid., 601.
28  See Article 54 ILC Articles on Responsibility of States for Internationally Wrongful Acts 2001.
29  C. Gray, *International Law on the Use of Force* (Oxford: Oxford University Press, 2008) 80–8.

but for a rebel movement that has not yet fully seized power then Cuba is relying on the less sure legal footing of supporting a people fighting for self-determination – a more controversial, but not clearly unlawful, form of support. While Cuba's record of external interventions is legally problematic, and may, in certain instances have justified proportionate countermeasures for the duration of the violation; there is no justification for continuing, disproportionate measures.

The post-1959 Cuban government has regularly violated the civil and political rights of individuals within its jurisdiction, for example in the Black Spring of 2003 when dissidents were jailed without due process and with disproportionately long sentences. The Inter-American Commission on Human Rights (IACHR) has asserted that Cuba is 'juridically answerable' to it in human rights matters, even during its exclusion from the OAS from 1962. Two reasons are given by the IACHR to justify its assertion of jurisdiction over Cuba: that although the Cuban government has been excluded from the OAS Cuba as a state has not, and that Cuba 'is party to the first international instruments established in the American hemisphere for the protection of human rights'.[30] It is true that Cuba was one of the founding states of the OAS that adopted the American Declaration of the Rights and Duties of Man 1948. However, neither Cuba nor the US became a party to the American Convention on Human Rights of 1969, which largely replaced the Declaration. While the Convention of 1969 contains binding obligations for state parties, the Declaration of 1948 is not binding in a treaty sense, although it has been treated as a source of obligations for OAS member states by both the IACHR and, to a lesser extent, the Inter-American Court of Human Rights. The latter has held that 'while it generally takes into account the American Declaration when interpreting the provisions of the Convention, its contentious jurisdiction was limited to finding violations of the American Convention only'.[31] Rivier doubts whether the IACHR can hold states responsible for human rights violations on the basis of the American Declaration of 1948 alone because of its lack of 'mandatory scope'.[32] This does not, of course, mean that Cuba has not committed human rights violations; it simply means that the IACHR can only point these out, not determine liability.

Nonetheless, this has not stopped the IACHR from receiving and upholding a number of individual complaints brought to it by Cuban citizens, basing its jurisdiction on the American Declaration. In recent years it has found violations of human rights of individuals (including rights to: life, liberty,

---

30  Inter-American Commission on Human Rights, Annual Report 2012, 308, para 12 (www.oas.org/en/iachr/docs/annual/2012/TOC.asp (accessed 10 February 2014)).

31  D. Rodríguez-Pinzón and C. Martin, 'The Inter-American Human Rights System: Selected Examples of its Supervisory Work' in S. Joseph and A. McBeth (eds), *Research Handbook on International Human Rights Law* (Cheltenham: Elgar, 2010) 353 at 372.

32  R. Rivier, 'Responsibility for Violations of Human Rights Obligations: Inter-American Mechanisms' in Crawford, Pellet and Olleson (n.6), 739 at 753.

personal security, privacy, family, due process, fair trial, assembly, association, to vote and participate in government, freedom of expression and freedom from arbitrary detention) during the crackdown on dissent in the 'Black Spring' of 2003.[33] The IACHR also found Cuba responsible for violating the rights to life, due process and fair trial of some of those individuals involved in the ferry hijack of 2003, by judging and sentencing them without due process and by subsequently executing them.[34] In a controversial decision in 1999, the IACHR determined that Cuba had violated the right to life of individuals flying two unarmed civilian aircraft belonging to 'Brothers to the Rescue' when the Cuban air force shot down the planes while in international airspace in 1996. The controversy over whether the victims were within the jurisdiction of Cuba in order for its human rights obligations to apply did not deter the Commission from finding against Cuba.[35] Cuba has been found liable by the IACHR for a number of violations of individuals' rights under the American Declaration over the years, but it has remained uncooperative, arguing that the Commission lacks legal jurisdiction over it.[36]

The 2012 Annual Report of the IACHR contains a synopsis of the Commission's reviews, recommendations and actions regarding Cuba. Cuba meets the IACHR's criteria for a state 'whose human rights practices merit special attention', for two reasons: the political rights enshrined in the American Declaration of Rights and Duties of Man are not observed, and 'structural situations persist that have serious and grave impact on the enjoyment and observance of fundamental rights enshrined in the American Declaration'.[37]

More specifically the IACHR found that:

> The restrictions on the political rights to association, freedom of expression, and dissemination of ideas, the lack of elections, the lack of an independent judiciary, and the restrictions on freedom of movement over the decades have come to shape a permanent and systematic situation of violation of human rights of the inhabitants of Cuba.[38]

---

33  *Oscar Elías Biscet et al v Cuba*, Report No. 67/06, Case 12.476, 21 October 2006.

34  *Lorenzo Enrique Copello Castillo et al v Cuba*, Report No. 68/06, Case 12.477, 21 October 2006.

35  *Armando Alejandre Jr, Carlos Costa, Mario de la Peña, and Pablo Morales v Cuba*, Report No. 86/99, Case 11.589, 29 September 1999. In contrast see European Court of Human Rights judgment in *Bankovic and others v 17 NATO states*, Admissibility Decision (Grand Chamber), 12 December 2001, paras 52–3.

36  Main examples are: *Victims of the Tugboat '13 de Marzo' v Cuba*, Report No. 47/96, Case 11.436, 16 October 1996; Resolution No. 2/82, Case 2300 (Armando F. Valladeres Pérez) Cuba, 8 March 1982; Resolution No. 46, Case 4429, *170 political prisoners held at the Prison 'Combinado Del Este'*, 25 June 1981; Case 1742, *American citizens unable to return to the US (1975)*; and Case 1805, *situation of political prisoners in Cuba (1975)*.

37  IACHR, Annual Report 2012 (n.30), para 13.

38  Ibid., para 14.

The IACHR found that the situation had not changed in 2012 and, while it had sent its findings to the Cuban government, it had not had a response.

The IACHR detailed the main examples of violations of human rights by the Cuban government. Regarding the right to life, guaranteed in Article I of the American Declaration, the IACHR was concerned that the death penalty was punishment for a 'significant number of crimes especially crimes against the security of the state', and, further, that it was available in summary proceedings thereby not affording the accused adequate protections. It welcomed the fact that in 2008 a number of death penalties had been commuted to life sentences but expressed concern that three individuals sentenced to death for supposed terrorist crimes appeared not to have had their death penalties commuted.[39] The IACHR noted that the death penalty did not seem to have been carried out in Cuba since 2003, when four individuals had been executed. It noted Cuba's explanation of its continued use of the death penalty, found in a response to a UN Human Rights Council review, that it had been 'forced, in the legitimate defence of our national security, to establish and apply severe laws against terrorist activities and crimes designed to destroy the Cuban state or the lives of its citizens, always adhering to the strictest legality and with respect for the most ample guarantees'.[40]

On the right to liberty and security of the person, also protected in Article I of the American Declaration, the IACHR was critical of the continued presence of Cuban laws prohibiting 'pre-delictive social dangerousness' ('conduct in manifest contradiction with the norms of socialist morality'), which, according to the IACHR, are based on a subjective concept whose 'vagueness constitutes a factor of juridical insecurity for the population, since it creates conditions for the authorities to commit arbitrary acts'.[41]

On political rights, the IACHR refers to the Inter-American Democratic Charter signed in 2001 (applicable to all active OAS member states and therefore not binding on Cuba), to the effect that 'representative democracy constitutes the system recognised and required in the OAS for the stability, peace, and development of the region'. This requires: free elections, the right to vote and to be elected, the presence of independent branches of government, respect for freedom of expression, and the 'rights of persons to constitute and participate in political groupings'.[42] The right to vote and participate in government is embodied in Article XX of the American Declaration of the Rights and Duties of Man. Cuba declared that 'Cuba's democratic system is based on the principle of government of the people, by the people and for the people', and that the restrictions provided by law on political rights are the minimum necessary to ensure self-determination in the face of anti-Cuban

39  Ibid., paras 18–19.
40  Ibid., para 20.
41  Ibid., paras 29, 33.
42  Ibid., paras 35–6.

aggressiveness.[43] Nevertheless, the IACHR declared that the 'lack of free and fair elections, based on universal suffrage and secret ballot as an expression of popular sovereignty, violates the right to political participation of the Cuban people'.[44]

Referring to previous Cuban violations of human rights in its practice of prosecution of dissidents under summary procedures during the Black Spring of 2003, the IACHR found that in 2012 the Cuban government continued to carry out 'political repression on the basis of systematic arrests for several hours or a few days, threats, and other forms of harassment directed against opposition activists'.[45] On freedom of expression, the IACHR has repeatedly found that 'Cuba is the only country in the Americas in which one can say that there is no guarantee whatsoever for the right of freedom of expression'.[46] Freedom of expression is protected by Article IV of the American Declaration. The IACHR urged Cuba to 'continue adopting all measures or reforms necessary to fully ensure the right of all Cubans to leave Cuba freely, to circulate freely inside Cuba, to freely choose their place of residence in Cuba, and to freely enter the country; it is clearly necessary to eliminate the restrictions on entry to and exit from the national territory'. At the same time the IACHR appealed to OAS states to guarantee human mobility and allow the entry of Cubans to their territories.[47] Freedom of movement is guaranteed by Article VIII of the American Declaration.

On fair trial guarantees, the IACHR pointed to the 'lack of independence and impartiality of the courts, and to the lack of judicial guarantees and due process guarantees in the trial of persons considered ideological dissidents, a particularly grave situation given the use of highly summary procedures',[48] in violation of Articles XVIII and XXVI of the American Declaration, which guarantee fair trial and due process rights.

In relation to economic, social and cultural rights, also protected in the American Declaration, the IACHR welcomed the economic reforms occurring in Cuba since 2008, especially relating to the right to buy property and motor vehicles.[49] In other respects, the IACHR applauded Cuba's record on economic, social and cultural rights, especially in education, health, social security and work.[50] These are protected by Articles XII, XI, XVI, and XIV of the American Declaration.

Cuba is not a party to either of the International Covenants – on Civil and Political Rights or on Economic, Social or Cultural Rights. Therefore Cuba

---

43  Ibid., para 39.
44  Ibid., para 41.
45  Ibid., para 47.
46  Ibid., para 70.
47  Ibid., para 106.
48  Ibid., para 107.
49  Ibid., para 125.
50  Ibid., para 129.

is not subject to the review of the respective quasi-judicial treaty committees – the Human Rights Committee and the Committee on Economic, Social and Cultural Rights. However, as a member of the United Nations, it is subject to review by the subsidiary organs of the General Assembly established with competence over human rights – first the Human Rights Commission and then, after 2006, its successor the Human Rights Council. The Human Rights Council, as with its predecessor, is a political body consisting of forty-seven state representatives and so reflects state opinion on Cuba's human rights record.

In response to the events of Black Spring in 2003, when the Cuban authorities clamped down on dissent, the Commission adopted a resolution in April 2004, which considered that Cuba 'should refrain from adopting measures which could jeopardise the fundamental rights, the freedom of expression and the right to due process of its citizens, and in that regard, deplores the events which occurred last year in Cuba involving verdicts pronounced against certain political dissidents and journalists'. Further, it expressed the hope that the government of Cuba 'will continue to boost religious freedom and will initiate measures designed to facilitate the transition towards the establishment of a fruitful dialogue with all schools of thought and organised political groups in Cuban society . . . with the aim of fostering the all-round development of democratic institutions and civil liberties'.[51] The resolution, however, was only adopted by the barest majority of twenty-two to twenty-one with ten abstentions.

One of the innovations developed by the UN General Assembly to distinguish the Human Rights Council from the somewhat tarnished record of its predecessor is the system of universal periodic reviews of the human rights record of all UN member states.[52] Cuba has been reviewed twice under this system, first in 2009, and then again in 2013. In the 2009 process, the Cuban representative commenced her presentation to the Working Group by concentrating on the right of self-determination; first by stating that the Cuban revolution of fifty years ago was not only a 'historic event that allowed all Cubans to enjoy all of their human rights' but, also, that the transformation caused by it 'ensured the eradication of the structural injustice inherited from the colonial and neo-colonial periods'. This allowed the Cuban people 'in the exercise of its right to self-determination' to establish a 'truly representative and genuinely autochthonous political system which would guarantee real participation by all the people in the exercise of public power'. In support she pointed to the following indicators of representativeness: the Cuban Constitution which established the Cuban state was approved by a vote of 98 per cent of the electorate; the National Assembly is the supreme body of state

---

51  UN Commission on Human Rights resolution 2004/11, 15 April 2004.
52  UNGA Res 60/251 (2006).

power expressing the sovereign will of the Cuban people having legislative competence; representatives to the Assembly are nominated by free, direct and secret vote; every Cuban citizen has the right to vote and be elected; the composition of the Assembly represents the diversity of the Cuban people (28 per cent workers; 43 per cent women; 36 per cent Afro-descendants; and 56 per cent born after the revolution); important decisions are passed only after the 'broadest possible public consensus has been reached', giving the example of the broad process of debate held about Cuban reality in 2008 involving 215,687 public meetings; and that human rights such as freedom of expression were protected by Cuban laws.[53]

Part of the inter-state dialogue under the UN's Universal Periodic Review Process involves recommendations made by other states to Cuba, a number of which were supported by Cuba in the 2009 process, others of which were to be considered by Cuba and responses given. The latter recommendations included one from Western states calling for Cuba to ratify and implement the International Covenants,[54] which contain guarantees on the right to vote and participate as well as freedom of expression, opinion and assembly; but interestingly none of the recommendations were directly concerned with the issue of self-determination or democracy in Cuba. The United States was not involved in this Universal Periodic Review, but its closest ally, the United Kingdom was. The UK concentrated its comments upon the detention of seventy-nine people in 2003 (the Black Spring), over fifty of whom remained in prison.[55]

In the UN's Universal Period Review of 2013 the Cuban representative again built his presentation on the issue of self-determination but this time focussing on the actions of the US. He pointed to the 'relentless attempts by the United States to impose a regime of change on the Cuban people', which was a 'serious violation of its right to self-determination', although it failed to prevent the democratic and direct representation of its citizens in government. Cuba also labelled the embargo as a 'mass, flagrant and systematic violation of human rights'.[56] The Cuban representative made it clear that it did not 'accept the existence of a unique or universal democracy model, much less the imposition of the political system of the western industrialised countries', although he did refer to modifications of the Cuban socio-economic model.[57] Cuba insisted that the rights enshrined in the UN's Universal Declaration of Human Rights of 1948, which contains an authoritative list

---

53 Human Rights Council, Report of the Working Group on the Universal Periodic Review: Cuba, A/HRC/11/22 (2009), paras 5–22.
54 Ibid., para 131 recommendation 1.
55 Ibid., para 64.
56 Human Rights Council, Report of the Working Group on the Universal Periodic Review: Cuba, A/HRC/24/16 (2013), paras 5–6.
57 Ibid., paras 11–12.

of civil-political and socio-economic rights,[58] were protected in Cuban laws. The dialogue and recommendations did not show any concerted effort by other states to challenge this position. The United States was involved in the dialogue,[59] as were many Western states. These states were critical of Cuba and made recommendations to it concerning: its failure to ratify the International Covenants and other human rights treaties; the continued presence of the death penalty, although the presence of a *de facto* moratorium on execution was noted;[60] the lack of protection for human rights defenders and journalists; the need for improvements in fair trial and in the treatment of prisoners; the need to guarantee the independence of the judiciary; the need to ensure access to legal representation; the need to remove restrictions on freedom of expression and association; and the need to ensure wider access to the internet and to stop censorship.[61]

Thus, from the perspective of other states, while the record of Cuba on human rights is problematic, especially in civil and political rights, there is little criticism of it in terms of self-determination. While Cuba's record on democracy can be criticised, it does not seem to reach the level of a denial of self-determination on the basis that its government is *so* unrepresentative as to violate that right. When it comes to state-based review world opinion is generally less critical of Cuba's human rights record when compared to more juridically-based mechanisms such as the IACHR. Cuba has a long way to go in protecting those rights contained in the UDHR, especially civil and political rights. There is little doubt that a combination of rights to association, assembly, expression, and the right to vote and to participate in government should produce a more open form of government than has been present in Cuba from the 1970s when the revolutionary government's hitherto broad-base of support started to erode.[62]

Although Cuba is not bound by any of the regional human rights treaties nor international treaties mentioned above (although it signed both International Covenants in 2008, it has yet to ratify them), this does not mean that Cuba has not violated human rights for clearly it has done so. Whether it has violated its human rights obligations under international law depends upon which of the rights reviewed have passed into customary international law and, therefore, bind all states irrespective of treaty commitments. Certainly the right to life, freedom from torture or other cruel, inhuman, or degrading treatment, and freedom from prolonged arbitrary detention, are all commonly regarded as customary according to the influential American Law Institute's 'Restatement of the Law', as is a 'consistent pattern of gross violations of

---

58  UNGA Res 217A (1948).
59  Human Rights Council Report 2013 (n.56), para 170, 138.
60  Ibid., para 170.
61  Ibid., para 170.
62  See discussion in Chapter 4.

internationally recognised human rights'.[63] It is worth noting that this US-based assessment of customary human rights does not include within it a denial of political rights such as expression, assembly and vote, unless there has been a 'consistent pattern of gross violations' of these rights.

Furthermore, according to the Committee on Economic, Social and Cultural Rights (operating under the International Covenant on Economic, Social and Cultural Rights) there are core socio-economic rights to: essential foodstuffs, essential primary health care, basic shelter and housing, and the more basic forms of education.[64] Socio-economic rights,[65] have also been defined as 'rights to the meeting of needs, among which the most important are the right to a minimum income, the right to housing, the right to health care, and the right to education'.[66]

Nonetheless, a lack of complete clarity as to what human rights have become customary makes it difficult to move the debate about Cuba's shortcomings forward more quickly, in the absence of more critical review by bodies such as the Human Rights Committee and the Committee on Economic, Social and Cultural Rights exercising their competence to review under the International Covenants. Clearly Cuba's track record in protecting socio-economic rights is strong, despite the hardship caused by the embargo, whereas its respect for civil-political rights is unconvincing especially for those disagreeing with the social and political direction and development of Cuba.

## 7.4 United States' conduct under international law

The continuing unilateral embargo against Cuba, effectively imposed and enforced by the US since 1960, has gone far beyond a temporary set of proportionate countermeasures against the Cuban government for its nationalisation of US-owned assets in the period following the revolution of 1959. Does this make the US action unlawful *per se*? Arguably a decision not to trade with Cuba, if it violates none of the international legal obligations of the US towards Cuba, might be viewed as an unfriendly but not, in itself, unlawful act, referred to in international legal doctrine as an act of retorsion. Retorsion is something that is essentially lawful, while countermeasures are inherently unlawful but if they are taken in response to a prior illegality then their imposition under strict limitations precludes wrongfulness. However, it would seem bizarre to conclude that while the US embargo is unlawful because it does not meet the

---

63 American Law Institute, 'Restatement of the Law, the Third, the Foreign Relations Law of the United States' (1987) vol. 2, 161, para 702. The Fourth Restatement is a work in progress.

64 Committee on Economic, Social and Cultural Rights, General Comment 3, 'The Nature of States Parties Obligations: Article 2(1) of the Covenant', UN Doc E/1991/23, para 10.

65 P. O'Connell, *Vindicating Socio-Economic Rights* (London: Routledge, 2012) 4.

66 C. Fabre, *Social Rights under the Constitution* (Oxford: Oxford University Press, 2000) 3.

temporary and proportionate conditions imposed on countermeasures, it might somehow be lawful conduct if it can be classified as retorsion.

Furthermore, the US measures did not simply amount to a ceasing of trade but they attempted to impose a type of blockade (*el bloqueo*) on the country. As stated in Chapter 1 such conduct did not amount to an unlawful pacific blockade, in the technical legal sense of the forcible seizure of the ships of the blockaded state as they try to enter port,[67] but in the sense that the US has tried to block other states and non-US actors trading with the 'enemy' by non-forcible means, for instance, the provisions of the Helms-Burton Act 1996, which gives a right of action against foreign enterprises trafficking in US-owned property that had been seized by the Cuban government.

The only workable interpretation of doctrine surrounding non-forcible measures of self-help is that any such response taken against a state responsible for a breach of international legal obligations owed to another state (the victim state), whether they amount to a suspension of the victim state's obligations (such as under trade agreements) or other acts directed against the responsible state (such as ceasing to trade and stopping others from trading), must be temporary, proportionate, and non-punitive. In addition, such measures must not affect the human rights of the population of the responsible state.[68] Furthermore, the direct linkage of the sanctions regime to the removal of the Castro government in Cuba represents a clear violation of the principle of non-intervention in international law, since they are directed at the political independence of a sovereign state. It must not be forgotten too that Cuba's seizure of US-owned assets was not illegal *per se*, though it has a duty to pay compensation equivalent to the fair market value of such assets. Thus, the actions which triggered the US counter-reaction in the form of the embargo do not clearly meet the requirement of being a wrongful act justifying even temporary and proportionate measures.[69] Nonetheless, there remains an unfilled obligation by Cuba to pay compensation. Furthermore, the US approach to expropriation, whereby the failure to pay compensation itself signifies illegality, meant that it viewed those expropriations as unlawful. Finally, there is the question of which side acted first in that period 1959–61 when relations broke down between the two states; the embargo was developed in this period as was the Cuban government's policy of nationalisation.

---

67  J.P. Grant and J.C. Barker, *Parry and Grant Encyclopaedic Dictionary of International Law* (Oxford: Oxford University Press, 2009) 66.

68  Article 50(1) Articles on the Responsibility of States for Internationally Wrongful Acts 2001. But see S. Borelli and S. Olleson, 'Obligations Relating to Human Rights and Humanitarian Law' in Crawford, Pellet and Olleson (n.6), 1177 at 1186, where it is suggested that the requirement that non-forcible measures should not affect human rights does not apply to acts of retorsion.

69  On the under-developed concept of liability for lawful acts see M. Montjoie, 'The Concept of Liability in the Absence of an Internationally Wrongful Act' in Crawford, Pellet and Olleson (n.6), 503.

The above analysis, though grounded in international legal doctrine, illustrates the problem with the unilateral enforcement of international law. The fact that there seems to be a 'tit-for-tat' relationship between the US and Cuba throughout the Cold War, and thereafter, does not mean that US action accords with international law (or that Cuba acted lawfully throughout). Furthermore, although countermeasures are seemingly of limited scope their inherent nature (involving auto-appreciation by each state of the legality of the conduct of the other state) has the potential to lead to spiralling episodes of action and reaction, which go way beyond the limits of the original doctrine. Without authoritative judgments to break the cycle of actions and reactions then both states continue to be locked into this struggle.

Indeed, the bilateral nature of international law enforcement almost encourages an escalation. The US embargo arguably precipitated Cuban interventions (some of which were unlawful) against US interests in Latin America and, later, in Africa. These in turn justified the continuation and extension of the embargo by the US. The same could be said of the illegal use of force by the US against Cuba by sponsoring the Bay of Pigs invasion in 1961. Clearly this could not be seen as any form of lawful countermeasure, neither was it taken in self-defence nor out of necessity and, therefore, did not qualify under the international law of responsibility as a circumstance precluding wrongfulness.[70] The failed invasion further escalated the dispute by pushing Cuba into an alliance with the Soviet Union, which peaked in the Missile Crisis in 1962. Legally the acquisition of nuclear missiles can be justified by Cuba, as equipping itself to act in self-defence against further attacks, but in terms of military escalation it was a hugely provocative and counter-productive act by Cuba. Although the naval quarantine emplaced by the US around Cuba to prevent the further acquisition of material was a violation of international law, given that it was neither taken in self-defence nor under UN authority, it was a measured response by the US that did lead to a climb down by the Soviet Union and the withdrawal of missiles. In contrast to the illegal use of force by the US in 1961, when the Bay of Pigs invasion created a threat to international peace, the illegal use of force in 1962 by the US in imposing a quarantine to prevent further missiles reaching Cuba served to defuse a threat to international peace and security. This illustrates that international law does not, by itself, provide the answer to dispute settlement, an issue returned to in the next chapter.

Nonetheless, Cuba's refusal to provide reasonable compensation for its expropriations carried out in the initial post-revolutionary period is a violation of a legal duty that remains unremedied. It is possible to see the initial embargo as a lawful countermeasure/act of retorsion at the time, particularly

---

70  Articles 21, 22, 25 Articles on the Responsibility of States for Internationally Wrongful Acts 2001.

as the law governing expropriation was in a state of development; but when it continued in a permanent and disproportionate form in the face of Cuban unwillingness to provide an effective remedy, it became a clear violation of international law. While the embargo was initially justified as a response to expropriation (which the US viewed as unlawful), it was also a reaction to Cuba breaking away from US imperialist influence in such an ideologically antagonistic manner.

The maintenance and strengthening of the embargo over the years, including its incorporation into legislation in the Helms-Burton Act of 1996, has been portrayed by the US as not only justified in response to those initial seizures but also, subsequently, by Cuba's external interventions and by the Cuban government's denial of human rights and democracy. Given that these alleged Cuban violations of international law were not directed at the US, but against various Latin American and African States as well as the citizens of Cuba itself, the traditional doctrine of non-forcible countermeasures seems inappropriate. Simply put, the US was not the victim of these wrongful acts. However, the International Law Commission, in its final articles on state responsibility, left the position of so-called 'collective countermeasures', whereby non-victim states can take countermeasures to uphold community norms, unresolved although there is some state practice to support such a doctrine.[71] Illegal uses of force and interventions, as well as systematic denials of human rights by Cuba, can be seen as violations of community norms so as to enable third states, whose rights have not been violated, to invoke responsibility on the part of the victims. Setting aside the question of whether this justifies collective countermeasures, it is clear that any such measures must be temporary and proportionate, aimed at a restoration of relations and not designed for punishment. By simply continuing the embargo as a blanket measure against Cuba, it is difficult to reconcile US conduct with international law.

The embargo, therefore, is itself a breach of international law given that it does not accord with the rules governing non-forcible measures. It also violates international law as a coercive form of intervention, in breach of the principle of non-intervention.[72] It is also directed at preventing the economic development of Cuba and at removing its legitimate government, a combination which amounts to a deliberate attempt to deny the self-determination of Cuba and the Cuban people. The irony is that by attempting to force Cuba towards democracy (the US's interpretation of what self-determination entails) the US has not only violated the Cuban peoples' right to make that decision, but it has also helped to entrench a one-party state.

---

71  Articles 48 and 54 Articles on the Responsibility of States for Internationally Wrongful Acts 2001.
72  UNGA Res 2131 (1965), 'Declaration on the Inadmissibility of Intervention in the Domestic Affairs of States and the Protection of their Independence and Sovereignty'.

There can be no doubt about US responsibility here, whether an objective or subjective approach is taken, in that the economic sanctions were deliberately aimed at the economic and political independence of Cuba – that intent is embodied in the wording of the Helms-Burton Act.[73]

However, whether it is possible to attach responsibility to the US for the devastating effects of the embargo on the health of the Cuban people is less straightforward. Although there is very little jurisprudence on causation in international legal doctrine,[74] the articles on state responsibility do require that any injury can only be remedied if it was 'caused by the internationally wrongful act'.[75] It has been stated that there will often be problems relating to proof of causation between the adoption of non-forcible measures against a state and the impact on human rights, 'which in most cases will be causally remote'.[76] However, the evidence reviewed in Chapter 6 was that the embargo has had a direct effect on the right to health in Cuba, an impact which would not have occurred 'but for' the embargo and its enforcement by the US.[77]

A further problem is whether the obligations on the US to protect and respect human rights can be owed to individuals outside the territory or jurisdiction of the US. The US signed both International Covenants on Human Rights in 1977. However, it has only ratified the Covenant on Civil and Political Rights in 1992. Thus, the treaty obligations found in the Covenant on Economic, Social and Cultural Rights are not binding upon the US. Furthermore, the US has taken a strong position against the extra-territorial application of its human rights obligations in response to the jurisprudence of the Human Rights Committee which has said otherwise.[78] Nevertheless, basic socio-economic rights, including the right to health, are customary and the indications are that the obligation to protect them is not limited to a state's own territory. Indirect evidence can be drawn from the Covenants themselves. While the Covenant on Civil and Political Rights is limited to a state party's territory and jurisdiction, the Covenant on Economic, Social and Cultural Rights is not.[79] Furthermore, the Committee on Economic, Social and Cultural Rights has suggested that obligations to respect and protect such rights apply extra-territorially in situations where sanctions have been imposed individually or collectively.[80] The US embargo of Cuba has

---

73  See analysis of the Helms-Burton Act 1996 in Chapter 6.
74  B. Stern, 'The Obligation to Make Reparation' in Crawford, Pellet and Olleson (n.6), 563 at 569.
75  Article 31 Articles on the Responsibility of States for Internationally Wrongful Acts 2001.
76  Borelli and Olleson (n.68), 1187–8.
77  On the problematic 'but for' test of causation see Crawford (n.12), 499.
78  General Comment No. 31, 'Nature of the General Legal Obligation on States Parties to the Covenant', UN Doc CCPR/C/21/Rev 1/Add 13 (2004) para 10.
79  Borelli and Olleson (n.68), 1187.
80  General Comment No. 8, 'The Relationship between Economic Sanctions and Respect for Economic, Social and Cultural Rights', UN Doc E/C.12/1997/8 (1997) paras 1, 11–12.

caused violations of the right to health in that country. Such conduct is directly attributable to the United States and, therefore, gives rise to responsibility and a duty to provide reparations.

Unfortunately, by not modifying its sanctions regime against Cuba towards one of a targeted nature thereby targeting the leaders of Cuba rather than the people of Cuba as a whole, the embargo violates a litany of other fundamental principles and rules of international law – of non-intervention, of self-determination and of core socio-economic rights, with a particularly clear causal link between the embargo and the deterioration of the right to health of the Cuban people, especially in that most vulnerable post-1991 period when Soviet support was removed. In a deliberate, almost vindictive act, the US tightened sanctions in its 1992 and 1996 pieces of legislation, knowing that such actions would cause serious suffering to Cubans. There is no excuse for such behaviour. Pointing to humanitarian loopholes in the embargo is not sufficient if they cannot be exploited in reality.

## 7.5   Access to justice in international law

Having established the responsibilities both of Cuba and the United States we turn to the issue of whether access to justice is possible for both sides, in particular for individual Cuban and US citizens who have suffered injury as a result of internationally wrongful conduct attributable to the US or Cuba. It will be seen that, at the moment, there is very little opportunity to access justice and it is essential to consider the form this might take within the broader context of a future settlement of the dispute by the two governments. This, in turn, necessitates a consideration of what is meant by 'access to justice' and why it should be part of a settlement.

Access to justice can be studied in a narrow way as the right to take a case to court to seek redress, but this is just the end of a long story about ideology, politics and justice in a broader sense. At the most abstract level the issue is what is meant by justice, involving a debate about the values political and legal systems should uphold and deliver; and, finally, how a particular system delivers and upholds justice, including the issue of how those who have suffered injustice can achieve redress.

Hilaire McCoubrey draws a distinction between 'justice according to the law' meaning the proper operation of the legal system, and 'justice' as an 'ideal form of dealing', in which an 'external standard is being advanced by reference to which the operation' of the legal and political system is evaluated.[81] Access to justice is not simply about procedural issues of how to bring a case or a claim before a court or another such type of body, it is also about how rights

---

81  J.E. Penner, *McCoubrey and White's Textbook of Jurisprudence* (4th edn, Oxford: Oxford University Press, 2008) 228–30.

and goods are allocated. Francesco Francioni follows this line when he writes that:

> As a term of art . . . access to justice has acquired a variety of meanings. In a general manner it is employed to signify the possibility for the individual to bring a claim before a court and have the court adjudicate it. In a more qualified meaning access to justice is used to signify the right of an individual not only to enter a court of law, but to have his or her case heard and adjudicated in accordance with substantive standards of fairness and justice.[82]

According to Alan Buchanan, a moral theory of international law must be able to explain how key values and principles fit together, otherwise there are just competing claims.[83] A moral theory must include an account 'of the most important moral goals' of international law: upholding both order and justice; the moral reasons for international law being a means of achieving those goals; the conditions under which the international legal order would be morally legitimate, including the conditions for participation of peoples, groups and individuals; and a 'statement of and the justification for the more fundamental substantive norms of the system'.[84]

It goes without saying that there are different philosophical and jurisprudential views and arguments about the external standard by which any legal order should be judged. John Rawls dominates much of the liberal literature. Rawls' two principles of justice give priority to civil and political freedoms, over economic and social goods, where inequalities are allowed as long as they benefit the least advantaged in society.[85] Such an approach is reflected to a certain extent in the two international human rights covenants where, although economic and social goods are cast as rights, the obligation on states is a qualified and progressive one in contrast to the absolute and immediate obligation found in the covenant on civil and political rights. Robinson has gone as far as stating that the right to food and the right to housing are not 'statements of rights' rather 'they articulate substantive conceptions of the good, which require much more than a statement of right to give them moral legitimacy'.[86]

---

82 F. Francioni, 'The Rights of Access to Justice under Customary International Law' in F. Francioni (ed.), *Access to Justice as a Human Right* (Oxford: Oxford University Press, 2007) 1 at 1.

83 A. Buchanan, *Justice, Legitimacy, and Self-Determination* (Oxford: Oxford University Press, 2004) 28.

84 Ibid., 60.

85 J. Rawls, *A Theory of Justice* (Oxford: Oxford University Press, 1973) 302.

86 F. Robinson, 'The Limits of a Rights-Based Approach to International Ethics' in T. Evans (ed.), *Human Rights Fifty Years on: A Reappraisal* (Manchester: Manchester University Press, 1998) 65. But see O'Connell (n.65), 199–208.

Given the state-dominated nature of the international legal system, justice is primarily for governments against governments so that in the dispute between Cuba and the US, mechanisms and remedies will be primarily for and against each state; although they will, in all likelihood, include access to justice for agreed groups of individuals and other non-state actors. In essence, the state parties to the dispute decide on which victims of wrongful acts are to be accorded access to justice and remedies. Such decisions will be a product of diplomacy between the two states, explored in Chapter 8, and not as a result of judicial settlement.

Certainly the International Court of Justice is of limited relevance to the US–Cuba situation as one of the legacies of its lineage from the Permanent Court of International Justice (created under the League of Nations' legal order) was that for many years the 'Court acted as if it were an arbitral tribunal of the nineteenth century and not as an integral part of the UN'.[87] The Court is thus somewhat restricted, in both its structures and powers, from developing into a powerful judicial organ of the UN. It is restricted in its contentious jurisdiction not only by the fact that its binding decisions are not enforceable but, more crucially, by the continuation of the need to ground each case on the consent of both parties.[88] Although an understandable restriction, the Court has stretched the meaning of 'consent' in a number of cases,[89] but has not yet yielded to arguments of breach of obligations owed *erga omnes* to found jurisdiction in the absence of consent. In the *East Timor Case* the Court, faced with a choice between the traditional paradigm of sovereignty and consent and the alternative paradigm of community and community values (in that case the right of the people of East Timor to self-determination), chose the more orthodox route.[90] This is balanced by its more adventurous advisory jurisprudence,[91] in which it has strongly upheld and developed the principle of self-determination in its 1971 *Namibia*, the 1975 *Western* Sahara, and 2004 *Security Wall* opinions.[92]

The question remains as to whether the International Court of Justice is a relevant forum for Cuba and the United States, since neither state is likely to agree to the jurisdiction of the Court as required by the ICJ's Statute. Christine Gray makes the point that the International Court of Justice is an acceptable forum for settlement of maritime and land boundary disputes,

---

87  G. Abi-Saab, 'The International Court as a World Court' in V. Lowe and M. Fitzmaurice (eds), *Fifty Years of the International Court of Justice* (Cambridge: Cambridge University Press, 1996) 3 at 6.

88  Article 36 Statute of the International Court of Justice 1945.

89  For example, *Nicaragua Case (Jurisdiction and Admissibility)*, (1984) ICJ Rep 392.

90  *Case Concerning East Timor (Portugal v Australia)*, (1995) ICJ Rep 90.

91  Article 65 Statute of the International Court of Justice.

92  *Namibia opinion*, (1971) ICJ Rep 16; *Western Sahara opinion*, (1975) ICJ Rep 1975, 12; *Legal Consequences of the Construction of a Wall in the Occupied Palestinian Territory*, (2004) ICJ Rep 136.

where the impact of its decision is mitigated by its tendency to rely on principles of equity and by the fact that both parties are looking for a genuine solution to a lack of clarity as to where the boundary lies. However, such limited conditions are absent in the US–Cuba dispute, where political and legal disagreements are far too deep for a rules-based decision of the Court. Gray questions the value of 'propaganda' type cases, such as the *Tehran Hostages Case* of 1980 brought by the US against Iran, and the *Nicaragua Case* 1986 brought by Nicaragua against the US,[93] in which the respondent state resists the jurisdiction and judgment of the International Court. These cases might help to develop international law in controversial areas, but they do little to settle the dispute between the states.[94]

At the level of state-to-state claims, cases before the International Court of Justice rarely concern remedies, at least in the sense of compensation. For instance, in the *Corfu Channel Case* of 1949, the UK sought a ruling that Albania had violated international law by mining, or permitting the mining, of the Channel, which led to the loss of one Royal Navy vessel and serious damage of another. Unusually in this case the ICJ appointed experts to assess the validity of the UK's figures for damages caused and, after investigation, they determined not only that they were accurate but that Albania should pay this amount.[95] However, Christine Gray concludes that:

> The World Court has not contributed much [to the law of remedies]. Its treatment of remedies seems somewhat perfunctory in contrast with its approach to substantive issues. For it, as for most writers, remedies are an afterthought. The conception of an international law of remedies seems weak; remedies are to be invented anew in each case.[96]

In the absence of a request by the UN General Assembly for an advisory opinion from the International Court on the legality of the US embargo under international law, settlement between the two countries will be achieved by non-judicial mechanisms as explored in Chapter 8. An issue discussed here, which may form part of that process, is whether and when non-state actors (individuals, peoples, and corporations from Cuba and the US) have access to

93 *US Diplomatic and Consular Staff in Tehran*, (1980) ICJ Rep 3; *Military and Paramilitary Activities in and Against Nicaragua*, (1986) ICJ Rep 14.

94 C. Gray. 'The Use and Abuse of the International Court of Justice in the Enforcement of International Law' in K. Koufa (ed.), *International Law Enforcement: New Tendencies* (Athens: Sakkoulas, 2010) 195 at 198, 202.

95 *Corfu Channel Case*, (1949) ICJ Rep, 17–22, 35. Settlement was only made in 1996 – see (1996) 67 *BYBIL* 818–19. See also *Gabčíkovo Case* discussed by R. Higgins, 'Introduction' in M. Evans (ed.), *Remedies in International Law: The Institutional Dilemma* (Oxford: Hart, 1998) 9–10.

96 C. Gray, *Judicial Remedies in International Law* (Oxford: Oxford University Press, 1987) 108.

justice under international law. Such issues can challenge the state-based foundations of the international legal order, although it has long been recognised that states can exercise diplomatic protection on behalf of their nationals, including seeking remedies on their behalf.

That the dispute between Cuba and the United States should be settled at the level of state and government by non-judicial means seems clear, and mechanisms for such will be explored in this chapter and the next, but it should be combined with access to justice for non-state actors, particularly individuals or groups of such. That access to justice could be provided by judicial or non-judicial means, or a combination of both. Although the ultimate control of the type of mechanisms and the causes of action will remain with the two states, there is increasing recognition that settlement should recognise the rights of individuals who have suffered loss as a result of internationally wrongful acts committed by states, not only in an abstract sense but in the shape of access to justice and, where applicable, remedies.

'Until the beginning of [the 20th] century the quality of the individual as a subject of public international law was not even raised as a question', but today that position has been significantly transformed.[97] Francioni points to three developments in allowing individual access to justice in international law. First, there is the law of state responsibility for injuries done to foreign nationals, second the emergence of *ad hoc* international mechanisms providing individual access to justice and, finally, the emergence of human rights law providing for a right to remedy.[98] The development, in the early part of the twentieth century, of customary law of state responsibility for injuries to foreign nationals provided some protection for foreign nationals whose rights were breached by a state. This is the basis upon which the US has insisted upon remedies for its nationals who suffered loss in Cuba in the immediate post-revolutionary period. Interestingly, there were a number of early twentieth century claims commissions established to address the mistreatment of US and other Western citizens and companies in South America.[99] The US claim against Cuba for uncompensated expropriations in the early 1960s is a continuation of this lineage. This area of judicial practice and law was largely developed by Western states whose nationals were investing in developing states. Successful claims were dependent upon the foreign national exhausting domestic remedies in the host state, but there was an international minimum standard expected by investing states in the treatment of their nationals, a denial of which would constitute a breach of international law. The foreign

---

97  A. Randelzhofer, 'The Legal Position of the Individual under Present International Law' in A. Randelzhofer and C. Tomuschat (eds), *State Responsibility and the Individual: Reparation in Instances of Grave Violations of Human Rights* (The Hague: Nijhoff, 1999) 231 at 232–4.

98  Francioni (n.82), 2.

99  Examples of commission cases: *Neer Claim* (*US v Mexico*), (1926) 4 RIAA 60; *Mallen Case* (*US v Mexico*), (1927) 4 RIAA 173; *Caire Claim* (*France v Mexico*), (1929) 5 RIAA 516.

national's claim was also dependent upon his state being willing to exercise diplomatic protection and bring a state-to-state claim, from which the individual could benefit if his national state so decided.[100] An outcome of that diplomacy might be the establishment of a claims commission. The justice that was done to the wronged individual was very much dependent upon the political and diplomatic prerogatives of his national state.

> The law on the protection of aliens is fundamentally different from human rights. It stems from an era of international law when the individual was totally mediatized by the State. The individual was in fact protected by the relevant rules, but the individual was and is not the holder of a corresponding right.[101]

The second trend identified by Francioni was the emergence, again in the early part of the twentieth century, of a number of separate *ad hoc* mechanisms such as war claims commissions giving private persons access to justice in relation to specific events or for specific wrongs. This development has continued apace since 1945 with the growing network of investment treaties that provide for directly enforceable rights belonging to individuals,[102] as well as regional courts such as the Central American Court (established as early as 1907) and the European Court of Justice. Other *ad hoc* mechanisms, which may be templates for a US–Cuba settlement, include the UN Compensation Commission set up to provide compensation for individuals who suffered loss as a result of the Iraqi invasion and occupation of Kuwait in 1990–1,[103] and the Iran–US Claims Tribunal that has provided an avenue for US citizens and companies to bring claims for loss and seizure of property and assets during the Iranian Revolution of 1979.

Third, as identified by Francioni, there has been the development of obligations on states imposed by human rights treaties to provide individuals with the right of access to justice. Even for internationally recognised human rights, the most effective remedies are available within states, with international bodies being a fall-back in the event of state failure.[104] Nevertheless, the 'more radical step of setting up international remedies open to individuals for the adjudication of claims against their own national state is an integral part of the development of the international law of human rights'.[105] However, these international mechanisms are not open to individuals within either the US or Cuba given that the US, while a party to the International Covenant

---

100 *Mavrommatis Palestine Concessions*, PCIJ Rep Series A No. 2 (1924) 12.
101 Randelzhofer (n.97), 234–5.
102 Ibid., 240.
103 Francioni (n.82), 16–17.
104 Ibid., 2, 7–9.
105 Ibid., 23.

on Civil and Political Rights, is not a party to the individual complaint optional protocol, and Cuba is not a party to the Covenant. In addition, neither state is a party to the International Covenant on Economic, Social and Cultural Rights. Nonetheless, access to justice is an emerging right in international law, one that applies within relevant domestic (and possibly regional) legal systems and, in the absence of established international mechanisms, should be protected by the establishment of *ad hoc*, bilateral or multilateral mechanisms. This should be a factor in the settlement of the dispute between Cuba and the US.

Neither the Universal Declaration of Human Rights of 1948 nor the International Covenants use the term access to justice, preferring to talk about state parties ensuring effective remedies,[106] which suggests that the right is not simply about victims of human rights abuse gaining access to a court or other forum such as a claims commission, but about gaining a remedy or remedies (which might include damages or compensation). The UN's Basic Principles on Reparations and Guidelines on the Right to a Remedy and Reparation for Victims of Violations of International Human Rights Law and International Humanitarian Law of 2005 defines a victim for the purposes of those areas of law in the following terms:

> Victims are persons who individually or collectively suffered harm, including physical or mental injury, emotional suffering, economic loss or substantial impairment of their fundamental rights, through acts or omissions that constitute gross violations of international human rights law, or serious violations of international humanitarian law. Where appropriate, and in accordance with domestic law, the term 'victim' also includes the immediate family or dependants of the direct victim and persons who have suffered harm in intervening to assist victims in distress or to prevent victimization.[107]

These Basic Principles further provide that:

> A victim of a gross violation of international human rights law or of a serious violation of international humanitarian law shall have equal access to an effective judicial remedy as provided for under international law. Other remedies available to the victim include access to administrative and other bodies, as well as mechanisms, modalities and proceedings conducted in accordance with domestic law. Obligations arising under international law to secure the right to access justice and fair and impartial proceedings shall be reflected in domestic laws.[108]

---

106 Article 8 Universal Declaration of Human Rights 1948; Article 2, International Covenant on Civil and Political Rights 1966.
107 GA Res 60/147, 16 Dec. 2005.
108 Ibid.

Where there are systematic violations of human rights, the victims are often groups of people and, given the continuing instability and mistrust prevalent in post-conflict or post-confrontation situations, 'remedies may have to be adjusted to achieve other goals'.[109] As Dinah Shelton states:

> Ascertaining and acknowledging the truth is an imperative, a first step that may be followed by a range of options: international prosecutions for international crimes, national prosecution, lustration or purging of individual wrongdoers, civil remedies, international or national compensation mechanisms, partial or total amnesties, and symbolic or other non-monetary remedies.[110]

While only some of these means and methods of remediation will be appropriate when the US–Cuban confrontation ends, the point is that the end of the period of confrontation will necessitate a range of mechanisms appropriate for the settlement of the dispute, possibly a combination of judicial and non-judicial bodies delivering both restitution for loss and restoration of relations.

As regards the types of remedies for individuals and groups, Shelton outlines the aims of substantive redress ranging from 'victim-oriented *restitutio in integrum* and full compensation for pecuniary and non-pecuniary losses to deterrence of violation for the benefit of all members of society', which can include retributive justice (punishment of wrongdoers).[111] Modern techniques of restorative justice or reconciliation primarily aim to 'bring together perpetrators and those affected by abuse and harm, and substantively restorative justice emphasises redress and reintegrating the offender'. As Shelton notes 'redress as a key element of restorative justice is associated with atonement, reconciliation, forgiveness, and reintegration i.e. healing', so that in this model, 'apologies and expressions of remorse are important to the process'.[112] This can find expression in the establishment of truth and reconciliation commissions but also in apologies for past injustices done to groups.[113]

Truth and reconciliation commissions 'investigate a past record of human rights or humanitarian law abuses in a particular country, in the end producing an official report'.[114] They generally 'examine both the causes and consequences of the pattern of abuses and are victim-centred in their approach'.[115]

---

109 D. Shelton, *Remedies in International Human Rights Law* (2nd edn, Oxford: Oxford University Press, 2005) 390.
110 Ibid.
111 Ibid., 12–13.
112 Ibid., 15.
113 See examples given by Shelton, ibid., 446–7.
114 Ibid., 259.
115 Ibid., 260.

Shelton states that by 2008, thirty such commissions had been created, the most well-known of which are found in Argentina, Chile, El Salvador and South Africa.[116] Their strengths are that they establish an 'authoritative record of abuses, and strengthen the rule of law'; they acknowledge the suffering of victims and their families, thus providing a healing effect; they provide moral condemnation which may lead to further (legal) sanctions; they establish human rights as a priority for current and future governments; they represent a clean break with the past; and, finally, unlike courts, they can make wider recommendations and so not just concerned with guilt or innocence.[117]

Whether there is a case for a modified form of truth and reconciliation commission in the context of the US–Cuba dispute will be returned to in Chapter 8. Although such bodies are almost exclusively used in the context of intra-state disputes, there may be a case for such a body in an inter-state dispute. Traditionally, however, the latter type of dispute is resolved by diplomacy between the parties, which may include the establishment of a fact-finding or conciliatory body. As shall be seen in Chapter 8, a commission is sometimes established to ascertain the facts and to make recommendations for settlement of the dispute.[118] Thus, traditional means of dispute settlement between states contain similar elements to modern forms deployed within states; both combine restitution with reconciliation and, it is by drawing upon ideas contained within both, that international law can be made relevant to the Cuba–US dispute.

## 7.6 Conclusion

Having identified violations of the primary rules of international law by both states involved in the dispute, and, furthermore, having determined their responsibilities to each other under the secondary rules as codified by the International Law Commission, we are now in a position to suggest a legal framework within which the parties can settle their dispute. This is attempted in Chapter 8, in which there is also a development of some of the suggestions made in this chapter about the types of processes and mechanisms that might be established to achieve dispute settlement, and to provide access to justice as well as remedies.

The above analysis has established that both states (Cuba and the US) bear responsibility in international law. The law on state responsibility is not concerned with punishing states for their wrongdoing. As stated by Kimberly Trapp in a different context, state responsibility is not about retribution or punishment, it is concerned with restoration of the relations between the

---

116 Ibid.
117 Ibid., 270–1.
118 J.G. Merrills, *International Dispute Settlement* (5th edn, Cambridge: Cambridge University Press, 2011) 58.

wronged state and the responsible state, a rationale which must be even stronger in situations where both states are wronged and wrongdoers. The law on state responsibility 'seeks to re-establish the primary legal relationship between states as a necessary element of their peaceful co-existence'.[119] Furthermore, Trapp states that:

> The possibility of punitive measures imposed on a wrongdoing state does not sit comfortably within an international legal paradigm built on the sovereign equality of states, and was rejected by the ILC in its consideration of a regime of criminal responsibility for states.[120]

Trapp points out that in the area of state-sponsored terrorism, the restoration of normal relations between two states (for example between Libya and the UK as regards the Lockerbie bombing of 1988), can involve the acceptance of state responsibility by the state sponsoring terrorism as well as measures taken to ascertain the criminal responsibility of individuals involved in terrorism. The latter was illustrated in the UK–Libya dispute by their agreement to the trial of the two Libyan agents suspected of the Lockerbie bombing before a Scottish constituted court situated in the Netherlands in 2000–1.

Thus, with the decriminalisation of state responsibility, we see the rise of individual criminal responsibility for breaches of international law, shown by the development of the International Criminal Court (ICC) for the most heinous crimes. State responsibility can arise for the same wrongful acts as give rise to individual responsibility, as shown in the *Bosnia Genocide Case* of 2003,[121] where Serbia was found responsible for failure to prevent genocide in contravention of the Genocide Convention, while individual Bosnian Serbs and Serb leaders were being tried for the crime of genocide before the ICTY. Establishing state responsibility between Serbia and Bosnia is to enable the restoration of state-to-state relations, while determination of individual criminal responsibility is primarily directed at retribution and punishment, although the criminal trials of individuals can also play a role in normalising state-to-state relations. The International Court of Justice was at pains to point out that it was not a criminal court but, rather, was concerned with establishing what primary rules had been breached by Serbia and the consequences of such breach.[122]

---

119 K. Trapp, *State Responsibility for International Terrorism* (Oxford: Oxford University Press, 2011) 263.
120 Ibid.
121 *Concerning the Application of the Convention on the Prevention and Punishment of the Crime of Genocide*, (2007) ICJ Rep 2007 43.
122 Ibid., paras 147–8, 167.

The next chapter examines the possible ways of restoring normal relations between Cuba and the US based on peaceful co-existence and mutual respect for state sovereignty. Most of these adjustments will be at the state-to-state level but with provision for access to justice for individuals. Part of the process of state adjustment may include criminal trials of individuals accused of 'terrorist' acts against Cuba, for instance for the destruction of a Cuba airlines plane with the loss of seventy-three lives in 1976,[123] or of those Cubans responsible for shooting down two 'Brothers to the Rescue' planes in 1996.[124] Criminal trials of individuals may form part of the restorative adjustment process between the two states, although, given the nature of the dispute, which has largely been of a state-to-state nature, albeit one with effects on individuals, most of the restoration will be at the governmental level. We now turn to a detailed analysis of the possible means and methods of adjustment between those governments.

---

123  R. Gott, *Cuba: A New History* (New Haven, CT: Yale University Press, 2004) 261.

124  One aspect of the dispute concerns the 'Cuban Five' convicted of spying against the US in 2001. Two of the five have been released by the US, but the case remains a source of tension between the two states. One of the five was also convicted of conspiracy to commit murder over the shooting down of two planes flown by the Cuban exile group – Brothers to the Rescue - in 1996; see 'Jailed Cuban Spy Fernando Gonzalez Freed from US Prison', BBC News 27 February 2014 – www.bbc.co.uk/news/world-latin-america-26373687 (accessed 17 March 2014).

# 8 Legal framework for peaceful settlement

## 8.1 Introduction

This chapter follows from the determination of state responsibility for breaches of international law uncovered in Chapter 7. It illustrates that although state responsibility can be determined, the legal framework for, and the means of, peaceful solution do not automatically follow; they must be negotiated and crafted by the parties with the help, if necessary, of third parties. Such a solution may create non-judicial and/or judicial bodies with jurisdiction over aspects of the dispute, which are able to deliver state, corporate and individual access to justice and remedies. It is argued further in this chapter that the theory of responsibility should, within limits, give way to the practicalities of dispute settlement. Rather than diminish the relevance of international law, it will be shown that this approach supports a central role for law in helping the parties to create an agreed framework within which they settle the dispute, in contrast to a more orthodox approach to rule application which results in law being peripheral when applied in a determinant manner under which one side loses and the other wins.

Even if a dispute does find its way to an authoritative judicial body, such as the International Court of Justice, there is little guarantee that the losing state will accept the judgment of the Court, especially in such a complex case as would be presented to the Court by Cuba and the US. If dispute settlement is to work in these circumstances it is essential that alternative understandings of the principles of international law,[1] as well as alternative mechanisms for dispute settlement, are considered by the parties if agreement is to be achieved. There is no magic formula that will solve the dispute and it is a mistake to consider that international law normally works in such a manner.

This chapter adapts Koskenniemi's idea of international law as the 'gentle civiliser of nations', which he posited generally in the following terms: 'between the arrogance of universality and the indifferences of particularity,

---

1 S. Allen and E. Guntrip, 'The Kosovo Question and *Uti Possidetis*: The Potential for a Negotiated Solution' in J. Summers (ed.), *Kosovo: A Precedent?* (Leiden: Nijhoff, 2011) 303 at 315.

what else is there apart from the civilised manner of gentle spirits?'.[2] This chapter applies such thinking within the context of a bilateral dispute. By so doing, it shows that when a political regime (such as that governing the US and Cuba since 1960) collapses, law plays a crucial role in establishing a new political regime. Furthermore, the chapter argues that, along with applicable principles of international law, the underpinning values of peace, justice and reconciliation must be delivered by the peace process. These values find current expression within modern ideas of transitional justice, a regime which has emerged most strongly within the context of post-conflict rebuilding. Transitional justice is based on the premise that without both a reckoning (as regards past abuses) as well as a reconciliation (between groups and individuals on different sides of the conflict), then the cycle of violence will only be broken temporarily.[3] Although actual armed conflict between the US and Cuba has been limited to the Bay of Pigs confrontation in 1961, the threat of violence and the level of hostility between the two countries have been such that, before normal relations between the two states can be established, a post-conflict (or post-confrontation) phase has to be passed through. Transitional justice and related arguments for a *jus post bellum*,[4] although not directly applicable to every dispute between states, serve to illustrate that international law has the potential to facilitate a dynamic environment in which both peace and justice can be built. Furthermore, the chapter demonstrates that the values most prominently found in transitional justice are also actually located in more orthodox and traditional methods of dispute settlement between states.

## 8.2 The role of law in the political settlement of disputes

Any student of international law must come to his or her own understanding of the relationship between international law and politics. Law, at any level, whether national, regional or international, is a product of politics, but we also expect it to govern politics – to create a legal framework within which political discretion can be exercised. The more law regulates politics the stronger the rule of law. However, it is more difficult to maintain that there exists an international rule of law, despite UN rhetoric to that effect.[5] The

---

2  M. Koskenniemi, *The Gentle Civilizer of Nations: The Rise and Fall of International Law* (Cambridge: Cambridge University Press, 2002) 515.

3  A.-M. La Rosa and X. Phillipe, 'Transitional Justice' in V. Chetail (ed.), *Post-Conflict Peacebuilding: A Lexicon* (Oxford: Oxford University Press, 2009) 368.

4  C. Stahn, J.E. Esterday and J. Iverson (eds), *Jus Post Bellum: Mapping the Normative Foundations* (Oxford: Oxford University Press, 2014) at 5 – 'it is still unclear whether *jus post bellum* is a construct, a strand of research, or a sub-discipline of existing paradigms'.

5  See for example UNGA Res 68/116 (2013), 'The rule of law at the national and international levels', which, at para 4, '*reaffirms* the imperative of upholding and promoting the rule of law at the international level in accordance with the principles of the Charter of the United Nations'.

reason for this is clearly exposed by the critical methodology of Martti Koskenniemi, who wrote in 1990, against the backdrop of a claimed new world order emerging in the radically changed circumstances at the end of the Cold War, that:

> I shall attempt to show that our inherited ideal of a World Order based on the Rule of Law thinly hides from sight the fact that social conflict must still be solved by political means and that even though there may exist a common legal rhetoric among international lawyers, that rhetoric must, *for reasons internal to the ideal itself*, rely on essentially contested – political – principles to justify outcomes to international disputes.[6]

The internal problem faced by international law is that the law, especially custom, is generated by state practice and so can be seen as an excuse or apology for state behaviour. Any attempt to depart from state practice can be dismissed as utopian and, therefore, irrelevant in that it will have no impact upon state behaviour. In order to achieve universal agreements in more formal documents, treaties or resolutions, norms are crafted in abstract and indeterminate terms. Thus, in these circumstances:

> Behind ritualistic references to well-known rules and principles of international law (the content of which remains a constant object of dispute), legal practice has increasingly resorted to resolving disputes by a contextual criterion – an effort towards an equitable balance. Though this has seemed to work well, the question arises as to whether such practice can be adequately explained in terms of the Rule of Law.[7]

In this way, law forms part of the debate and discussion within which disputes can be resolved but, in the end, abstract and often indeterminate universal rules can only provide guides towards an equitable solution which is politically just.[8] The growth, since 1990, of specialist international legal regimes, with greater precision in terms of rules, does not remove political choices,[9] given that disputes refuse to neatly fit within only one legal regime. The US–Cuba dispute involves issues of forcible and non-forcible measures, sovereignty and self-determination, democratic and socio-economic rights, as well as trade and investment. Resort to human rights norms and mechanisms will produce a different range of answers to one brought within a trade regime. The problem is exacerbated when the disputants' participation in different regimes does not overlap significantly or even marginally.

---

6  M. Koskenniemi, 'The Politics of International Law', (1990) 1 *EJIL* 4 at 7.
7  Ibid., 14.
8  Ibid., 31.
9  M.Koskenniemi, 'The Politics of International Law – 20 Years Later', (2010) 20 *EJIL* 7 at 11.

Furthermore, despite problems with indeterminacy, Koskenniemi admits that international laws can, at certain crucial points, have a significant role to play even within highly politicised regimes concerning the security of states. Realism foresees security being achieved in such circumstances by states acting out of self-interest and, eventually, by achieving a balance of power.[10] Koskenniemi argues that a purely pragmatic approach still contains normative premises involving stylised and abstract understandings of concepts such as 'interest' (as in the national 'interest'), 'security' (as in national 'security') and 'power' (as in balance of 'power'). In addition, he argues that the legal justifications invariably put forward by states for their actions under a balance of power or similar system are not simply excuses but meaningful justifications and explanations for action.[11]

According to Koskenniemi, when the political context is stable, as it largely was during the superpower confrontation of the Cold War, law primarily plays a pragmatic role, for example, in helping shape the text of Security Council resolutions to be in broad conformity with the UN Charter. Politics are in effect poured into a variety of legal vessels (treaties, resolutions, soft laws). However, when the political context radically changes and becomes unstable the Charter and international law more generally take on a central role in shaping the boundary between law and politics. In these circumstances, international law acts as a constraint on discretion, not in a fully 'constitutional' sense,[12] rather in a 'political' sense. International law performs the function of being a container within which politics are confined. This signifies that within a new political context international law provides the parameters for political action, but international law is not a strong or rigid enough framework to fully constrain political considerations. In these circumstances, the legal framework is significantly expanded and developed by interpretation and subsequent practice.[13]

In this way, at the end of the Cold War, international law was reinterpreted to apply to new circumstances, for example, in the Badinter Commission's interpretations of self-determination in the context of the break-up of Yugoslavia in the early 1990s.[14] Faced with the break-up of a different type of empire the Commission, established by the European Community, extended the idea of external self-determination, which in the Cold War period was

---

10 J.J. Mearsheimer, 'Back to the Future: Instability in Europe after the Cold War' in M.E. Brown, O.R. Cote, S.M. Lynn-Jones and S.E. Miller (eds), *Theories of Law and Peace* (Boston, MA: MIT Press, 1998) 3.

11 M. Koskenniemi, 'The Place of Law in Collective Security', (1996) 17 *Michigan Journal of International Law* 455 at 465, 469, 472, 476.

12 Ibid., 473, 478, 480.

13 Subsequent practice is recognised as a means of interpretation in Article 31(3)(2)(b) Vienna Convention on the Law of Treaties 1969.

14 See M. Craven, 'The European Community Arbitration Commission on Yugoslavia', (1995) 66 *BYBIL* 333.

applied to colonial territories, to cover new states emerging from the federal units within a collapsing Communist state.

According to Koskenniemi, law took on a shaping role in the 1990 crisis that followed the Iraqi invasion of Kuwait. The end of the Cold War meant that:

> The traditional patterns of Council decision making had become irrelevant and inapplicable. There was no anterior political agreement, no long-standing negotiation with fixed positions, and no routine language to cover events. The situation was canvassed nowhere but in the Charter itself. As the debate took on a legal style and an engaged aspect, the rest of formalism followed suit.[15]

This took place, for example, in the search for legal precedent in the management of sanctions, in which the comprehensive regime against white Rhodesia 1965–79 was clearly the template, while the mandating resolution for force in 1950 against North Korea was used as the template for Resolution 678 (1990), which authorised member states to enforce the Security Council's demand for Iraqi withdrawal from Kuwait and 'to restore international peace and security to the area'.

The move to law was evidenced in the way these precedents were put together with other legally based responses, including declaring Iraq's annexation of Kuwait as null and void, in a suite of resolutions whereby the Council used its full range of Chapter VII powers in a unique way in 1990, but one clearly in accordance with the UN Charter of 1945. It started with a determination of a breach of the peace under Article 39 and a demand for Iraqi withdrawal under Article 40 (in Resolution 660), then the Security Council: imposed comprehensive sanctions against Iraq under Article 41 (Resolution 661); determined that Iraq's annexation of Kuwait was null and void (Resolution 662); authorised naval forces to enforce sanctions in a limited application of Article 42 (Resolution 665); then it authorised full-scale force to remove Iraq (Resolution 678), with many fine-tuning resolutions in between. The war was brought to an end by a unique Resolution (687 of 1991), which imposed severe conditions upon Iraq including supervised disarmament and a mechanism for providing compensation to victims of its aggression. Resolution 687 illustrates the malleability of international law in changed political conditions, but this does not mean that the Resolution was *ultra vires*, for if the Security Council is empowered to authorise the waging of war on a state it is equally empowered to bring it to an end.

The consensus within the five permanent members enabled the Council to develop a legal framework for its post-Cold War actions (implicitly acting

---

15 Koskenniemi (n.11), 476–7.

under Charter Article 41's open-ended list of non-forcible measures) that would have been unimaginable during the Cold War. In addition to imposing post-war conditions upon Iraq, this enabled it to create international criminal tribunals for Yugoslavia and Rwanda, and post-conflict administrations for Kosovo and East Timor. However, that consensus had dissipated by 2003, with the US and the UK, bridling against Iraq's perceived lack of compliance especially with the disarmament provisions of Resolution 687 (1991), taking unilateral military measures culminating in the full-scale invasion of Iraq in 2003.

In 2003 law once again took a back seat to politics, evidenced by the unconvincing attempts by the UK, in particular, to justify the use of force against Iraq on the basis that Resolution 678 of 1990 was somehow still a legally valid authorisation to use force. The 'revival' argument, as it came to be known, only came to the fore once it became clear that a follow-up resolution that would have allowed for the enforcement of the WMD inspection regime re-established by Resolution 1441 (2002), was not going to be achieved due to French and Russian reticence.[16]

After the terrorist attacks on New York and Washington of 11 September 2001 in which the world's remaining superpower was significantly wounded by a relatively small non-state terrorist group, the political context changed to a 'war on terror'. Arguably again international law, this time on self-defence, provided a constraint on the US reaction, but at the same time self-defence was adapted to a new form of threat. However, even after that paradigm seemingly became accepted after 9/11, the expansion of the right of self-defence suffered from abuse in that it was used as a justification for a continuing war of self-defence against al-Qaida from 2001 to the present day. From gaining world-wide support for its initial use of force against Afghanistan in October 2001, US actions moved from those of a lawman towards those of a badman due to its ill-considered prosecution of a global war on terror.

Iraq and Afghanistan raise the question of whether in general terms international law has settled back into being a handmaiden to pragmatism in issues of security, or whether it plays an external role to politics, challenging and perhaps controlling politics despite it being, in a sense, inside social practices? We also have to consider whether the wider political context affects the role international law plays in bilateral dispute settlement as in the Cuba–US confrontation embodied in the continuing embargo. Bearing in mind Koskenniemi's warning against viewing the weaknesses of international law's claims to universality as an argument for simply dealing with particularities, it is contended that his analysis does apply to a bilateral

---

16 See Parliamentary Written Answer to House of Lords given by the Attorney General Lord Goldsmith, *Hansard* HL, vol. 646, WA2-3, 17 March 2003.

dispute. We are not guilty of reducing international law to particularities in doing this, rather we are making the claim that it is actually easier to make the universalities of international law work within a bilateral context than it is within a collective context where the achievement of inter-subjective agreement is more difficult,[17] especially once the opportunities provided by the collapse of an existing political regime have passed.

## 8.3  The political context

It follows that for international law to take a shaping role in any process of dispute settlement between the US and Cuba, there must be a significant break in the prevailing political context. The end of the Cold War created new conditions enabling the revitalisation of existing (and seemingly exhausted) principles of law such as self-determination in the context of the former Yugoslav and Soviet Republics, and self-defence in the context of the terrorist attacks of 9/11. In addition, this period saw further innovations in collective measures against international crimes (for example, the international criminal tribunals for the former Yugoslavia and Rwanda),[18] and terrorism (for example, Security Council 'legislation' prohibiting support for terrorism).[19] Arguably the end of the Cold War should have been the context-breaking event that led to the end of the US–Cuban confrontation, given the removal of Soviet support for Cuba and the opening of the Cuban economy to wider trade. However, the US decision was to continue the same political framework and, indeed, to re-enforce it by tightening the embargo in order to remove one of the few remaining Communist regimes. In effect, by 1991 the Cold War had ended between the superpowers but continued across the Florida Straits. The attacks of 11 September 2001 served to strengthen this resolve as Cuba was (wrongly) categorised as a continuing threat and was grouped by the US as a pariah state along with Iran and North Korea.

Thus, it appeared that the window of opportunity that had briefly opened at the end of the Cold War had been firmly shut by US legislation in 1992–1996. However, it is contended that in bilateral disputes, while the broader international political conditions remain a factor, of more importance is the political relationship between the two states. As has been shown the mainstay of US policy towards Cuba, the embargo, has long ceased to be a tool of foreign policy and is really a product of domestic American politics.

---

17  I. Johnstone, 'Legislation and Adjudication in the UN Security Council: Bringing Down the Deliberative Deficit', (2008) 102 *AJIL* 275. See J. Habermas, *Between Facts and Norms: Contributions to a Discourse Theory of Law and Democracy* (Oxford: Polity, 1996) at 107 where Habermas writes 'just those action norms are valid to which all possible affected persons could agree as participants in rational discourses'.

18  UNSC Res 827 (1993); UNSC Res 955 (1994).

19  UNSC Res 1373 (2001).

Furthermore, the animosity Cuba has consistently shown towards the US, to the extent of closing any opportunity for rapprochement, was largely practised during the leadership of Fidel Castro, which, enmeshed in the history of Cuba's struggle for independence, was strongly anti-imperialist and anti-American. If those domestic political contexts change and converge on the issue of the embargo and the wider relationship between the two countries, then there is the possibility of a settlement process, in which international legal principles will provide a shared language enabling common ground to be found.

For a peace process to start it is essential that the prolonged political stalemate that has gripped US–Cuban relations since 1960 comes to an end. This will possibly happen upon the deaths of both the Castro brothers, or maybe when this is combined with a change in electoral configurations in the US, especially when the Cuban–American vote in Florida becomes less important; or maybe if Raúl Castro and his successor continue their 'glasnost' policies and the embargo becomes less and less relevant (for example, even though it might continue to exist on the statute books but not in practice in terms of enforcement).

Furthermore, changes in the wider geopolitical context might help push the US towards a more constructive approach to Cuba. China's involvement in the hemisphere might provoke a US reaction in favour of trying to normalise its relations with Cuba and other left-wing Latin American countries such as Venezuela. China has been steadily lending and investing in a number of Latin American countries with left-leaning governments, particularly Venezuela, Ecuador, Cuba and Brazil. While the US remains a global hegemon favouring unilateral military interventions, China is trading and investing on the basis of respect for national sovereignty and by claiming to support a multi-polar world, thereby aligning its policies with Latin American countries that have broken free from US influence in the last fifteen years.[20] At some point the US will realise that its liberal interventionist policies (as practised in Iraq and Afghanistan) are neither legitimate nor effective and will resort to quieter diplomacy on the basis of respect for sovereign equality and the principle of non-intervention, as laid out in Articles 2(1) and 2(7) of the UN Charter,[21] and Articles 1 and 3(e) of the Charter of the OAS.[22]

---

20  'US Leaves Door Open for China', *Guardian Weekly*, 7 February 2014. There is also the problem for Cuba of its dependency on Venezuela for oil and trade, a relationship that looks precarious following the death of Venezuela's President Hugo Chávez – 'Cuba Contemplates Life After Venezuela', *Guardian Weekly*, 30 May 2014.

21  Article 2(1) UN Charter states that the UN 'is based on the principle of sovereign equality of all its members'; while Article 2(7) states that 'nothing contained in the present Charter shall authorise the United Nations to intervene in matters which are essentially within the domestic jurisdiction of any state . . .; but this principle shall not prejudice the application of enforcement measures under Chapter VII'.

22  Article 1 OAS Charter reads, in part, that the OAS is established to 'achieve an order of peace and justice, to promote their solidarity, to strengthen their collaboration, and to

The recent dominance of left-wing ideology in Latin America has led to a shift away from the OAS (based in Washington) as the dominant regional organisation, towards the Community of Latin American and Caribbean States (CELAC), which was established as an alternative regional organisation of thirty-three states,[23] and does not include the US or Canada. While Cuba remains outside the OAS, it is worth noting that the Second Summit of CELAC was held in Havana in January 2014, at the end of which the Havana Declaration was adopted, the opening paragraph of which reiterated that the:

> Unity and integration of our region must be built gradually, with flexibility, with respect for pluralism and the sovereign right of each of our peoples to choose their own political and economic system. Reiterate that our Community is founded on the unrestricted respect for the Purposes and Principles of the United Nations Charter and International Law, the peaceful settlement of disputes, the prohibition of the use and threat of use of force, respect for self-determination, sovereignty, territorial integrity, non-interference in the internal affairs of each country, protection and promotion of all human rights, the Rule of Law at the national and international levels, promotion of active citizenship, and democracy. Likewise, pledge ourselves to work together for the sake of prosperity for all, in such a way as to eradicate discrimination, inequalities and marginalization, violations of human rights and transgressions of the Rule of Law.[24]

If the US does not want to lose all its influence and prestige in Latin America it will need to be less interventionist and look to cooperate with the states of the region in trade and security. There is plenty in the Havana Declaration of 2014 that the US, as well as Cuba, could agree to.

## 8.4 The importance of reciprocity and restoration

There has been an absence of peaceful relations between Cuba and the US since 1960. Although armed conflict has been limited there has been coercion by both sides, although more so on the part of the US. The situation has been one of confrontation or conflict in a broad sense so that there is a clear need for a peace process that leads to a peace agreement. Peace agreements in the

---

defend their sovereignty, their territorial integrity, and their independence'. Article 3(e) reads, in part, that 'every state has the right to choose, without external interference, its political, economic and social system and to organize itself in the best way suited to it, and has the duty to abstain from interfering in the affairs of another state . . .'.

23 'Right has Little Appeal', *Guardian Weekly*, 31 January 2014.

24 Havana Declaration, II Summit CELAC, Havana 2014, http://celac.cubaminrex.cu/sites/default/files/ficheros/havana_declaration_celac.pdf (accessed 13 February 2014).

post-Cold War period have shown a number of similarities to the extent that it has been argued that what is emerging is a form of *lex pacificatoriae*.[25] Although most of these agreements have brought to an end intra-state conflicts, those common principles are mainly applicable to an inter-state dispute which, in part, raises concerns about the conditions within one of the states involved in the dispute (Cuba), as well as relations between the two states.

Common features of peace accords include agreement by the parties on methods of achieving peace and security, self-determination and human rights, transitional justice (to address wrongful acts committed), and providing for access to justice. In addition, a peace agreement between the US and Cuba should include a process of normalising trade relations between states over a period of years so as to allow the Cuban economy to adjust to free trade without being overwhelmed by American enterprises (with the danger that this could lead to a return of US dominance and, possibly, imperialism). Without such an agreement covering peace and justice between the two states the cycle of confrontation and conflict between the US and Cuba will not be broken.

Transitional justice addresses the legacy of a violent past, which, as has been stated, represents the condition of US–Cuban relations going back to 1898. Transitional justice is based on 'adherence to applicable law', inter-national, regional and domestic, and an 'integrated approach to justice where the victim is at the heart of the process', involving judicial and non-judicial elements to ensure the goals of 'truth seeking, reparation, enforcement and sanctions' are attained.[26] Many would add restoration to this list of goals. Shelton writes that:

> Restorative justice has a procedural aspect and a substantive one. In terms of process, restorative justice aims to bring together perpetrators and those affected by abuse and harm. Substantively, restorative justice emphasizes redress and reintegrating the offender, not punishing him. Redress as a key element of restorative justice is associated with atonement, reconciliation, forgiveness, and reintegration i.e. healing. In this model, apologies and expressions of remorse are important to the process.[27]

We mostly speak of restorative justice in the context of individual (criminal) responsibility, as a different approach to 'retributive justice', which involves 'the application of punishment . . . or it can take the form of fines or exemplary or punitive damages'.[28] State responsibility, if anything, is even more firmly

---

25   C. Bell, 'Peace Agreements: Their Nature and Legal Status', (2006) 100 *AJIL* 373 at 373–5.

26   La Rosa and Philippe (n.3), 368.

27   D. Shelton, *Remedies in International Human Rights Law* (2nd edn, Oxford: Oxford University Press, 2005) 15.

28   Ibid., 12.

grounded on restoration, of normal relations between two states, which have been disrupted by internationally wrongful acts. Indeed, the criminalisation of state behaviour has not been the route taken by the ILC in its drafting of Articles on the Responsibility of States for Internationally Wrongful Acts in 2001. If restoration of friendly relations is combined with an understanding of peaceful settlement between states, which combines peace and justice, then it is not necessary to stretch modern mechanisms of transitional justice, such as truth and reconciliation commissions, that have developed *within* post-conflict states to apply them, by analogy, to disputes *between* states. It will be seen that commissions of inquiry can play a similar role to truth and reconciliation commissions in the context of bilateral disputes between states. The principles of peace and justice underpinning transitional justice are the same as those that underpin international law.

When most transitional justice processes and mechanisms are directed at achieving truth, reconciliation and at establishing individual criminal responsibility for crimes arising from an internal conflict or crisis,[29] the bilateral nature of the US–Cuba dispute suggests that any mechanism should address the issue of responsibility primarily at the level of states. The purpose of such mechanisms would not be to establish individual criminal responsibility, but to address the responsibilities of both states with the aim of restoration of normal relations between them, and with the further aim of providing access to justice and remedies for citizens of both countries who have suffered loss as a result of the wrongful acts of the two states. According to Shelton:

> The primary function of corrective or remedial justice is to rectify the wrong done to the victim, that is, to correct the injustice. As such remedies serve moral goals. Law and its institutions are the instruments through which fault is determined and its consequences are assessed in order to redress harm caused. . . . Remedies aim to place an aggrieved party in the same position as he or she would have been had no injury occurred.[30]

The principles of transitional justice provide inspiration for any modern peace process, whether internal or international, since they are founded upon achieving both peace and justice. While the traditional methods of dispute settlement applicable to inter-state disputes are normally characterised as being concerned with the attainment of peace, a deeper analysis (below) of the more successful processes reveals that they have a concern for justice as well.

---

29 UNSG's Report, 'The Rule of Law and Transitional Justice in Conflict and Post-Conflict Societies', UN Doc S/2004/616 (2004) para 8.
30 Shelton (n.27), 10.

Traditional methods facilitate a reciprocal exchange of rights and duties between the parties as well as a restoration of normal relations between sovereign states based on mutual respect and cooperation. Both theories of transitional justice and state responsibility point to restoration rather than retribution as the guiding principle.[31] It follows that one path a peace agreement between Cuba and the US could take would be to establish an independent commission of inquiry to establish a historical record, and to make recommendations for normalisation, as well as a quasi-judicial or non-judicial compensation commission to assess claims from individuals for losses suffered as a result of internationally wrongful acts by both states on the basis of reasonable or equitable compensation rather than punitive damages.

The contention is that a holistic peace process and agreement is essential if the cycle of confrontation between the US and Cuba is to come to an end. A piecemeal approach may bring temporary relief but will not produce a sustainable peace between the two countries. For example, if the result of agreement between the US and Cuba is limited to the establishment of a judicial body to hear complaints being brought by US citizens for loss of property rights in Cuba in the immediate post-revolutionary era, then this will be inadequate as a means of settling the wider dispute. This is best illustrated by the creation, work and impact of the Iran–US Claims Tribunal.

The Iran–US Claims Tribunal was established to remedy losses arising out of the Islamic Revolution in Iran of 1979, when a US-friendly regime was ousted by one antagonistic towards the West. The Tribunal was established in January 1981, as a result of mediation by Algeria, culminating in the Algiers Accords. The purpose of the Tribunal was to resolve claims between the United States and Iran, as well as between their nationals, and cases were to be decided 'on the basis of respect for law', including principles of commercial law and general principles of international law. The costs of the tribunal were borne equally by Iran and the US. Iran, uncooperative at first, complied due to billions of dollars of its assets being frozen by the US. Furthermore, there was the threat of litigation in the US if the Tribunal did not work, which helped to induce Iran into cooperation in setting up the Tribunal and complying with its decisions. To date about 4,000 claims have been settled, which is a remarkable achievement given the continuing state of hostility between the two governments.[32]

Nonetheless, despite the successes of the Iran–US Claims Tribunal, the underlying tensions and confrontation between the two countries have not

---

31  Crawford states that 'there is little or no state practice to support "punitive" or "penal" consequences for breaches of international law' – J. Crawford, *State Responsibility: The General Part* (Cambridge: Cambridge University Press, 2013) 52.

32  See further C. Gray, *Judicial Remedies in International Law* (Oxford: Clarendon, 1987) 181–5; J.R. Crook, 'Applicable Law in International Arbitration: The Iran-U.S. Claims Tribunal Experience', (1989) 83 *AJIL* 278.

been resolved, showing that a broader approach to dispute settlement will be necessary if success is to be achieved in the Cuba–US dispute. The Iran–US Claims Tribunal was created in a politically difficult and unfavourable environment after the revolution in Iran had 'deeply disturbed the relationship between Iran and the US at the end of the 1970s'.[33] Parallels with the Cuban revolution, and expropriations of US-owned property and assets in 1959–60, can be seen. It is true to say that the Tribunal became an 'exceptional arbitration mechanism' rich in jurisprudence on state responsibility for expropriations.[34] In many ways it was a successor to the mixed claims commissions established at the beginning of the twentieth century,[35] although it more clearly gave individuals access to justice by enabling them to file claims directly, rather than relying on their national states exercising diplomatic protection on their behalf.[36] However, there is little evidence that the Iran–US Claims Tribunal has helped with reconciliation between the US and Iran, whose relationship has remained one of confrontation, up to the level of threats of force and limited uses of force.[37] Indeed, in 1981 the Iran–US Claims Tribunal made a decision (by majority) that Article II of the claims settlement declaration did not include a right to bring claims against US nationals on the grounds that a 'clear formulation' of that provision excluded Iranian claims from the jurisdiction of the Tribunal. Although the majority could draw support for this interpretation from a textual reading of the Article, the minority pointed out that this undermined any reciprocity underpinning the agreement.[38] By disregarding that reciprocity, the Tribunal has provided only one-sided justice and, although that is some justice, it is not one upon which to build reconciliation and restoration between the two countries.

## 8.5  Setting up a peace process

The importance of diplomacy was made clear by the International Court of Justice in a 1980 case concerning US hostages being held in Iran, another

---

33  D. Müller, 'Other Specific Regimes of Responsibility: The Iran-US Claims Tribunal' in J. Crawford, A. Pellet and S. Olleson (eds), *The Law of International Responsibility* (Cambridge: Cambridge University Press, 2010) 843.

34  Ibid.

35  See I. Scobbie, 'The Permanent Court of Arbitration, Arbitration, and Claims Commissions in the Inter-War Period', in M. Fitzmaurice and C.J. Tams (eds), *Legacies of the Permanent Court of International Justice* (The Hague: Martinus Nijhoff, 2013) 203.

36  Müller (n.33), 844–5.

37  See *Oil Platforms (Islamic Republic of Iran v United States of America)*, (2003) ICJ Rep 161. In 2010 there was an unattributed cyber-attack using Stuxnet against Iran's nuclear plants resulting in the destruction of centrifuges essential for the enrichment of uranium.

38  Iran–US Claims Tribunal, *Interpretation of the Algerian Declaration of 19th January 1981*, (1982) 62 ILR 599–600.

aspect of the dispute between the US and Iran. The Court described diplomacy as an:

> Instrument essential for effective cooperation in the international community, and for enabling states, irrespective of their differing constitutional and social systems, to achieve mutual understanding and to resolve their differences by peaceful means.[39]

Bearing in mind the importance of establishing a basis of reciprocity in order to achieve restoration of normal relations between the US and Cuba, the chapter now turns to the methods of dispute settlement normally deployed in international law and relations.

The whole process of negotiation towards an agreement with reciprocal rights and duties is premised on the obligation to settle disputes peacefully, a basic principle of international law as reflected in the UN Charter,[40] as well as the OAS Charter.[41] Indeed, the latter instrument provides as one of its principles that 'controversies of an international character arising between two or more American states shall be settled by peaceful procedures'.[42] The purposes of the UN Charter prominently include the admonition to 'bring about by peaceful means, and *in conformity with the principles of justice and international law*, adjustment or settlement of international disputes or situations which might lead to a breach of the peace'.[43] It is that combination of justice and law which enables an equitable interpretation and application of legal principles within a new or emerging political context.

Chapter VI of the UN Charter, which concerns the peaceful settlement of disputes, obligates disputant states to 'seek a solution by negotiation, enquiry, mediation, conciliation, arbitration, judicial settlement, resort to regional agencies or arrangements, or other peaceful means of their own choice', before resorting to the Security Council.[44] These methods of settlement are not necessarily mutually exclusive. All settlement processes commence with negotiation, and in relatively confined issues, this may be sufficient to produce agreement.[45] In relation to intractable disputes, an unwillingness by the parties to meet face-to-face, or the lack of progress in 'talks about talks', might lead the parties to allow for third party intervention in the settlement process. At one end of a spectrum third party involvement may simply take the form of 'good offices' or a 'channel for communication', while the other end involves

---

39 *Tehran Hostages Case*, (1980) ICJ Rep 3 at 91.
40 Article 2(3) UN Charter 1945.
41 Articles 24 and 25 of the OAS Charter.
42 Article 3(i) OAS Charter.
43 Article 1(1) UN Charter 1945, emphasis added.
44 Article 33(1) UN Charter 1945. See also Article 25 OAS Charter.
45 J.G. Merrills, *International Dispute Settlement* (5th edn, Cambridge: Cambridge University Press, 2011) 22–5.

the 'assignment' to the third party or body 'to investigate the dispute and to present the parties with a set of formal proposals for its solution'. The latter is known as 'conciliation', whereas 'mediation' is situated somewhere between good offices and conciliation.[46] The mediator is an 'active participant authorised, and indeed expected, to advance fresh proposals and to interpret as well as transmit, each party's proposals to the other'.[47]

Given the historical animosity between Cuba and the US, rather than face-to-face negotiations, mediation may represent a suitable method, also bearing in mind that neither state would necessarily want to be faced with a concrete set of proposals for peaceful settlement coming from a conciliation commission. Mediation accords with the idea of a settlement process that operates within an equitable framework of law and justice, underpinned by reciprocity and aiming for restoration. Finding an appropriate and willing mediator in the US–Cuba dispute would be difficult. The US would be unwilling to accept the UN Secretary General or his appointed representative given the reluctance of the US to accept UN intervention generally and, even more so, given the General Assembly's regular condemnation of its embargo. Similarly, the Cuban government might not accept an OAS-appointed mediator given that organisation's decisions on Cuba in the past. A bold move by both states might be to accept an EU mediator, perhaps Catherine Ashton who is currently the High Representative of the Union for Foreign Affairs and Security Policy, and who was widely praised for bringing about an agreement and, moreover, an on-going normalisation process in relation to Iran's nuclear programme in November 2013.[48] The EU has shown itself to be sufficiently independent from the US as regards its policy on Cuba, but is also politically acceptable to the US. Ultimately, however, it is up to both parties to agree on a mediator. According to John Merrills:

> What of the mediator's substantive contribution? The aim . . . must be to satisfy both parties. In some situations it will be possible to do this by giving each state all or most of what it wants. This is because the aims of the parties in an international dispute are rarely identical and often quite different. Of course, the fact that there is a dispute indicates that the parties' aims are not entirely compatible, but unsuccessful negotiations may cause these differences to become the exclusive focus of attention. A mediator who can remind the parties of their essential objectives (or cause them to be redefined) may therefore be in a position to suggest a mutually satisfactory arrangement.[49]

46 Ibid., 26.
47 Ibid.
48 'Iran nuclear: EU's Ashton Hails Deal as a "First Step"', BBC News, 24 November 2013 – www.bbc.co.uk/news/world-middle-east-25074663 (accessed 28 March 2014).
49 Merrills (n.45), 35.

Alternatively, or possibly in addition, the parties might be encouraged to agree on another traditional method of inter-state dispute settlement – inquiry. Inquiry involves bringing in a third party or body to 'provide the parties with an objective assessment'.[50] Traditional inquiries have, on occasions, gone beyond providing an independent assessment of the facts underlying or leading to the dispute, and have made recommendations towards settlement of the dispute and reconciliation of the parties. For example, the Dogger Bank Inquiry of 1904–5, consisting of admirals from the UK, Russia, France, US and Austro-Hungary, was established to report on the circumstances and issues of responsibility and blame surrounding the damage done to the Hull trawler fleet by the Russian navy in the North Sea. The Inquiry's report helped to avoid conflict and normalised relations between the UK and Russia.[51] The value of such an independent inquiry can be contrasted with the sinking of the US battleship *Maine* in Havana harbour in 1898. This incident led to both states (Spain and the US) establishing their own inquiries each of which blamed the other state.[52] This precipitated both states towards conflict which ended the period of Spanish colonisation of Cuba, and the start of US occupation and then domination of Cuba.

Before discussing what proposals and mechanisms might be produced by a Cuba–US peace process, the chapter returns briefly to discuss the legal issues that arise in the dispute, not to repeat the determinations of wrongful acts that were covered in Chapter 7, but to discern common ground upon which agreement can be built.

## 8.6 Common legal ground

The analysis in Chapter 7 showed that, despite the origins of the dispute, self-determination and human rights are at its heart, and disagreement on their meaning and application continue to fuel the dispute. Disagreements on self-determination and human rights represent the core of the dispute and, therefore, they form the general framework for any dispute settlement. The aim of any peace process between the US and Cuba will be for those states to achieve common understandings on self-determination and human rights in the context of the bilateral relationship between them. The genuine consent of the two states in achieving this agreement will reconcile the common understanding of the two states in the concrete dispute between them, with general principles of international law in their abstract form, unless any agreement conflicts with a norm of *jus cogens*.

50  Ibid., 41.
51  Ibid., 42–3.
52  Ibid., 41–2.

Consent cannot be used as an excuse in the face of a violation of a norm of *jus cogens*.[53] This principle is further contained in the Vienna Convention on the Law of Treaties 1969 to the effect that any peace treaty adopted in violation of a peremptory norm of international law will be seen as null and void.[54] Orakhelashvili has demonstrated that self-determination is a peremptory norm of international law accepted by the international community as allowing of no derogation.[55] However, this has to be placed within the context of the indeterminacy that haunts the principle of self-determination in international law, in both its political and economic aspects, allowing states a significant degree of room to negotiate as to how it will be protected and implemented. As Rein Müllerson points out in relation to another norm of *jus cogens* – the prohibition on the use of force – while states agree that the prohibition is *jus cogens* they are not agreed on its precise content or the content of the exceptions to it.[56] More generally, it has been accurately stated that 'one of the criticisms of *jus cogens* is that they lack sufficiently robust meaning to provide effective constraints on decision making'.[57]

Finding common legal ground involves a recognition that international laws often do not give black and white answers, for example, as to: whether sovereignty is absolute or mediated; whether non-intervention covers all forms of interference; whether self-determination is a purely external one-off event or whether it is internal (and the meaning of this); and whether civil and political rights have priority over socio-economic rights. Such uncertainty signifies that alternative choices can be made by states, and be agreed upon (bilaterally or multilaterally) by them. This means that while legal principles frame discussions, they cannot determine the dispute without common agreement on their meaning and application in the context of potentially new political context. Drawing upon the works of Jürgen Habermas, Steven Wheatley depicts such an approach as 'deliberative diplomacy',[58] where the aim is to establish a 'communicative consensus' about the parties' 'understanding of a situation as well as justifications for the principles and norms guiding their actions'.[59] Parties refer to a common system of norms

---

53 Articles 20 and 26 Articles on the Responsibility of States for Internationally Wrongful Acts 2001.

54 Article 53 Vienna Convention on the Law of Treaties 1969.

55 A. Orakhelashvili, *Peremptory Norms in International Law* (Oxford: Oxford University Press, 2006) 51–3.

56 R. Müllerson, 'Jus Ad Bellum: Plus Ça Change (Le Monde) Plus C'est La Même Chose (Le Droit)?', (2002) 7 *JCSL* 149.

57 M. Del Mar, 'System Values and Understanding Legal Language', (2008) 21 *LJIL* 29 at 58.

58 S. Wheatley, *The Democratic Legitimacy of International Law* (Oxford: Hart, 2010) 138.

59 T. Risse, '"Let's Argue": Communicative Action in World Politics', (2000) 54 *International Organization* 1 at 9.

and rules,[60] with international law providing the 'rules of the game'.[61] This signifies that 'once international relations are framed in terms of law, they operate within the disciplinary constraints of an interpretive community'.[62] Legal discourse involves 'appeals to legal norms as they are understood not by each actor individually (subjectively) or in some abstract sense (objectively) but together as a collective law-interpreting body (inter-subjectively)'.[63] While powerful states have greater leverage within diplomatic relations they 'cannot change those rules (and shift the terms of the debate) instantaneously and at will'.[64] Powerful states have to respect the 'conventions of argument, persuasion and justification associated with the particular enterprise in which the deliberations occur'.[65] However, given the problems of indeterminacy in a number of applicable principles and rules of international law, there is scope for 'divergent legal arguments'.[66]

In effect, international law operates as the common language for diplomacy not as a system of readily applicable rules. This allows the parties to achieve understanding upon which a peaceful solution can be built. When the political relationship governing two states comes to an end international law operates to fill in the space vacated by politics but it does not do so by providing a ready solution or answer. International law must be discussed, interpreted, agreed upon in formal or informal terms and, finally, implemented. If common ground has been successfully captured in that agreement subsequent political relations can be framed by international law as encapsulated in that agreement.

In the context of self-determination, it is possible for the parties to find common ground, despite the appearance of being poles apart, given that US arguments are premised on a liberal democracy while Cuban arguments are that its socialist government has always embodied the will of the people. Without fully accepting either argument, it can be agreed between them that even if the Cuban government is denying the right to self-determination of the Cuban people that does not justify external intervention to help the people achieve this, as such intervention would be, by its very nature, a denial of the right to self-determination. Non-consensual intervention cannot protect the right of self-determination because it will lead to a state set up in the image of the interventionists (for example, following the US invasion of Grenada in 1983, and the US/UK invasion of Iraq in 2003). Even consensual UN

---

60  Ibid., 10.
61  J. Habermas, 'Does the Constitutionalization of International Law Still Have a Chance?' in C. Cronin (ed.), *The Divided West* (Cambridge: Polity, 2006) 115 at 119.
62  Wheatley (n.58), 143.
63  I. Johnstone, 'The Plea of "Necessity" in International Law Discourse: Humanitarian Intervention and Counter-Terrorism', (2005) 43 *Columbia Journal of Transnational Law* 337 at 381.
64  Ibid., 383.
65  Ibid.
66  Wheatley (n.58), 149.

interventions have been criticised, particularly in the immediate post-Cold War period, as promoting the liberal state.[67]

Modern peace agreements within states have moved away from requiring immediate elections and representative democracy which have, despite intentions to the contrary, tended to consolidate military elites.[68] However, to accord with human rights norms such agreements have incorporated 'broader notions of participation',[69] labelled 'consociational democracy'.[70] In these agreements 'power sharing, proportional representation and mutual vetoes replace "pure" representative democracy, and so respond to the idea that majoritarian voting systems do not work in situations of conflict, where they stand to exacerbate rather than channel political divisions'.[71] According to Christine Bell:

> Once the concept of participation is accepted as a measure of democracy, other innovations can be tolerated more easily. It is logically a short move to require participation of groups other than those at the heart of the conflict, who have similar claims to exclusion but have been unwilling or unable to assert themselves through the use of violence.[72]

Elections may be held in the longer term but in the transitional period 'governance must rely on a concept of "participation" rather than representation'.[73] What does this mean in a bilateral relationship between a liberal democratic state (the US) and one that is not (Cuba), although it claims to have a broadly representative government. Consociational democracy demonstrates that it is possible to have an alternative to representative democracy at least as a transitional step. Indeed, some have applied the consociational model to the international system of states where 'each political community has a voice'.[74] Thus, both parties could agree to respect their versions of representative government but allow their systems to be subject to international scrutiny and criticism – by both states becoming parties to the two main human rights treaties as well as regional human rights instruments. By subjecting themselves to the same human rights obligations, the peace agreement would be underpinned by that essential element of

---

67 R. Paris, 'International Peacekeeping and the "Mission Civilisatrice"', (2002) 28 *Review of International Studies* 637 at 638–9.

68 C. Bell, *On the Law of Peace: Peace Agreements and the Lex Pacificatoria* (Oxford: Oxford University Press, 2008) 213.

69 Ibid, 210.

70 Wheatley (n.58), 138.

71 Bell (n.68), 210.

72 Ibid., 211.

73 Ibid., 213.

74 M. Moore, 'Globalization and Democratization: Institutional Design for Global Institutions', (2006) 37 *Journal of Social Philosophy* 21 at 38. But see Wheatley (n.58), 139.

reciprocity. This would accord with international law where democracy is actively promoted by both the UN,[75] and the OAS,[76] but it is not required.

Whereas self-determination is a fundamental principle of international law applicable to both parties, democracy – at least the multiparty version practised by Western, and increasingly non-Western, states – is not. Although the 'idea of a government representative of its people is the underlying principle of both democracy and the concept of self-determination',[77] the term 'representative government', as found in the 1970 UN Declaration on Friendly Relations,[78] does 'not presuppose any particular political system'. International law 'does not prescribe how exactly the right of self-determination is to be consummated internally'.[79] Raic identifies the following characteristics of a representative government that would satisfy the principle of self-determination:

> A minimum requirement seems to be that the claim to representativeness by a non-oppressive government is not contested or challenged by (part of) the population. Thus, the notion of 'representativeness' assumes that government and the system of government is not imposed on the population of a state, but that it is based on the consent or assent of the population and in that sense is representative of the will of the people, regardless of the forms or methods by which the consent or assent is freely expressed.[80]

Both sides have their own view of government but still can agree that self-determination is the key to the solution of the dispute, and can utilise

---

75  N.D. White, 'The United Nations and Democracy Assistance: Developing Practice within a Constitutional Framework' in P. Burnell (ed.), *Democracy Assistance: International Co-operation for Democratization* (London: Frank Cass, 2000) 67 at 74–6.

76  Article 2(b) OAS Charter – one of the purposes is 'to promote and consolidate representative democracy, with due respect for the principle of nonintervention'. The principles upon which the OAS is based contain more contradictory statements, however. Article 3(d) contains the principle that the 'solidarity of the American states and the high aims which are sought through it require the political organization of those states on the basis of the effective exercise of representative democracy'; where Article 3(e) states that 'every state has the right to choose, without external interference, its political, economic, and social system and to organize itself in the best way suited to it . . .'. Article 9 provides for measures to be taken 'when a democratically constituted government has been overthrown by force'.

77  J. Vidmar, 'The Right of Self-Determination and Multiparty Democracy: Two Sides of the Same Coin?', (2010) 10 *Human Rights Law Review* 239 at 239.

78  UNGA Res 2625 (1970), 'Declaration on Principles of International Law Concerning Friendly Relations and Co-Operation Among States in Accordance with the Charter of the United Nations' refers to states conducting themselves in accordance with the principle of self-determination 'and thus possessed of a government representing the whole people belonging to the territory without distinction as to race, creed or colour'.

79  Vidmar (n.77), 253, 257.

80  D. Raic, *Statehood and the Law of Self-Determination* (The Hague: Kluwer, 2002) 279.

international laws and mechanisms, such as the two international human rights covenants and their supervisory committees, to provide for implementation of that understanding. Cuba could, of course, object that issues of Cuban self-determination should not be of concern to the US. The Cuban government does not insist on the US government taking a certain form. However, this does not take account of the fact that self-determination is an *erga omnes* obligation, which all states have a stake in seeing implemented.[81] More importantly, within the context of a bilateral dispute between the US and Cuba, the self-determination of the Cuban people is at its heart. Indeed, it can be argued that the origins of the dispute, the events at the very beginning, were disagreements about both economic and political self-determination. The nationalisation of US properties and assets was part of Cuba claiming sovereignty over its own resources. The embargo was imposed, initially, as punishment for this assertion of self-determination, which at the time was very controversial in international law. That seizure by the revolutionary government was just an aspect of its struggle to free itself from alien domination that could be traced back from 1959 to the US military occupation at the turn of the twentieth century and, before that, to centuries of Spanish colonialist occupation. Subsequent to the Cuban revolution, the US has increasingly focused on the denial of political self-determination (meaning democracy) and civil and political rights of the Cuban people pointing, in part, to the thousands of Cubans leaving or fleeing the island and seeking asylum in the US, and it has continued and tightened the embargo to this end. So this is clearly a dispute in which the US is involved, and is a dispute which will require finding common ground on self-determination and human rights in Cuba, if the embargo is to be lifted and normal relations restored.

A further objection to this approach would be to argue that this would be rewarding what is essentially an unlawful act of intervention (the embargo), moreover one causing human suffering. In response, the history of the dispute points to violations of international law on both sides, with Cuba intervening in other states in addition to its liability for failure to compensate US owners of Cuban property and assets that were expropriated in the early 1960s. Nonetheless, any peace agreement based on consent and reciprocity must recognise all those illegal acts and provide for their remediation. It is very important that any peace agreement is not a product of the embargo but represents an agreement, in part, on ending the embargo and providing for its remediation as well as reparation for other wrongful acts committed by both states. Although the Vienna Convention on the Law of Treaties does not invalidate treaties arrived at through economic coercion,[82] the legitimacy

---

81  The International Court of Justice has determined that self-determination has an *erga omnes* character – *East Timor Case*, (1995) ICJ Rep 90 at 102.

82  Article 52 Vienna Convention on the Law of Treaties 1969 renders void those treaties that are gained by coercion through the threat or use of force.

of any peace agreement between Cuba and the US would be undermined if it were, or were seen to be, a product of the embargo.

Post-colonial practice shows that once the period of external self-determination of colonial territories had passed, then the meaning of self-determination is contested, with the US viewing it as representative democracy, while Cuba sees it as continuing independence and freedom from imperialism. In the early 1990s, democracy was the model being promoted by the UN, whereas after the Brahimi Report in 2000, the model is one of peace-building in which elections are not the starting point, although they will play a part in ensuring that a people of a state has a representative government.[83] Even then the UN is operating in a post-conflict situation, where the peace agreement is designed to rebuild the state, whereas Cuba is a stable and peaceful state. In these circumstances, it is strongly contended that the normal processes and development of a state's engagement with international law be recognised in any peace agreement between the US and Cuba. One element of the agreement could be that within a specified period Cuba agrees to ratify the International Covenant on Civil and Political Rights and be subject to a review of its implementation of the obligations, including Article 1 (on self-determination),[84] and Article 25 (on elections) of the Covenant,[85] by the Human Rights Committee. Cuba would then be subject to the same process of human rights review, including criticism and recommendations for reform, that other state parties are subject to (including the United States).[86] In order to fulfil its obligations in terms of democratic rights contained in the Covenant, Cuba would be subject to that treaty regime and to the supervision mechanisms contained therein. This should lead to Cuban adjustments of its form of government over time. The Cuban government should be free to decide whether to become a party to the First

83  Report of the Panel on United Nations Peace Operations (Brahimi Report), UN Doc A/55/305-S/2000/809, paras 10–13.
84  Which states in paragraph 1 that: 'All people have the right to self-determination. By virtue of that right they freely determine their own political status and freely pursue their economic, social and cultural development'.
85  Which includes the right of every citizen 'to vote and to be elected at genuine periodic elections which shall be by universal and equal suffrage and shall be held by secret ballot, guaranteeing the free expression of the will of the electors'. The Human Rights Committee General Comment No. 25, 'The Right to Participate in Public Affairs, Voting Rights and the Right of Equal Access to Public Service', CCPR/C/21/Rev.1/Add.7 (1996) para 9 – 'genuine periodic elections in accordance with [Article 25(b)] are essential to ensure the accountability of representatives for the exercise of the legislative or executive powers vested in them. Such elections must be held at intervals which are not unduly long and which ensure that the authority of government continues to be based on the free expression of the will of the electors'.
86  See Human Rights Committee, 'Concluding Observations on the Fourth Report of the United States of America', adopted by the Committee at its 110th session, 10–28 March 2014 (CCPR/C/USA/CO/4).

Optional Protocol to the International Covenant on Civil and Political Rights allowing for individual complaints of violation. Given that the US has not become a party to the Optional Protocol it would undermine the reciprocity of a peace agreement to require Cuba to do so.

Thus, a peace process could find common ground on protecting self-determination and civil–political rights through Cuban ratification of the International Covenant on Civil and Political Rights. Although this would not provide any guarantee that Cuba would protect all the rights contained therein, by means of a Cuban government representing all the people of Cuba, it would bring Cuba into the international human rights regime. The dialogue would then shift to the Human Rights Committee on how self-determination and civil and political rights should be better protected. It might be difficult for Cuba to resist free and fair elections, at least after a period of adjustment; but it should be able to insist, in a bilateral peace agreement, on those elections being free from outside interference – for example in the shape of funding for opposition parties by the US, given that the dispute, in part, revolves around interventions by both sides but, specifically and continuously since 1898, by the US in Cuban affairs. Genuine self-determination should reflect the will of the Cuban people. To achieve that not only depends on the absence of outside interference but also on allowing the Cubans themselves their civil and political rights – freedom of expression, opinion, association, and the right to take part in elections and in government. To reassure the US of the genuineness of the elections, any peace agreement should allow for outside observers to any future elections in Cuba, possibly from the OAS and CELAC. What this means is that a democratic process could produce a socialist or a free market-oriented government, but whichever is successful (or indeed a coalition of groups), will be the legitimate government of Cuba. To ensure that elections do not lead to a tyranny of the majority (and therefore a failure to respect the right of self-determination of the Cuban people), minority and group rights will have to be fully protected within the Cuban constitution, laws and practices. US insistence on a future Cuban government not including either Fidel or Raúl Castro is no longer necessary in practice but also is overtly interventionist and flies in the face of a vast amount of practice in which revolutionary leaders become or remain parts of governments. There is also no justification for any equivalent of the de-Ba'athification process that was carried out in Iraq in 2003, and members of the Communist Party of Cuba, as well as the party itself, should be able to freely take part in any future elections. To do so, however, the Communist Party must separate itself from the state, but this and the full integration of human rights protections into the Cuban constitution and laws would be subject to supervision by the Human Rights Committee. Furthermore, for complete human rights supervision both states could agree to ratify the International Covenant on Economic and Social Rights and, therefore, subject themselves to the jurisdiction and supervision of the Committee on Economic, Social and Cultural Rights. However, while this would fulfil the equal treatment of both civil-political and socio-economic rights that is claimed (but not always followed) in human rights jurisprudence,[87] within the context of the Cuba–US dispute arguably it would not be essential for the provision of a reciprocal basis upon which to build a peace process.

## 8.7  Compensation for losses suffered

Cuban expropriation of US-owned property and the US imposition of an embargo can be viewed narrowly as (unremediated) measure and (unlawful) countermeasure, or slightly more broadly as an exercise in the freedom to trade by the United States amounting to an (unlawful) coercive intervention with the aim of subordinating the sovereign rights of Cuba;[88] and even more broadly still they can be viewed as measures arising out of a dispute about the meaning and application of the principle of self-determination in the context of Cuba and its close proximity to the US. The US embargo was implemented in response to the expropriation of US property by the Cuban government and then, later, to force change in Cuba towards democracy. The Cuban government on the other hand seized US assets to further its own socialist view of self-determination. Given the longevity of the dispute over the original nationalisations and expropriations carried out by the Cuban government in the early part of the revolution (and, bearing in mind, any interest accruing to date from any losses) on the one hand, and the damage done to the Cuban economy, infrastructure and population by the embargo on the other, the two sides would be unlikely to unilaterally agree to the other side's demands (for instance the Cuban government's claim that it has suffered $1 trillion damage as a result of the embargo). This impasse calls for some form of moderation or mediation that might be supplied, for instance, by a commission of inquiry tasked to investigate and quantify such losses.

It is possible that both parties could effectively agree the equivalent of an 'amnesty' here, meaning that in return for the Cuban government dropping any possible claim to damages caused by the embargo, the US government would not only bring an end to the embargo but call a halt to all claims arising from the revolutionary government's nationalisation programme. However, just as amnesties for acts of individual criminality have been curtailed in the development of transitional justice, it would fly in the face of the growing recognition in international law for access to justice to deny remedies for individuals suffering loss, if Cuba and the United States were to write off such losses. Instead of an amnesty, however, both governments could

---

87  See a critical evaluation of this 'equality' – C. Chinkin, 'International Law and Human Rights' in T. Evans (ed.), *Human Rights Fifty Years on: A Reappraisal* (Manchester: Manchester University Press, 1998) 105.

88  E. Katselli, *The Problem of Enforcement in International Law: Countermeasures, the non-injured state and the idea of international community* (London: Routledge, 2010) 94–6.

agree to establish a mechanism to address these issues and could either choose a judicial mechanism equivalent to the Iran–US Claims Tribunal, or choose a non-judicial mechanism similar to the UN Compensation Commission established in 1991 by the Security Council to provide compensation for losses suffered as a result of Iraq's invasion of Kuwait.

Although the Iran–US Claims Tribunal has been criticised above, the criticism was directed at the lack of reciprocity underpinning it which was clearly linked to the inability of the Tribunal, *per se*, to restore normal relations between Iran and the US. This indicates that an arbitral body could be part of a peace agreement between the US and Cuba if it were based on reciprocity and was keyed into a restoration and reconciliation process. Arbitration does not normally involve the straightforward application of international laws to claims. It is normal in arbitration that the parties frame the issues, terms of reference and jurisdiction of any arbitral body.[89] Furthermore, it is common for arbitral bodies to be directed to apply equitable considerations, for example in calculating the levels of compensation, alongside international laws.[90] According to Merrills, this signifies that arbitrators are 'no longer simple adjudicators, applying the relevant rules, but begin to assume the role of legislators, creating law for the case in hand'.[91] Ratner takes this further by arguing that 'political arbitration allows a panel the freedom to balance interests rather than applying legal rules'.[92] Allen and Guntrip, however, argue that this 'might be over emphasising the political nature of arbitral decision-making rather than the political conditions within which the arbitral panels operate'. They conclude that 'arbitral panels do strive to apply legal rules; however, there is often a degree of flexibility in their decision-making that is rarely apparent, for instance, in the decisions of the International Court of Justice'.[93]

An arbitral body might prove attractive to Cuba and the United States, given that they can exercise a considerable degree of control over its creation. However, the experience of the Iran–US Claims Tribunal suggests that control can be lost once such a body is created. Given the longevity of the dispute between the US and Cuba, an alternative mechanism, and one that would allow the parties some control over its operation as well as its creation, would be a non-judicial administrative-type compensation commission. The UN Compensation Commission established in 1991 by Security Council Resolution 687 is controlled by a Governing Council consisting of the member states of the Security Council. That body ultimately approves payments made.

---

89  Merrills (n.45), 91.
90  Ibid., 98.
91  Ibid.
92  S.R. Ratner, 'Land Feuds and Their Solutions: Finding International Law Beyond the Tribunal Chamber', (2006) 100 *AJIL* 808 at 825.
93  Allen and Guntrip (n.1), 335.

In addition, there is a body of commissioners who, in panels of three, examine claims and make recommendations on the amounts awarded under each claim. Commissioners apply rules laid down in Resolution 687, by the Governing Council and, where applicable, international law. In addition, the national governments identify claimants first and, therefore, act as a filter. If this were applied to the US–Cuban dispute, it might seem a step backwards, towards forms of diplomatic protection rather than access to justice for victims.[94] However, the reality is that both states have orthodox approaches to international law based on strong conceptions of sovereignty and, therefore, are more likely to accept more indirect forms of access to justice. The combination of pragmatism and justice embodied in the UN Compensation Commission was neatly captured by the UN Secretary General in 1991:

> The Commission is not a court or an arbitral tribunal before which the parties appear; it is a political organ that performs an essentially fact-finding function of examining claims, verifying their validity, evaluating losses, assessing payments and resolving disputed claims. It is only in this last respect that a quasi-judicial function may be involved. Given the nature of the Commission, it is all the more important that some element of due process be built into the procedure. It will be the function of the commissioners to provide this element.[95]

Given the trend away from amnesties (in the general sense of excusing illegalities) and the move towards the provision of access to justice for individuals, the parties could negotiate a compensation commission before which US and Cuban citizens could bring claims: against Cuba for failure to compensate for seizures of US property and assets in the immediate post-revolutionary period, and against the United States for violation of the right to health (amounting to serious personal injury or death)[96] in Cuba (perhaps limited to the immediate post-1991 period when the embargo was tightened and the impact of the embargo in the absence of Soviet support was most felt). In reality there would have to be some limitations upon claimants, balancing the longevity of the dispute against the requirements of justice. This suggests that the appropriate mechanism would be a joint US–Cuban Compensation Commission consisting of separate panels (composed of US, Cuban and third party commissioners) to consider claims made by US citizens for losses incurred as a result of expropriation by the Cuban government in the immediate post-revolutionary era, and to consider claims for long-term

---

94  D. Petrović, 'The UN Compensation Commission' in Crawford, Pellet, and Olleson (n.33), 849 at 850–2.
95  Report of the Secretary-General pursuant to para 19 of Security Council Resolution 687 (1991), UN Doc S/22559 (1991) para 20.
96  Petrović (n.94), 853.

damage to health caused by the continuation of the US embargo in the immediate post-Cold War period. Both governments could set maximum limits to claims and specify the evidence needed (for example as regards title to property and medical evidence) and, indeed, agree on a detailed set of terms of reference for any such Commission. This will enable the two states to balance the need for access to justice against the danger of creating an open-ended mechanism which, in time, would not serve the purposes of reciprocity and restoration.

## 8.8 Conclusion: towards a peace agreement

What is envisaged in this chapter is that the parties will, at some point in the (near) future, seize the moment when there is a dramatic break in the political context that has governed their relations since 1960, thereby setting off a process of diplomacy whereby a mediator guides the parties, through discussion of general issues down to specific mechanisms, towards a peace agreement under which the parties agree to normalise diplomatic, political and economic relations over a period of time. A peace process and peace agreement between the US and Cuba should primarily be aimed at restoring and normalising peaceful relations between the two states. It has been shown in this chapter that the concept of 'restoration' is not just embodied in modern notions of transitional justice as applied within conflict-ridden states, but is also found within the primary and secondary rules of international law and mechanisms that are available to states to provide for accountability for breach of those rules.

The parties could move into the post-conflict stage or, more accurately, the post-confrontational stage, by negotiating (with the help of mediation) a framework peace agreement which, alongside broad reciprocal obligations as regards non-intervention, non-use of force, restoring normal trading relations, and on respect for human rights and self-determination (by, at a minimum both states being parties to the International Covenant on Civil and Political Rights), should also provide for the establishment of joint US–Cuban mechanisms of inquiry and compensation. Principles of equity and justice, as well as the more detailed rules of international law, should help frame the agreement and the mechanisms.

This may seem to be some distance from the formal application of the rules of international law, as a basic form of universalism would indicate should happen but, as has been argued in this chapter, those rules are at the disposal of states when settling disputes within the broad framework of the fundamental principles of international law. Indeed this is reflected in those most formal and abstract secondary rules on responsibility of states as discussed in Chapter 7. All state disputes and, indeed, any situation where a state is responsible for breach of the primary rules of international law, are governed by the articles on state responsibility of 2001, which, provide that 'full reparation for the injury caused by the internationally wrongful act shall take the form of restitution, compensation and satisfaction, either singly or in combination'.[97] Compensation shall 'cover any financially assessable damage including loss of profits insofar as it is established'.[98] However, the articles also provide that the 'state responsible for an internationally wrongful act is under an obligation to give satisfaction for the injury caused by that act insofar as it cannot be made good by restitution or compensation'; and that 'satisfaction may consist in an acknowledgement of the breach, an expression of regret, a formal apology or another appropriate modality'.[99] The point is that even under the formal rules of state responsibility there is a range of remedies that can be adjusted as appropriate to the situation under consideration. As with remedies for states, remedies for individuals and companies are adaptable to the circumstances and to the model of justice being aimed for. In the case of Cuba and the US, remediation (by individuals and companies bringing claims to a compensation commission) should be combined with restoration (between the governments of the states). Certain retributive elements, in the form of national criminal trials, could also form a part of a peace agreement to cover significant unresolved acts of violence or sabotage by individuals from either state.

The peace agreement itself should act as a deterrent for further violations of sovereignty by either state by, for example, providing for reference of any dispute over its terms to conciliation, arbitration or, indeed, ultimately to the International Court of Justice. This may appear to be a contradiction, or a certain irony at least, by referring to the International Court of Justice in this context but, once normal relations are established between the US and Cuba, the political and normative framework should be stable enough to allow disputes to be settled by judicial means.

---

97  Article 34 Articles on the Responsibility of States for Internationally Wrongful Acts 2001.
98  Ibid., Article 36(2).
99  Ibid., Article 37.

# 9 Concluding remarks on the relevance of international law

Cuba has been through a number of stages in its relationship with external powers: discovery (more accurately conquest) and colonisation by Spain (1511–1898), occupation by the US (1898–1902 and again in 1906–9), imperialism by the US (1902–59), independence and sovereignty (1959–68/70), a further period of imperialism or at least dependence on the Soviet Union (1970–91) and, finally, 'pariah-status' in relation to the US (from 1991 onwards). The Cuban revolution of 1959 brought US imperialism to an end but the geopolitical context of the Cold War meant that the path towards securing the independence and self-determination of the Cuban people was disrupted by Cuba's dependence upon the Soviet Union and its turn towards Communism. Whether it became a Soviet satellite is debatable given that it survived the end of the Cold War, unlike those eastern European satellites closer to the Soviet Union. Despite being in the backyard of the United States, the Cuban revolution survived the end of the Cold War and, furthermore, adapted by returning to the inspiration of José Martí, the embodiment of the Cuban struggle for independence, rather than the strictures and structures of Marxism. Nonetheless, it is treated as a 'pariah' by the US and, moreover, the US has tried to impose this status on Cuba in its relations with other trading states (in the Torricelli and Helms-Burton Acts of the 1990s). This pariah status is a matter of dispute. It enables the US to treat Cuba, along with other states it has so labelled, as having limited sovereignty and, therefore, as being legitimate targets of what would otherwise be seen as illegal intervention in a sovereign state. In other words it is an attempt to continue to see Cuba's sovereignty as curtailed, just as it has been during all the episodes of Cuban history listed above. Moreover, it serves to justify the continuance of the principal weapon of intervention against Cuba – the embargo – and it being maintained until Cuba adopts a political and economic system the US views as acceptable.

Despite such immense political pressure on the inter-state relations between Cuba and its superpower neighbour, international law survives at least in the form of condemnation, shown by the hardening of the General Assembly's position on the illegality of the embargo during the post-Cold War period.

Despite problems with indeterminacy,[1] international law has relevance as a standard against which we can judge behaviour, or rather it enables states to achieve agreement on when behaviour is violative of international law, for example as to when non-forcible measures are so coercive and intrusive that they violate the norm of non-intervention. However, a developed legal system not only consists of primary rules which are used to judge and condemn misbehaviour, it must also provide for secondary rules allowing for effective dispute settlement.[2] In the international legal order there are an increasing number of judicial bodies, but the Cuba–US dispute shows that none of these has any jurisdiction over the dispute (in the absence of agreement by the parties) and, besides which, would be counterproductive. The argument has been made that for intractable, multilayered and complex disputes, a combination of politics and law is essential. For international law to work as a framework for dispute settlement in Cuban–American relations, we await further changes in US and/or Cuban domestic politics, and for them to come into line with broader geopolitical movements, for example, with new world powers such as China playing a more influential and, apparently, benign role in Latin America. Once the political deadlock is broken, international law will provide the framework within which the parties can negotiate to settle the dispute, and it will provide precedents for mechanisms to facilitate this, primarily through mediation, inquiry and a compensation commission. In this way international law has relevance in dispute settlement.

International law performs the dual function of upholding Cuba's sovereignty and freedom of choice, while gently encouraging it towards internal self-determination, civil-political rights protection, as well as applauding its undoubted socio-economic strengths. Furthermore, it enables states and other actors to condemn the embargo as a breach of international law, whether it is viewed as a monstrously disproportionate countermeasure, a major and on-going act of 'unfriendly' retorsion or, what it really is, a sustained and punitive policy of economic coercion that violates Cuba's sovereignty and the self-determination of its people. It also enables us to recognise that the exporting of the Cuban revolution to Latin America and Africa was at least controversial and, in a number of situations, involved violation of those very same norms of sovereignty and, on occasions, self-determination.

Since 1991, the US embargo rests on a particular vision of democratic government for Cuba, the denial of which the US sees as an on-going violation of international law. The embargo is also continued as a punishment for past wrongs done to the US relating to the failure to remediate US citizens and companies for seizures of properties in the immediate post-revolutionary

---

1  J. Crawford, *Chance, Order and Change: The Course of International Law* (The Hague: Hague Academy of International Law, 2014) 177–8.

2  H.L.A. Hart, *The Concept of Law* (Oxford: Clarendon, 1961) 91, 94.

period. Despite international law's abstract nature and its struggle with indeterminacy it is possible, when confronted with actual events, to discern clear violations of the primary rules of international law but, probably more importantly, to discern where behaviour is unacceptable to the international community of states and other actors. In this book it is argued that it is equally important to recognise the applicability and flexibility of the secondary rules of international law, which seek to restore ruptured international relations. The secondary rules on state responsibility create a framework within which the parties have to negotiate and agree on ways to implement, adjust to, or remediate breaches of the primary rules of international law based on recognising and strengthening their reciprocal rights and obligations under international law. In this way international law has relevance by gently nudging states towards conformity with norms of international law.

In his assessment of Philip Allott's contribution to international legal theory, David Kennedy writes:

> We have always thought politics was everywhere and what we needed was law; Philip was, I think, the first to say clearly that we have got law everywhere, and how did we come to be governed with so little politics.[3]

It is true that there are plenty of international legal principles and rules in existence, both general and specialist; the problem lies in their interpretation, application and enforcement. Universal international laws are drafted at an abstract level in order to achieve maximum consensus, but this leaves laws floating at a huge distance from the events on the ground that they are meant to control. Thus, a great deal of law does not necessarily mean a system under the rule of law. With the difficulty, if not impossibility, of achieving an international rule of law in the currently state-dominated system of international relations and law, we must not only accept the inevitability of the dominance of politics, but also appreciate the sentiment contained in the above quote, that it is in politics that ideas for justice and law are forged and developed. Furthermore, within a bilateral relationship it is politics that hold the key to dispute settlement, moreover, to dispute settlement in accordance with international law.

Although a state-based system may not be the ideal in which justice and peace can be achieved,[4] it is what we have and, moreover, this book has

---

3 D. Kennedy, 'Thinking of Another World', (2005) 16 *EJIL* 255. See P. Allott, *The Health of Nations: Society and Law Beyond the State* (Cambridge: Cambridge University Press, 2002). See generally I. Scobbie, 'The Holiness of the Heart's Affection: Philip Allott's Theory of Social Idealism' in A. Orakhelashvili (ed.), *Research Handbook on the Theory and History of International Law* (Cheltenham: Elgar, 2011) 168.

4 See Allott's rejection of the Vatellian conception of international law and relations based on the interests of states and their ruling elites. Allott (n.3), ch. 13; Scobbie (n.3), 179–83. See E. de Vattel, *Le Droit des Gens, ou Principes de La Loi Naturelle* (1758).

attempted to show that it is possible not only to harness law to consolidate a political settlement, but also that law can provide a framework within which new political contexts can be legitimated. If we do not recognise that politics and law have to work together then lasting settlement will not be achievable. A purely political solution will be in danger of collapsing in the longer term as the political context changes; while a purely 'black and white' legal solution will probably alienate one party and, thereby, serve to prolong the dispute.

In intractable disputes involving, as examples, Israel and Palestine over the Occupied Territories, Iran and the US over Iran's nuclear ambitions, the UK and Argentina over the Falklands, and Cuba and the US over the embargo, simply analysing state (mis)behaviour in the light of the primary rules of international law in order to determine the responsibilities of the two countries will only get us as far as establishing the broad legal framework within which dispute settlement should occur. Congruent political will, achieving common understanding on key politico-legal terms and concepts, and mutually agreed and legally constituted mechanisms, will all contribute to a peaceful solution.

While Martii Koskenniemi's thesis on the relationship between politics and international law was used to unlock an intractable dispute in Chapter 8, the full implications of the indeterminacy thesis have not been accepted. As James Crawford states: 'international legal language is not so open-ended or mutable to justify just anything: there comes a point at which a particular argument or interpretation becomes untenable'.[5] In a sense the weakness of international law is its strength in that the flexibility contained within its broad provisions: on general principles such as non-intervention, self-determination, sovereignty (including over natural resources), forcible and especially non-forcible measures; also on specific regimes governing civil-political and socio-economic rights; and, moreover, in the secondary rules on state responsibility, gives states significant room for negotiation, compromise and agreement in their disputes with other states. This enables states to achieve political solutions within a broad framework of relevant primary and secondary international laws.

International human rights organs and other legitimate bodies have identified violations of human rights in relation to particular practices, both on the Cuban side regarding civil-political rights of its citizens (particularly due process rights, freedom of expression and freedom of movement), and on the part of the US regarding the socio-economic rights of Cubans (especially the right to health).[6] The Cuban people are, in effect, being doubly punished.

---

5  Crawford (n.1), 172.
6  There is also the issue of serious violations of basic rights and freedoms of detainees at the US base at Guantánamo Bay in Cuba following the events of 9/11 (2001). The base has been under US jurisdiction since it gained a perpetual lease over it in 1902. See J. Fitzpatrick, 'Speaking Law to Power: The War Against Terrorism and Human Rights', (2003) 14 *EJIL* 241 at 249–55; A. Roberts, 'Righting Wrongs or Wronging Rights? The

The cruel irony, what is really the dark heart of international law, is that it is only the very sources of those violations – the governments of Cuba and the US – who can remedy this in a meaningful way by entering into a constructive dialogue and agreeing a process whereby relations between the two states are normalised and human rights protections are thereby improved (and past ones remediated).

International relations and international law demand that law, justice and political reality are considered together in order to achieve solutions that are legitimate as well as effective. Law and justice by themselves might indicate one solution or, indeed, separate solutions, but without considering the broader political context, such solutions will often fail. For example, in a different context, while law and justice dictate that amnesties for crimes should not be permitted and individual criminal responsibility enforced, political reality, in particular the need to achieve peace, suggests that amnesties have to play a part. A solution is to accept conditional or conditioned amnesties, where there are acceptable alternative mechanisms which operate to record, reconcile and, if appropriate, remediate the victims.[7] In the context of the Cuban–US dispute, while wrongdoing by both states and their agents should not go unrecognised, responsibility and remedies should be adjusted to achieve a peaceful solution while providing for reasonable compensation to victims in cases of clear breach by either side.

The Cuban people have been subject to violations of international law for over fifty years, including a punitive and cruel embargo imposed by the US, suffering for the perceived and actual sins of their leaders, some of which also constituted violations of international law both externally and internally. The embargo has been imposed to punish Cuba for violations of international law but it is, in itself, a violation of international law. It follows that the embargo is at the heart of the bilateral relationship between Cuba and the US and symbolises its abnormal and confrontational nature, placing the relationship itself outside international law. The removal of the embargo would be a significant part of normalising, restoring and, thereby, legalising peaceful relations between the two countries, but it should also be part of an agreement between the two countries that would enable Cuba to fulfil its human rights obligations over a period of time. That it is time to end the embargo is recognised by Cuba, increasingly by the US, and certainly by the rest of the world. The political conditions are falling into place; now it is time for international law to show its worth, not just as a means of condemning behaviour, but as a method for effective and legitimate dispute settlement.

---

United States and Human Rights Post-September 11', (2004) 15 *EJIL* 721 at 724–6, 731–3; H. Duffy, *The 'War on Terror' and the Framework of International Law* (Cambridge: Cambridge University Press, 2005) 379–442.

7 L. Mallinder, *Amnesty, Human Rights and Political Transitions* (Oxford: Hart, 2008) 373–7; M. Freeman, *Necessary Evils: Amnesties and the Search for Justice* (Cambridge: Cambridge University Press, 2009) 110–36.

# Bibliography

Abi-Saab, G. (1996), 'The International Court as a World Court' in V. Lowe and M. Fitzmaurice (eds), *Fifty Years of the International Court of Justice* (Cambridge: Cambridge University Press) 3.

Acheson, D. (1963), 'The Cuban Quarantine – Implications for the Future', 14 *American Society of International Law Proceedings* 14.

Alland, D. (2002), 'Countermeasures of General Interest', 13 *EJIL* 1221.

Alland, D. (2010), 'The Definition of Countermeasures' in J. Crawford, A. Pellet and S. Olleson (eds), *The Law of International Responsibility* (Oxford: Oxford University Press) 1127.

Allen, S. and Guntrip, E. (2011), 'The Kosovo Question and *Uti Possidetis*: The Potential for a Negotiated Solution' in J. Summers (ed.), *Kosovo: A Precedent?'* (Leiden: Nijhoff) 303.

Allott, P. (2002), *The Health of Nations: Society and Law Beyond the State* (Cambridge: Cambridge University Press).

Anghie, A. (2004), *Imperialism, Sovereignty and the Making of International Law* (Oxford: Oxford University Press).

Anghie, A. (2010), 'Basic Principles of International Law: A Historical Perspective' in B. Cali (ed.), *International Law for International Relations* (Oxford: Oxford University Press) 46.

Barker, J. (2010), 'The Different Forms of Compensation: Reparation' in J. Crawford, A. Pellet and S. Olleson (eds), *The Law of International Responsibility* (Oxford: Oxford University Press) 599.

Bederman, D.J. (2002), 'Counterintuiting Countermeasures', 96 *AJIL* 817.

Bell, C. (2006), 'Peace Agreements: Their Nature and Legal Status', 100 *AJIL* 373.

Bell, C. (2008), *On the Law of Peace: Peace Agreements and the Lex Pacificatoria* (Oxford: Oxford University Press).

Boisson de Chazournes, L. (2010), 'Other Non-Derogable Rights' in J. Crawford, A. Pellet and S. Olleson (eds), *The Law of International Responsibility* (Oxford: Oxford University Press) 1205.

Borelli, S. and Olleson, S. (2010), 'Obligations Relating to Human Rights and Humanitarian Law' in J. Crawford, A. Pellet and S. Olleson (eds), *The Law of International Responsibility* (Oxford: Oxford University Press) 1177.

Borowy, I. (2011), 'Similar but Different: Health and Economic Crisis in 1990s Cuba and Russia', 72 *Social Science and Medicine* 1489.

Bowett, D.W. (1972), 'Economic Coercion and Reprisals by States', 13 *Virginia Journal of International Law* 1.

Bowett, D.W. (1972), 'Reprisals Involving Recourse to Armed Force', 66 *AJIL* 1.

Brierly, J.L. (1928), 'The Lotus Case', 44 *Law Quarterly Review* 154.

Brierly, J.L. (1946), 'The Covenant and the Charter', 23 *BYBIL* 83.

Buchanan, A. (2004), *Justice, Legitimacy and Self-Determination* (Oxford: Oxford University Press).

Calvo, C. (1896), *Le Droit International* (5th edn).

Calzón, F. (1998), 'El embargo a debate: Persistir en el embargo', 1 *Revista hispano cubano* 54.

Calzón, F. (2003), 'USA-Europa: los Estados Unidos y el embargo contra Cuba', 17 *Revista hispano cubano* 30.

Cárdenas, J.R. (1998), 'El embargo a debate: La política de los Estados Unidos hacia Cuba: Una defensa', 1 *Revista hispano cubano* 46.

Cass, D. (2000), *The Constitutionalization of the World Trade Organization: Legitimacy, Democracy and Community in the International Trading System* (Oxford: Oxford University Press).

Cassese, A. (2005), *International Law* (2nd edn, Oxford: Oxford University Press).

Castro, F. (2002), *History Will Absolve Me: Speech at the Court of Appeals of Santiago de Cuba October 16, 1953* (Havana: Editora Política).

Chayes, A. (1974), *The Cuban Missile Crisis* (Oxford: Oxford University Press).

Chinkin, C. (1998), 'International Law and Human Rights' in T. Evans (ed.), *Human Rights Fifty Years On: A Reappraisal* (Manchester: Manchester University Press) 105.

Chomsky, N. (2003), 'Commentary: Moral Truisms, Empirical Evidence, and Foreign Policy', 29(4) *Review of International Studies* 605.

Craven, M. (1995), 'The European Community Arbitration Commission on Yugoslavia', 66 *BYBIL* 333.

Craven, M. (2010), 'Statehood, Self-Determination, and Recognition' in M. Evans (ed.), *International Law* (3rd edn, Oxford: Oxford University Press) 203.

Craven, M. (2012), 'Colonialism and Domination' in B. Fassbender and A. Peters (eds), *The History of International Law* (Oxford: Oxford University Press) 862.

Crawford, J. (2001), 'The Relationship Between Countermeasures and Sanctions' in V. Gowlland-Debbas (ed.), *United Nations Sanctions and International Law* (The Hague: Kluwer) 57.

Crawford, J. (2001), 'The Right to Self-Determination in International Law: Its Development and Future' in P. Alston (ed.), *Peoples' Rights* (Oxford: Oxford University Press) 7.

Crawford, J. (2002), *The International Law Commission's Articles on State Responsibility* (Cambridge: Cambridge University Press).

Crawford, J. (2012), *Brownlie's Principles of International Law* (8th edn, Oxford: Oxford University Press).

Crawford, J. (2013), *State Responsibility: The General Part* (Cambridge: Cambridge University Press).

Crawford, J. (2014), *Chance, Order and Change: The Course of International Law* (The Hague: Hague Academy of International Law).

Crook, J.R. (1989), 'Applicable Law in International Arbitration: The Iran-U.S. Claims Tribunal Experience', 83 *AJIL* 278.

David, E. (2010), 'Primary and Secondary Rules' in J. Crawford, A. Pellet and S. Olleson (eds), *The Law of International Responsibility* (Oxford: Oxford University Press) 27.

Del Mar, M. (2008), 'System Values and Understanding Legal Language', 21 *LJIL* 29.

Dore, I.I. (1984), *International Law and the Superpowers: Normative Order in a Divided World* (New York: Rutgers University Press).

Duffy, H. (2005), *The 'War on Terror' and the Framework of International Law* (Cambridge: Cambridge University Press).

Elagab, O.Y. (1988), *The Legality of Non-Forcible Counter-Measures in International Law* (Oxford: Oxford University Press).

Evans, T. (1998), 'Power, Hegemony and the Universality of Human Rights' in T. Evans (ed.), *Human Rights Fifty Years On: A Reappraisal* (Manchester: Manchester University Press) 2.

Fabre, C. (2000), *Social Rights under the Constitution* (Oxford: Oxford University Press).

Falcoff, M. (2003), 'Presente y futuro en las relaciones Estados Unidos-Cuba: un ejercicio de análisis y especulación', 173 *Foro internacional* 693.

Fitzpatrick, J. (2003), 'Speaking Law to Power: The War Against Terrorism and Human Rights', 14 *EJIL* 241.

Francioni, F. (2007), 'The Right of Access to Justice under Customary International Law' in F. Francioni (ed.), *Access to Justice as a Human Right* (Oxford: Oxford University Press) 1.

Franck, T.M. (1992), 'The Emerging Right to Democratic Governance', 86 *AJIL* 46.

Franck, T.M. (2008), 'On Proportionality of Countermeasures in International Law', 102 *AJIL* 715.

Freeman, M. (2009), *Necessary Evils: Amnesties and Search for Justice* (Cambridge: Cambridge University Press).

Fukuyama, F. (1992), *The End of History and the Last Man* (London: Penguin).

Ghandour Z.B. (2010), *A Discourse on Domination in Mandate Palestine* (London: Routledge).

Gilmore, W.C. (1984), *The Grenada Intervention: Analysis and Documentation* (London: Mansell).

Glennon, M. (2010), *The Fog of Law: Pragmatism, Security and International Law* (Chicago, IL: Stanford University Press).

Gott, R. (2004), *Cuba: A New History* (New Haven, CT: Yale University Press).

Grant, J.P. and Barker, J.C. (2009), *Parry and Grant Encyclopaedic Dictionary of International Law* (Oxford: Oxford University Press).

Gray, C. (1987), *Judicial Remedies in International Law* (Oxford: Oxford University Press).

Gray, C. (2008), *International Law on the Use of Force* (Oxford: Oxford University Press).

Gray, C. (2010), 'The Use and Abuse of the International Court of Justice in the Enforcement of International Law ' in K. Koufa (ed.), *International Law Enforcement: New Tendencies* (Athens: Sakkoulas) 195.

Guilfoyle, D. (2009), *Shipping Interdiction and the Law of the Sea* (Cambridge: Cambridge University Press).

Habermas, J. (1996), *Between Facts and Norms: Contributions to Discourse Theory of Law and Democracy* (Oxford: Polity).

Habermas, J. (2006), 'Does the Constitutionalization of International Law Still Have a Chance?' in C. Cronin (ed.), *The Divided West* (Cambridge: Polity) 115.

Haney, P.J. and Vanderbush, W. (2005), *The Cuban Embargo: The Domestic Politics of an American Foreign Policy* (Pittsburgh, PA: University of Pittsburgh Press).

Harris, D.J. (2010), *Cases and Materials on International Law* (7th edn, London: Sweet and Maxwell).

Hart, H.L.A. (1961), *The Concept of Law* (Oxford: Clarendon Press).

Higgins, R. (1994), *Problems and Process: International Law and How We Use it* (Oxford: Clarendon Press).

Higgins, R. (1998), 'Introduction' in M. Evans (ed.), *Remedies in International Law: The Institutional Dilemma* (Oxford: Hart) 9.

Holmes, O.W. (1897), 'The Path of the Law', 10 *Harvard Law Review* 457.

Hunter-Miller, D. (1928), *The Drafting of the Covenant Volume I* (London: Putnams).

Johnstone, I. (2005), 'The Plea of "Necessity" in International Law Discourse: Humanitarian Intervention and Counter-Terrorism', 43 *Columbia Journal of Transnational Law* 337.

Johnstone, I. (2008), 'Legislation and Adjudication in the UN Security Council: Bringing Down the Deliberative Deficit', 102 *AJIL* 275.

Katselli, E. (2009), 'Countermeasures: Concept and Substance in the Protection of Collective Interests' in K.H. Kaikobad and M. Bohlander (eds), *International Law and Power: Perspectives on Legal Order and Justice* (Leiden: Nijhoff) 401.

Katselli, E. (2010), *The Problem of Enforcement in International Law: Countermeasures, the Non-Injured State and the Idea of the International Community* (London: Routledge).

Kelsen, H. (1967), *Principles of International Law* (New York: Rinehart and Winston).

Kennedy, D. (2005), 'Thinking of Another World', 16 *EJIL* 255.

Kennedy, P. (2006), *The Parliament of Man: The Past, Present and Future of the United Nations* (London: HarperCollins).

Kennedy, R. (1969), *Thirteen Days: A Memoir of the Cuban Missile Crisis* (New York: Norton).

Kirkpatrick, A.F. (1996), 'Role of the USA in Shortage of Food and Medicine in Cuba', 348 *The Lancet* 1489.

Klein, P. (2002), 'Responsibility for Serious Breaches of Obligations Deriving from Peremptory Norms of International Law and United Nations Law', 13 *EJIL* 1241.

Koskenniemi, M. (1990), 'The Politics of International Law', 1 *EJIL* 4.

Koskenniemi, M. (1996), 'The Place of Law in Collective Security', 17 *Michigan Journal of International Law* 455.

Koskenniemi, M. (2002), *The Gentle Civilizer of Nations: The Rise and Fall of International Law* (Cambridge: Cambridge University Press).

Koskenniemi, M. (2010), 'The Politics of International Law – 20 Years Later', 20 *EJIL* 7.

Koskenniemi, M. (2010), 'Doctrines of State Responsibility' in J. Crawford, A. Pellet and S. Olleson (eds), *The Law of International Responsibility* (Oxford: Oxford University Press) 45.

Koskenniemi, M. (2010), 'What is International Law For?' in M. Evans (ed.), *International Law* (3rd edn, Oxford: Oxford University Press) 32.

Krinsky, M. and Golove, D. (1993), *United Nations Economic Measures Against Cuba: Proceedings in the United Nations and International Law Issues* (Northampton, MA: Aletheia Press).

La Rosa, A.-M. and Phillipe, X. (2009), 'Transitional Justice' in V. Chetail (ed.), *Post-Conflict Peacebuilding: A Lexicon* (Oxford: Oxford University Press) 368.

Lamrani, S. (2013), *The Economic War Against Cuba: A Historical and Legal Perspective on the US Blockade* (New York: Monthly Review Press).

Lauterpacht, H. (1933), 'Boycott in International Relations', 14 *BYBIL* 125.

Lawrence, T. (1895), *The Principles of International Law* (Boston, MA: D.C. Heath).

Leyva de Varona, A. (1994), *Propaganda y realidad: análisis del embargo económico de los Estados Unidos contra la Cuba castrista* (Washington DC: Fundacion Nacional Cubano Americana).

Lillich, R.B. (1975), 'Economic Coercion and the International Legal Order', 51 *International Affairs* 358.

Liriano de la Cruz, A. (2005), *Cuba, El Caribe y el post embargo* (Santo Domingo: FLASCO).

Lowe, V. (2007), *International Law* (Oxford: Clarendon).

Lowenfeld, A.F. (2001), 'Unilateral Versus Collective Sanctions: An American Perspective' in V. Gowlland-Debbas (ed.), *United Nations Sanctions and International Law* (The Hague: Kluwer) 95.

McDougal M.S. (1963), 'The Soviet-Cuban Quarantine and Self-Defense', 57 *AJIL* 597.

McNair, A.D. (1930), 'The Functions and Different Character of Treaties', 11 *BYBIL* 100.

Mallinder, L. (2008), *Amnesty, Human Rights and Political Transition* (Oxford: Hart).

Mearsheimer, J.J. (1998), 'Back to the Future: Instability in Europe After the Cold War' in M.E. Brown, O.R. Cote, S.M. Lynn-Jones and S.E. Miller (eds), *Theories of Law and Peace* (Boston, MA: MIT Press) 3.

Merrills, J.G. (2011), *International Dispute Settlement* (5th edn, Cambridge: Cambridge University Press).

Montjoie, M. (2010), 'The Concept of Liability in the Absence of an Internationally Wrongful Act' in J. Crawford, A. Pellet and S. Olleson (eds), *The Law of International Responsibility* (Oxford: Oxford University Press) 503.

Moore, M. (2006), 'Globalization and Democratization: Institutional Design for Global Institutions', 37 *Journal of Social Philosophy* 21.

Morgenthau, H.J. (1940), 'Positivism, Functionalism and International Law', 34 *AJIL* 260.

Müller, D. (2010), 'Other Specific Regimes of Responsibility' in J. Crawford, A. Pellet and S. Olleson (eds), *The Law of International Responsibility* (Oxford: Oxford University Press) 843.

Müllerson, R. (2002), 'Jus ad Bellum: Plus Ça Change (Le Monde) Plus C'Est La Même Chose (Le Droit)?', 7 *JCSL* 149.

Murphy, D. (2008), *The Island that Dared: Journeys in Cuba* (London: Eland).

Neff, S. (2010), *Justice in Blue and Grey: A Legal History of the Civil War* (Cambridge, MA: Harvard University Press).

Nuccio, R.A. (1998), 'El embargo a debate: Castro es quien mantiene aislada a Cuba', 1 *Revista hispano cubano* 55.

O'Connell, P. (2012), *Vindicating Socio-Economic Rights* (London: Routledge).

Oppenheim, L. (1912), *International Law: A Treatise* (2nd edn, London: Longmans).

Orakhelashvili, A. (2006), *Peremptory Norms under International Law* (Oxford: Oxford University Press).

Pahuja, S. (2011), *Decolonising International Law: Development, Economic Growth and the Politics of Universality* (Cambridge: Cambridge University Press).

Paris, R. (2002), 'International Peacekeeping and the Mission Civilsatrice', 28 *Review of International Studies* 637.

Paust, J. and Blaustein, A.P. (1974), 'The Arab Oil Weapon – A Threat to International Peace', 68 *AJIL* 410.

Pellet, A. (2010), 'The Definition of Responsibility in International Law' in J. Crawford, A. Pellet and S. Olleson (eds), *The Law of International Responsibility* (Oxford: Oxford University Press) 3.

Penner, J.E. (2008), *McCoubrey and White's Textbook on Jurisprudence* (4th edn, Oxford: Oxford University Press).

Pérez, L. (2008), 'Reflections on the Future of Cuba', 39 *Cuban Studies* 85.

Pérez-Stable, M. (1999), *The Cuban Revolution: Origins, Course and Legacy* (2nd edn, Oxford: Oxford University Press).

Petrović, D. (2010), 'The UN Compensation Commission' in J. Crawford, A. Pellet and S. Olleson (eds), *The Law of International Responsibility* (Oxford: Oxford University Press) 849.

Provost, R. (2002), *State Responsibility in International Law* (Aldershot: Ashgate).

Purcell, S.K. (2003), 'La Ley Helms-Burton y el embargo estadounidense contra Cuba', 173 *Foro internacional* 704.

Raic, D. (2002), *Statehood and the Law of Self-Determination* (The Hague: Kluwer).

Randelzhofer, A. (1999), 'The Legal Position of the Individual under Present International Law' in A. Randelzhofer and C. Tomuschat (eds), *State Responsibility and the Individual: Reparation in Instances of Grave Violations of Human Rights* (The Hague: Nijhoff) 231.

Ratner, S.R. (2006), 'Land Feuds and their Solutions: Finding International Law Beyond the Tribunal Chamber', 100 *AJIL* 808.

Rawls, J. (1973), *A Theory of Justice* (Oxford: Oxford University Press).

Reinisch, A. (1996), 'A Few Public International Law Comments on the Cuban Liberty and Democratic Solidarity (LIBERTAD) Act of 1996', 7 *EJIL* 545.

Reisman, W.M. (1984), 'Coercion and Self-Determination: Construing Charter Article 2(4)', 78 *AJIL* 642.

Risse, T. (2000), '"Let's Argue": Communicative Action in World Politics', 54 *International Organization* 1.

Rivier, R. (2010), 'Responsibility for Violations of Human Rights Obligations: Inter-American Mechanisms' in J. Crawford, A. Pellet and S. Olleson (eds), *The Law of International Responsibility* (Oxford: Oxford University Press) 739.

Roberts, A. (2004), 'Righting Wrongs or Wronging Rights? The United States and Human Rights Post-September 11', 15 *EJIL* 721.

Robinson, F. (1998), 'The Limits of a Rights-Based Approach to International Ethics' in T. Evans (ed.), *Human Rights: Fifty Years On: A Reappraisal* (Manchester: Manchester University Press) 65.

Rodríguez-Pinzón, D. and Martin, C. (2010), 'The Inter-American Human Rights System: Selected Examples of Its Advisory Work' in S. Joseph and A. McBeth (eds), *Research Handbook on International Human Rights Law* (Cheltenham: Elgar) 353.

Roy, J. (2003), 'Las dos leyes Helms-Burton: contraste de la actitud de los Estados Unidos ante la Unión Europea y ante Cuba', 173 *Foro internacional* 719.

Russell, R. (1958), *A History of the United Nations Charter: The Role of the United States 1940–1945* (Washington DC: Brookings).

Schachter, O. (1984), 'The Legality of Pro-Democratic Invasion', 78 *AJIL* 645.

Schermers, H.G. and Blokker, N.M. (2011), *International Institutional Law* (5th edn, Leiden: Nijhoff).

Schoultz, L. (2010), 'Benevolent Domination: The Ideology of US Policy Toward Cuba', 41 *Cuban Studies* 1.

Scobbie, I. (2011), 'The Holiness of the Heart's Affection: Philip Allott's Theory of Social Idealism' in A. Orakhelashvili (ed.), *Research Handbook on the Theory and History of International Law* (Cheltenham: Elgar) 168.

Scobbie, I. (2013), 'The Permanent Court of Arbitration, Arbitration, and Claims Commissions in the Inter-War Period' in M. Fitzmaurice and C.J. Tams (eds), *Legacies of the Permanent Court of International Justice* (The Hague: Martinus Nijhoff) 203.

Seriocha Fernandez Pérez, S. (2000), *Las nacionalizaciones cubanas y el bloqueo de los Estados Unidos: una historia ajena a la guerra fría* (Madrid: Escuela Diplomatica).

Sheeran, S. (2011), 'International Law, Peace Agreements and Self-Determination: The Case of Sudan', 60 *ICLQ* 423.

Shelton, D. (2005), *Remedies in International Human Rights Law* (2nd edn, Oxford: Oxford University Press).

Sicilianos, L.-A. (2010), 'Countermeasures in Response to Grave Violations of Obligations Owed to the International Community' in J. Crawford, A. Pellet and S. Olleson (eds), *The Law of International Responsibility* (Oxford: Oxford University Press) 1137.

Simpson, G. (2004), *Great Powers and Outlaw States: Unequal Sovereigns in the International Legal Order* (Cambridge: Cambridge University Press).

Stahn, C., Esterday J.E. and Iverson, J. (2014), *Jus Post Bellum: Mapping the Normative Foundations* (Oxford: Oxford University Press).

Stanger, A. (2009), *One Nation Under Contract: The Outsourcing of American Power and the Future of Foreign Policy* (New Haven, CT: Yale University Press).

Stern, B. (2010), 'The Obligation to Make Reparation' in J. Crawford, A. Pellet and S. Olleson (eds), *The Law of International Responsibility* (Oxford: Oxford University Press) 563.

Szurek, S. (2010), 'The Notion of Circumstances Precluding Wrongfulness' in J. Crawford, A. Pellet and S. Olleson (eds), *The Law of International Responsibility* (Oxford: Oxford University Press) 427.

Thouvenin, M. (2010), 'Circumstances Precluding Wrongfulness' in J. Crawford, A. Pellet and S. Olleson (eds), *The Law of International Responsibility* (Oxford: Oxford University Press) 455.

Trapp, K. (2011), *State Responsibility for International Terrorism* (Oxford: Oxford University Press).

Treitschke, H. von (1963), *Politics* (Hans Kohn ed).

Vásquez, I. and Rodríguez L.J. (1999), 'Es hora de levanter el embargo contra Cuba', 4 *La Ilustración liberal: revista española y americana* 44.

Vattel, E. de (1758), *Le Droit des Gens, ou Principes de La Loi Naturelle.*

Vidmar, J. (2010), 'The Right of Self-Determination and Multiparty Democracy: Two Sides of the Same Coin?', 10 *Human Rights Quarterly* 239.

Vitoria, F. de (1917), *De Indis at de Ivre Belli Relectiones* (Ernest Nys ed, John Pawley Bate trans., Washington DC: Carnegie Institution of Washington).

Waltz, K. (1959), *Man, the State, and War: A Theoretical Analysis* (New York: Columbia University Press).

Wheatley, S. (2010), *The Democratic Legitimacy of International Law* (Oxford: Hart).

Wheaton, H. (1866), *Elements of International Law* (Boston, MA: Little, Brown and Co).

White, N.D. (2000), 'The United Nations and Democracy Assistance: Developing Practice within a Constitutional Framework' in P. Burnell (ed.), *Democracy Assistance: International Cooperation for Democratization* (London: Frank Cass) 74.

White, N.D. (2014), *Advanced Introduction to International Conflict and Security Law* (Cheltenham: Elgar).

White, N.D. and Abass, A. (2014), 'Countermeasures and Sanctions' in M. Evans (ed.), *International Law* (4th edn, Oxford University Press) ch.18.

Wilson, H.A. (1988), *International Law and the Use of Force by National Liberation Movements* (Oxford: Clarendon).

Young, J.C. (2001), *Postcolonialism: An Historical Introduction* (Oxford: Blackwell).

Zaldívar Dieguez, A. (2003), *Bloqueo: el asedio económico más prolongado de la historia* (La Habana: Capitán San Luis).

Zanders, J.P., French, E.M. and Pauwels, N. (1998), 'Chemical and Biological Weapon Developments and Arms Control', *SIPRI Yearbook* 586.

# Index

Terms in **bold** refer to extended discussions or terms highlighted in the text. Terms followed by 'n' can be found in the footnotes.